Library of Congress Cataloging in Publication Data:
Technology licensing strategies / [edited] by Russell L. Parr, Patrick
   H. Sullivan.
         p.   cm.—(Intellectual property library)
      Includes bibliographical references.
      ISBN 0-471-13081-8 (cloth : alk. paper)
      1. License agreements—Economic aspects.   2. Technology transfer—
   Valuation.   3. Royalties.   I. Parr, Russell L.   II. Sullivan,
   Patrick H.   III. Series: Intellectual property library (John Wiley &
   Sons)
   HF1429.T43   1996
   338'.064—dc20   95-53195
                                                               CIP

Printed in the United States of America

10 9 8 7 6 5 4 3 2

INTELLECTUAL PROPERTY SERIES

About the Editors

Russell L. Parr, CFA, ASA is Senior Vice President of AUS Consultants where he assesses the value of intellectual property and intangible assets and advises his clients about the investment value of patents, trademarks, and copyrights. He has advised banks about the collateral value of intangible assets and provides expert witness testimony regarding intellectual property infringement damages. Specializing in royalty rates, Mr. Parr is often called on by his international clientele to help fashion complex and critical licensing negotiations. A sampling of his clients include AT&T, Battelle, Pfizer, Silicon Graphics, TRW, Exide Corp., Hechingers, and The Estate of *Dr. Seuss*.

Mr. Parr is publisher of the highly respected *Licensing Economics Review* which is dedicated to reporting detailed financial information about strategic alliances involving intellectual property. A frequent speaker at Licensing Executive Society conferences, Mr. Parr holds a BS in Electrical Engineering, a Masters in Business Administration and is presently working on a PhD in International Business Strategies at Rutgers. In addition to his formal education he also holds the professional designations of *Chartered Financial Analyst* from the Association for Investment Management and Research and *Accredited Senior Associate* from the American Society of Appraisers.

Mr. Parr frequently speaks and writes about new techniques, based on investment rate of return analysis, for determining intellectual property values and royalty rates. He is a member of The Licensing Executives Society, The Technology Transfer Society, and The Planning Forum. He also serves on the advisory board of *The Licensing Journal* and *The IP Litigator*.

Mr. Parr's writings include authoring or co-authoring the following books:

- *Valuation of Intellectual Property & Intangible Assets, 1st & 2nd Editions*
- *Intellectual Property: Licensing & Joint Venture Profit Strategies*
- *Intellectual Property Infringement Damages: A Litigation Support Handbook*
- *Investing In Intangible Assets: Funding & Profit From Hidden Corporate Value*

- *The Royalty Rate Report for the Pharmaceutical & Biotechnology Industries*
- *The Royalty Rate Report for the Medical Products Industry*

Patrick H. Sullivan, DBA, MS is an expert at developing profits from intellectual assets. He is founding partner in The ICM Group, a consulting company focused on extracting value from intellectual capital. His consulting practice involves assessing and creating decisions processes for extracting value from intellectual assets; developing business, financial, and technology strategies for technologically based enterprises; and valuing intellectual assets for business and management use. He is also co-founder and convener of the prestigious ICM Gathering, comprised of managers of intellectual capital for large, diverse international companies who meet to exchange information on new and innovative management techniques.

Dr. Sullivan is affiliated with the Law & Economics Consulting Group, an expert testimony firm comprised largely of economists and faculty from major business schools around the country. He testifies as a court approved expert in matters involving intellectual property valuation and damages. Dr. Sullivan has an undergraduate degree in engineering, a Masters in R&D Management and a doctorate in Business Administration.

Dr. Sullivan has worked as an engineer on the launch team of the Saturn/ Apollo project at Cape Kennedy and following graduate school as the chief financial officer at two research universities. He has been a Principal Consultant at SRI International where he managed the firm's general consulting practice in Europe. A sampling of his clients include Dow Chemical, Xerox, NASA, General Motors, and University of Chicago.

Dr. Sullivan is a frequent speaker, giving talks on a range of intellectual management issues including management, valuation, royalties, and profiting from intellectual capital. He is a Fellow of the American Council on Education and is a member of the American Bar Association Intellectual Property Section, the Licensing Executives Society (LES), and the World Intellectual Property Trade Forum. He is included in Who's Who and Who's Who in California. He is a regular contributor of articles to the LES Journal, *les Nouvelles*.

About the Contributors

Joseph J. Daniele is Corporate Manager of Intellectual Property at Xerox Corporation. He is responsible for all aspects of licensing of Xerox's intellectual property portfolio including 6,000 patents and related know-how. He is Corporate Manager of Intellectual Property responsible for corporate review and approval for all Xerox licenses and intellectual property transfers worldwide. Previous to his current position Mr. Daniele was Principal and Corporate Strategist in the Xerox Corporate Strategy Office with responsibility for Xerox's core products including copiers, printers, and systems reprographics (Docutech). As a CSO Principal he was a member of the elite team that developed the Xerox 2000 Strategy and was advisor to senior management for technology and organization. Mr. Daniele joined Xerox in 1980 and has held line management positions in laser and ink jet printing, scanning, and image analysis. He was also previously Manager of the Technology Strategy Office. Prior to working at Xerox Mr. Daniele was at NA/NV Philips where he held line management positions in R&D for compact disc, compact optical recorder and diode laser development. He earned a BSEE and PhD from the Massachusetts Institute of Technology and an MBA from the University of Rochester. He has published over 20 papers and holds 21 patents.

Leif Edvinsson is Corporate Director of Intellectual Capital at Skandia Insurance Co., Ltd., a Swedish financial services company. He has studied economics and international business both in Sweden and the United States. He holds an MBA from the University of California, Berkeley. He pioneered the management of intellectual capital through his work at Skandia where he has implemented learning organizations and created intellectual capital supplements to the firm's annual report. He is now setting up a series of "future centers" that will bring together three generations of Skandia managers to create new methods for managing in the future.

Edward Kahn is founder and president of EKMS, Inc., a technology development and partnering firm based in Cambridge, Mass. Since 1986 EKMS has provided a wide variety of tech transfer services to organizations ranging from Fortune 100 industrial corporations to emerging high-tech companies to major universities and teaching hospitals. Mr. Kahn is Membership Chairman of the Licensing Executives Society (LES) North America and co-chair of the Greater Boston Local Meetings Committee of LES.

Steven P. Fox is Associate General Counsel and Director of Intellectual Property at Hewlett-Packard Company, headquartered in Palo Alto, California. In 1986 he was given overall responsibility for the Intellectual Property Section of the Legal Department comprised of 65 professionals in Europe, Japan and the United States. He received a bachelor's degree in electrical engineering from Northwestern University in 1964. In 1968 he earned his Juris Doctorate from George Washington University Law School. Mr. Fox joined Hewlett-Packard directly after graduating from law school and has been with the company for 27 years. He is a member of the American Bar Association Intellectual Property Section, American Intellectual Property Law Association, the Licensing Executives Society and the Association of Corporate Patent Counsel.

Peter Grindely, Ph.D., MBA is a Senior Economist at Law & Economics Consulting Group, Berkeley, California, where he specializes in the economics of innovation, intellectual property, licensing, and competitive policy. He has particular experience in electronics and telecommunications. He has been a Visiting Professor of Economics at the University of California, Berkeley and previously was an Assistant Professor of Economics at London Business School. While at London Business School, in addition to teaching in the areas of business strategy and innovation, Dr. Grindely was co-principal investigator of a major research program on *Technology and the Firm*. He is author of *Standards, Strategy and Policy: Cases and Stories* published by Oxford Press in 1995. Prior to his academic career he spent several years in the US electronics industry with management positions in engineering and finance based in Germany, Singapore, and the United States. Dr. Grindely has a first degree in electrical engineering from Cambridge University, an MBA from Stanford University, and a doctorate in economics from the London School of Economics

Michael Merwin is a Senior Manager in the Midwest Region International Business Group of Ernst & Young. He specializes in the economic and financial analysis of intercompany transfer pricing. He works primarily with US multinational companies to develop and implement practical transfer pricing regimes that not only comply with US and foreign tax laws, but also allow for clients to grow their businesses abroad. With many years of tax consulting experience Dr. Merwin has found that an important aspect of intercompany pricing is the determination of arm's-length royalties for transfers of technology. Utilizing public available filings, as well as financial analysis, he assists multinational companies with establishing appropriate royalty rates for these transfers. He has experience working with companies in a wide range of industries including medical technology, mining equipment, and computer peripherals. Additionally, he has industry experience in forecasting competitive intelligence, and actuarial and compensation analysis. Dr. Merwin holds a BS from Bradley University and a Ph.D. in Economics from the University of Illinois at Chicago.

Jack A. Nickerson, MBA is an Assistant Professor at the John M. Olin School of Business, Washington University in St. Louis. He has worked for over four years as a Senior Economist at Law & Economics Consulting Group where he conducted economic analyses in support of intellectual property litigation, particularly where licensing was involved. He has pioneered in the development of new analytical techniques for analyzing licensing structures and royalty rates. Mr. Nickerson is the recipient of the prestigious Licensing Executives Society North America Fellowship. His areas of academic interest include management of technology, business strategy, and organization theory. He expects to receive his Ph.D. in the spring of 1996.

James P. O'Shaughnessy is Vice President and Chief Intellectual Property Counsel, Rockwell International Corporation. Before assuming that position, Jim was a Senior Partner at Foley & Lardner, where he was a leader in the growth of the firm's intellectual property practice. Jim also was a founder of Innovatech Co., a company devoted to the development of innovation strategies. The material contained in Jim's contribution to this book is drawn from his experiences while at Foley & Lardner and Innovatech.

Jim is a frequent lecturer and an author on a wide range of intellectual property topics. He was graduated from Rensselaer Polytechnic Institute and received his law degree from Georgetown University Law Center.

Suzanne Sullivan is Managing Partner of The ICM Group LLC, a consulting firm focused on helping clients extract value from their intellectual capital. She has worked for over seven years in the emerging field of intellectual capital management (ICM). Prior to her current assignment, she was with Coopers & Lybrand's Financial Advisory Services as a financial consultant, specializing in intellectual property issues. She has also worked for Hewlett-Packard as a financial analyst and for The MAC Group as a litigation analyst. She has conducted economic and financial analyses in support of intellectual property litigation and has advised clients on maximizing value from their patent portfolios. Ms. Sullivan is a recipient of the Licensing Executives Society North America Fellowship. She holds an undergraduate degree in economics from the University of California and a masters degree in business administration from the University of Chicago.

Colleen W. Warner, a Manager with the Midwest Region International Business Services Group of Ernst & Young, is a research expert and has worked on over 50 different transfer pricing and corporate tax engagements. She has extensive experience in intellectual property research. She directs a staff of associates who use more than a dozen different on-line global data bases for comparable searches and retrieval of industry and company specific financial data. She has also developed a series of data bases for internal use which provide information on license and service agreements. Ms. Warner specializes in the use of intellectual property licensing agreements to support comparable analyses and for academic oriented research. She holds a BA in communications from DePaul University and is currently pursuing her MM in accounting from Northwestern University.

Contents

Part II   Royalty Rates

Part III   Intellectual Capital

Preface

We are pleased to present this anthology of technology licensing strategies as practiced by some of the best corporations in the world. No longer a peripheral activity, technology licensing, intellectual property management, and technology portfolio management are becoming central to the success of global corporations. Our primary focus in this book is technology licensing, one of the most important elements of intellectual property management. The strategies and practices presented in this book are those found in corporations as well as those recommended by seasoned consulting professionals. Each chapter in this book is unique and addresses different strategies, practices, goals, and needs. We have found that a one-size-fits-all strategy does not adequately treat the complexities and subtleties of technology licensing. Yet we have definitely found some guiding principals that should be considered when determining the strategy that is right for you.

We have found that patent management strategies, solely for the purpose of protecting market positions, is giving way to strategies where optimization of a variety of opportunities is the central goal. We discuss the forces bringing about this change. Among them is the increased value accruing to patents as a result in the shift of US policy toward patent rights. In 1982 the US created the Court of Appeals for the Federal Circuit designed to focus on intellectual property issues. Decisions by the court have strengthened the rights of intellectual property ownership and the value of patent holdings has soared. Companies now view their patents as basic elements of corporate value and are seeking to maximize this valuable corporate asset in new ways. We have also found new interest in technology management from new places. Typically CEOs focus on broad strategic issues. The reason for their growing interest in technology management is not that CEOs have narrowed their focus. The reason is that technology management has become one of the most important strategic issues of our time. Corporate strategies are focusing on extracting value from patents in a variety of ways.

As you read the different chapters of this book you may find conflicting ideas. This is how it is and should be. Technology licensing is complex and challenging. As such, opinions are bound to conflict. Our goal for this book has been to set forth some of the best ideas we could find without diluting them by trying to bring them into harmony.

We deeply hope that this book will contribute to defining and implementing successful technology licensing strategies.

Russell L. Parr   Patrick H. Sullivan
Yardely, Pennsylvania   *Santa Cruz, California*

Acknowledgments

The most important thanks must go to the people that took time from their busy schedules to contribute to this book. This book would not have been possible without the enthusiasm, time, and effort given to it by the chapter contributors. We appreciate the collaboration that brought together the ideas of extremely talented professionals who had pressing schedules well before they agreed to participate in this project. We are very complimented that they would add this project to their work load and our most sincere thank you is extended to each contributor.

For their intellectual curiosity and interest in furthering the state of knowledge about management of intellectual property we also wish to thank Gordon Petrash of Dow Chemical Company, Leif Edvinsson of Skandia, Richard Razgaitis of Bellcore, Bruce E. Sanderson of AT&T, Karl Jorda of Franklin Pierce Law Center, Gordon V. Smith of AUS Consultants, Fred F. Nazem of Nazem and Company, and Melvin Sharp of Sharp, Comfort & Merrett. Their interest and willingness to create as well as challenge new thoughts has been an invaluable intellectual as well as personnel resource. We also wish to acknowledge all of the members of the ICM Gathering for their inquisitiveness, foresight and frankness. Without such insight and dedicated people, the field of intellectual property management would not be experiencing its explosive pace. Special thanks are also extended to John Osterhout of Kodak and Gaylord P. Haas, Jr. of AlliedSignal. If not for their generosity and openness important aspects of this book would not have been possible.

Russell L. Parr would like to thank his beautiful wife for enduring him— Thanks Jane. He would also like to thank his sons, John and James, for growing into fine young men.

Patrick H. Sullivan would like to thank his entire family, in particular his children Christine, Suzanne, and Patrick. They are a neverending source of pride, inspiration, and love.

Most importantly, both of us would like to thank our mothers for having and nurturing us—Thanks Mom.

Part I

Licensing Strategy

1

Vital Resources of the Future—Knowledge

Russell L. Parr

AUS Consultants and Intellectual Property Research Associates

Patrick H. Sullivan

The ICM Group

Knowledge is the new strategic raw material for creating wealth. The source of commercial power has shifted from capital resources to knowledge resources. In fact the definition of capital resources itself is shifting. No longer does it only bring to mind balance sheets of cash or pictures of sprawling manufacturing plants. The definition of capital now includes knowledge capital—intellectual assets—including technology, patents, and trade secrets along with the means to create more inventions and innovations. Corporations once dominated industries by acquiring and managing extensive holdings of natural resources and manufacturing facilities. Barriers to entry were high because enormous amounts of fixed asset investments were required to displace well-entrenched players. Today, companies that once dominated fixed asset industries are finding themselves fighting for survival. Upstart companies are creating new products and services based not on extensive resource holdings or on accumulated cash, but on knowledge resources. Management of knowledge-based resources will distinguish winners from losers in the decades ahead. This book focuses on developing winning licensing strategies that both create and extract value from a firm's intellectual capital.

Intellectual capital is a topic of increasing interest to firms that derive their profits from innovation and knowledge-intensive services. Intellectual capital may be minimally defined as the firm's stock of focused, organized information available for some positive purpose. Companies deriving their

3

profits largely from the commercialization of innovation are called "knowledge firms." In many cases these "knowledge firms" find that equity markets value them at a price far higher than their balance sheets warrant. But the existence of intellectual capital is not enough to explain the high value the marketplace places on many knowledge companies. We believe this extra measure of value represents the market's perception not only of the firm's stock of intellectual capital but also its ability to leverage that capital into profits.

We define intellectual capital as "knowledge that can be converted into profits." Traditionally, the mechanisms available for converting ideas into cash include: sale, donation for tax benefit, license, joint venture, strategic alliance or integration of the innovation into the firm's current business. This book focuses on how firms may extract value from one of the most-often used of these conversion mechanisms: licensing.

THE TECHNOLOGY SPIRAL

Technology has created opportunities and initiated change throughout history. The Industrial Revolution of the mid-18th century revolutionized all aspects of economics, society, and lifestyles. It caused migration to the cities. It eliminated local craftspeople from the mainstream and replaced handtools with large-scale industrial machinery powered by water or steam. Companies began to specialize, they began to focus not just on products but on sub components. The Industrial Revolution transformed Society from its agricultural base into a technology-oriented business economy. Now dramatic changes are again in the wind. The continuing advances of technology are once again shifting all aspects of economics, society, and lifestyles. More people are working at home. Not since our country was based on agriculture have so many people been able to work at their living place. Cities are no longer the center of economic power. Large industrial complexes are being replaced by single-story structures that house well lighted and clean operations producing very specialized products and small manufacturing shops that are located thousands of miles away in newly developed countries.

Advancing technology presents and responds to new competitive pressures. To address the threat of new competitive products more technology is needed and access time is critical (access time is the amount of time required to identify and develop a new technology). The development of specific new technologies to help meet specific new business challenges accelerates the overall development pace and requires even greater advances in technology. There is an upward spiral of technology development. The spiral accelerates because in order to keep pace, a corporation's technology must be managed to allow it to quickly gain access to more technology. The problem becomes more complex as new competitive products and services become based on a number of divergent technologies. Companies cannot rely on their own core competencies to remain market competitive. They must understand the interrelations of all the basic sciences beyond their own specialties. They must understand subatomic physics, advanced mathematics, computer simulation, biology, and materials engineering but more than just a basic understanding is needed. Expertise in divergent technological know-how is required to remain competitive.

ECLECTIC SCIENCE

Dr. Leroy Hood, recently featured in a story in *The Wall Street Journal*, is in the business of automating the process biotechnology scientists use to find the defective genes underlying cancer. The search must be conducted among the 100,000 genes that can be found in our species. Making matters more complicated, the current process is slow and tedious because precisely measured solutions must be manually shuttled among hundreds of test tubes. Dr. Hood is changing the process by combining a broad range of technologies. One of his machines identifies the sequence of the three billion molecules that make up human DNA and does it 60 times faster than manual methods. He has accomplished this by bringing biotechnology together with computer science, mechanical engineering, physics, liquid science, optics, and electronics. Dr. Hood exemplifies the trend that all businesses must not follow if they are to be successful. He marries established ideas and technologies from far-flung fields.

In less than ten years corporations have been faced with technological advances including the continued miniaturization of electronics and widespread wireless communications. Surgical equipment manufacturers are facing increased use of non invasive surgical techniques. Computer makers have seen their mainframes literally reduced to, and replaced by, tabletop models. CD ROMs are seriously eroding traditional encyclopedia sales. All of these changes are technology based. As a result, corporations need even more technology and what they need is often what they do not have.

The new world order is defined by change. The leaders in this tumultuous environment will be those who embrace change. Change is coming fast and it keeps coming—and it is all driven by technology. There is no time to gain expertise in all the different technologies necessary to compete if a company is in the marketplace. There is no room for not-invented-here mindsets. The pace of change does not afford any company the luxury of developing expertise in all the divergent technologies that it needs. It is not even clear if such a wide-ranging goal could be accomplished.

SELF-SUFFICIENCY IS DEAD

Compare two industries, one based on the old paradigm and the other based on the new. Compare automobiles and computers. The heyday of auto manufacturing represents the model where one company had its finger on the pulse of all aspects and components of the final product. One company would design and build all critical components of the product. Auto makers designed and built the engine, chassis, transmission, axles, steering mechanism interiors, window levers, radios, and even batteries for their cars. They custom-designed and manufactured shock absorbers, body panels, and brakes. Computer makers, on the other hand, take critical components from many independent providers. The author's Dell computer uses a processer built by *Intel*. Its sound card is made by *Soundblaster*, *US Robotics* build the modem, the video card came from a company called *Number Nine*, the CD ROM player was manufactured by *Creative*, and the speakers were made by *Peavey*. Printed documents arrive on the desk compliments of *Epson*, and the software used on the system came mostly from *Microsoft*. It's the same with all computer makers. None have the time, inclination, or core competencies to design and make each of the complex components that integrate to form a personal computer. Dell is a large and successful company with over a billion dollars in annual sales, but is far from being characterized as an independent. It relies on many other companies, not only to supply them with computer components but to keep it on the leading edge of product offerings. These companies are interdependent.

Interdependence is at the root of the paradigm shift taking place. Technology management in the future will center on leveraging technology that a company owns to gain access to technology that it needs. Sharing technology is a concept many will find difficult to accept, but accept it they must. Dennis Waitley writes in *Empires of the Mind,*[1] "The leaders of the present and the future will be champions of cooperation more often than of competition. While the power to maintain access to resources will remain important, 'the survival of the fittest' mentality will give away to survival of the wisest, a philosophy of understanding, cooperation, knowledge, and reason." Access to vital resources has changed because the nature of the most important resources is no longer embodied in fixed material assets. Gaining access to technology means cooperating with other companies, even with competitors, in order to gain access to their knowledge-based resources. Independence is again being replaced by interdependence. Waitley succinctly explains, "The future leaders will only get what they want by helping others get what they want."

---

[1]Dennis Waitley, *Empires of the Mind—Lessons to Lead and Succeed in a Knowledge-Based World*, William Morrow and Company, Inc., New York, 1995, page 8.

Along with the demise of self-sufficiency is the death of "captive internalization" of technology. In the past technology was commercialized solely by the company owning it. Corporations conducted research and focused efforts on promising discoveries. Additional effort brought about innovative new products and the new products were brought to market by their originator. The advantages inherent in the technology were exploited by three primary methods: price premium, cost savings, and market expansion. All of these methods bring enhanced profitability. For example, premium prices are charged for the inherent advantages that new technology brings to products or services. When new utility is attached to existing products, premium prices may also be charged and additional profits can be enjoyed. Cost savings also translate into profits. Technological advances sometimes allow existing products to be manufactured at lower cost. The technological advantages of enhanced product performance may even be offered in the marketplace without a premium price. As more customers are attracted to the enhanced product additional profits are enjoyed from the economies of scale that are derived from volume production. These methods of exploiting technology are all alive and well but must be modified as independence gives way to interdependence. The value derived from technology goes far beyond those just discussed. Besides the enhancement of profits, technology will be required in order to gain access to other technologies that will allow companies to keep up with competitive pressures. Technology has become more than a tool for making better products and services, it has become valuable currency that is happily accepted all over the world.

ONLY TECHNOLOGY HAS LASTING VALUE

Paul Romer, a U.C. Berkeley economist, maintains that technology is a fundamental source of value in industrialized society. He believes there is a new or emerging world-wide economy driven not just by traditional economy theory's two factors of production: labor and capital, but also a third: technology. The effect of technology on business, Romer believes, is to leverage investments. "Investments can make technology more valuable and technology can make investments more valuable."[2]

The value of any technology does not last forever, however. New innovations can replace old. But more than any other capital asset, technology has unique attributes, the following lists several:

1. The research programs that create technology are often expensive to establish and maintain. These programs, because of their inher-

---

[2]Forbes ASAP, p. 67.

ent risk provide a significant barrier to competitive entry. There are
no guarantees that large expenditures of time and money will regularly, if ever, give birth to a valuable invention. Therefore, maintaining technological incubators is an effective, although expensive,
barrier to competitive entry in many industries. An additional barrier
exists in the specialized competencies possessed by many corporations that would take decades for another to duplicate, regardless of
the research and development effort required.

2. Patent protection affords unique proprietary rights. The limited monopoly that accompanies a patent allows companies to extract premium profits from the market and build other competitive barriers
   during the protection period. During that period corporations can
   also add onto already patented technology to create additional
   patented technologies, allowing the proprietary protection to carry
   forward after the first patent expires.

3. Possession of advanced technology represents a peerless form of
   currency. It can be used to gain access to other technologies or
   shared with foreign countries to gain access to entirely new markets. Its proprietary nature makes it powerful because of its
   scarcity.

TECHNOLOGY LICENSING

Licensing is already a frequently used and efficient method for leveraging
the value of technology. It is used to obtain access to the technology of others
and to provide access to one's own technology. It is used as a mechanism
for establishing and monitoring joint ventures as well as strategic alliances.
Already an important mechanism for converting innovations into profit,
licensing will become even more important in the future as companies seek
to gain extra value from their store of innovation, their intellectual capital.

Licensing will become a more frequently-used strategic alternative for
companies as the more sophisticated of them become aware of its power to
help them achieve their business objectives. Look at any corporate mission
statement and you will find the seeds of a strategy-based technology licensing program. Mission statements often promise to provide ever-improving
products and services to meet the needs of customers. This goal will be increasingly difficult to accomplish if based only on one's own technology.
More often, increasingly complex products for increasingly more sophisticated markets will require ever more interdependent technologies and company relationships to develop them. Gaining access to needed technologies
will require strong strategy-based technology management programs with
licensing as an integral if not a key component.

OVERVIEW OF THIS BOOK

The ideas found in this book reflect the sweeping changes effecting the way companies compete now and will compete in the future. Most of the ideas presented here defy the old models of self-sufficiency and independence. A technology management strategy that reflects interdependence may be abhorrent to those who built their careers during periods when outmoded attitudes reigned supreme. Introduction of the new thinking or the strategies discussed in this book to entrenched management will not be accepted happily. Negative reactions are to be expected and will take time to overcome, but it can't take too long because delay might contribute to the death of laggard corporations. If someone tells you your ideas are radical or crazy, keep going. You are on the right track!

This book is divided into three parts. The first part contains discussions of different licensing and patent portfolio strategies. In the second part, methods for pricing technologies are presented, along with royalty rate models for readers involved in licensing negotiations. Real-life questions: for example, what would you as a deal maker do if you needed to know a royalty rate in five minutes? If you have more than five minutes but you were working with a limited budget what would you do? A series of accurate options are presented to help in those situations. If time, money, and financial expertise are abundantly available, then what are more precise alternatives for deriving royalty rates?

In part three we present several views of the future of intellectual capital management. Here we bring to the reader some of the most current thinking of theorists and practitioners about what lies beyond the horizon of current practice and into the future.

For those interested in more information on current licensing practice, we have included an appendix containing information about recent technology licenses for a variety of industries. This section also contains information about license fees and running royalties. This section on actual licensing is included to provide readers with insights into current practice: what is being transferred, who is involved, and how much is being paid for technologies.

PART ONE—LICENSING STRATEGY

Chapter 2   Key Terms & Strategic Positions

Patrick H. Sullivan introduces licensing as an integral part of business strategy, identifying terms frequently found in licensing agreements, and discussing the importance of each to licensing negotiations. He suggests that when entering licensing negotiations, the firm's strategic position may have a major impact on the kind of outcome that can be expected. Finally, he offers suggestions on how to use strategic position to a firm's advantage in licensing negotiations.

Chapter 3   Portfolio Types and Strategies

Patrick H. Sullivan and Joseph J. Daniele, having surveyed a number of major international corporations, identify and define a range of different kinds of intellectual property portfolios and how they are managed. They discuss the ways in which these portfolios are used, either directly in business negotiations or indirectly, define direct and indirect strategies and cite their advantages and disadvantages. In addition, the chapter continues the discussion of positioning and key terms that began in Chapter 2.

Chapter 4   TQM for IMM (TM): Applying the TQM Model to Intellectual Property Management

Edward Kahn explains how the Total Quality Management programs used to enhance corporate operations can enhance intellectual property management. He points out some of the ways that intellectual property management is more than the traditional practice of patent management and that the job of maximizing intellectual property value extends far beyond that of the patent office or licensing department.

Chapter 5   Strategic Objectives Supported by Licensing

Jack A. Nickerson introduces recent research suggesting that four general types of license exist. These license types have evolved over time and each carries some unique implications for licensing strategy. He details the uses, strengths, and weaknesses of each type of license along with an identification of the business situations in which it applies as well as providing some strategies for its use.

Chapter 6   Establishing An Out-Licensing Activity

Patrick H. Sullivan and Stephen P. Fox list and discuss the results of their research into the lessons learned by a group of major corporations who have either implemented or at least considered implementing an out-licensing office. They identify the reasons why corporations do or do not establish out-licensing offices, the conditions that lead up to such a decision, the conditions under which out-licensing offices tend to succeed as well as the conditions under which they don't. They share the results of their informal conversations with more than twenty companies and provide profiles of the out-licensing perspectives of eight major U.S. corporations.

Chapter 7   Licensing and Business Strategy in the Chemical Industry

Peter C. Grindley and Jack A. Nickerson discuss the unique business conditions in the chemical industry and the licensing policies that have evolved and using that as a basis they seek to develop a general model that will be helpful to practitioners. They focus on the chemical industry because of its importance as an initiator of licensing practice and its role as the industry that first embraced licensing as a strategic element of business management. The strategies developed in this industry, and outlined in this chapter, may be instructive to practitioners in other industries where licensing is in its infancy.

Chapter 8   Central Control of Technology Licensing

Russell L. Parr explores the role of central control as practiced at Allied Signal Corp and the Eastman Kodak Company. He examines central control at the corporate level as it pertains to intellectual property management. Through interviews with top executives at these two companies he explains the importance of business judgment and the insights of business-unit managers to the success of the firm's out-licensing activities.

Chapter 9   Gaps Analysis

Russell L. Parr describes a method used by DuPont for identifying their future technology needs in relation to the business and technology trends in their industry. A licensing strategy must address the future technology needs of the organization and DuPont's Gaps Analysis is presented as a way to determine those needs.

Chapter 10   Developing the Complete Portfolio: The Case for Market Strategic Technology

Jim O'Shaughnessy discusses the components of patent portfolios and how to manage keystone technology to support market strategies. The focus of this chapter, which includes case studies, is market-oriented and complements the other chapters in Part 1.

PART TWO—ROYALTY RATES

Chapter 11   The Importance of Context in the Derivation of Royalty Rates

Suzanne P. Sullivan provides an overall view of royalty rate derivation. She discusses the importance of context, time, money, and knowledge constraints, and opens the discussion for the remainder of this book. Her description of the basic methods for deriving royalty rates overviews the strengths and weaknesses of each. The summary chart at the end of the chapter provides an instructive recap of available royalty rate methods.

Chapter 12 Techniques for Obtaining and Analyzing External License Agreements

Michael Merwin and Colleen Warner explain how market evidence of royalty rates can supply some of the best information for use in negotiating the royalties for a new deal. They use data disclosed to the Securities and Exchange Commission to explain how to go about finding information for specific circumstances. They include a discussion of the key characteristics to consider when deciding the relevance of marketplace information to specific technologies under negotiation. An example, using trademarks for purposes of demonstration, is outlined in the chapter.

Chapter 13 Advanced Methods for Royalty Rates

Russell L. Parr discusses many popular royalty rate derivation models. He presents qualitative models that have come from intellectual property infringement court decisions and contrasts them with investment rate of return models that have evolved from financial theory. He concludes that more royalty rate precision than that provided by rules of thumb and industry standards is available and must be considered in light of the accelerating value associated with technology.

PART THREE—THE FUTURE

Chapter 14 A Model for Managing Intellectual Capital

Patrick H. Sullivan and Leif Edvinsson begin this section with an overview of the broader issues suggested by the earlier chapters in this book: the management of intellectual capital. In this chapter they describe and define intellectual capital and discuss the issues that surround its management. They provide the reader with a model of intellectual capital derived from the experience of eight industry leaders in intellectual capital management (ICM) and provide a glimpse into the unique and powerful insights managers can obtain through the use of an ICM perspective on day-to-day problems.

Chapter 15 Intellectual Capital Management at Skandia

Leif Edvinsson, Director of Intellectual Capital at Sweden's Skandia Corporation, discusses the evolution of the Skandia experience. His discussion includes the thinking of the corporation as well as the lessons he has learned from implementing ICM at Skandia.

Chapter 16 The Future of Intellectual Capital Management

Russell L. Parr and Patrick H. Sullivan discuss their views about the future of intellectual capital management. This final chapter summarizes much of what has been discussed in earlier chapters, the extensive interviews the authors conducted as part of their research for this book as well as their own perspectives drawn from their respective litigation and consulting practices. Finally, this chapter includes some predictions for the future of ICM and the importance of licensing in the business strategy of knowledge companies.

APPENDIX
RECENT TECHNOLOGY TRANSFERS AND ROYALTY RATES

Russell L. Parr summarizes the financial terms associated with technology licensing transactions as reported in *Licensing Economics Review*.

CONCLUSION

This book presents current thinking and practice on licensing and licensing strategies by thoughtful, successful corporations. The ideas presented here are collected from practitioners who are developing and testing new ideas in the marketplace. Virtually every company or individual interviewed for this book would agree that we are already into a new age of technology management. The opinions may vary about how the new age may be described or defined but they are unanimous that we are deep into it. Few were sanguine about the new age, but none feared it. All are excited about what they are doing and what they are learning from each other. We hope that the ideas presented here are as exciting to the reader as they were to those of us who have presented them to you.

2

Key Terms
and Strategic Positioning

Patrick H. Sullivan

The ICM Group

The licensing of technology has become an area of increasing profitability for knowledge-based companies. Recent court decisions upholding the rights of innovators have led not only to reimbursements and back payment for patent infringements but also to substantial damages awards. The *financial* importance of technology licensing has alerted business as well as technology managers in knowledge-based companies to the need for well-conceived and concisely articulated licenses that contribute to the bottom line.

In the past, the commercialization of technology, of which licensing was a major component, was usually accomplished by the CEO or the corporate attorney, working on instinct. There were few guidelines or norms, and success depended directly on the background and experience of the person directing the commercialization activity. As long as licensing held only limited importance to the firm, such a hit-or-miss approach was acceptable. Today, however, the business environment for knowledge-based companies means that licensing, both in-licensing and out-licensing, has become a fundamental part of the firm's business strategy. And to be a solid part of the firm's business strategy, licenses must reflect a wide range of considerations, external as well as internal.

LICENSING AS A CONVERSION MECHANISM

At the conceptual level, the commercialization of intellectual assets involves two kinds of activities. The first is the evolution of a marketable concept from initial thought through research, product development, manufacturing, distribution, and finally sale to the end-user. The second aspect of commercialization is called the conversion mechanism. Simply stated, conversion mechanisms are the devices that companies along the commercialization chain use to convert their knowledge or service into cash.

Consider a research company. It has no manufacturing facilities, no distribution capability, and no retail function. It makes its contribution by creating marketable innovations. This company converts its innovations to cash by licensing them to manufacturers. In this case, the mechanism used to convert the firm's asset (the innovation) to cash is a license. Another firm may have innovations as well as manufacturing capability but no ability to distribute or sell to end-users. For a company such as this, the conversion mechanism might be the sale of manufactured goods to a distributor. Equally, the manufacturer could convert its assets into cash through a joint venture with a company that has both distribution and sales capabilities.

The point is that there are several different conversion mechanisms that firms may use to convert their knowledge or services into dollars. The typical list of conversion mechanisms contains a number of possibilities. Sale of the rights to the innovation is the most obvious way of converting knowledge into cash. A second alternative is to license the innovation, thereby retaining the basic ownership but allowing someone else the right to use it. A third alternative is a joint venture with one or more companies. Typically joint ventures are undertaken when the owner of the rights to an innovation has some but not all of the business assets required to commercialize it fully. In this case, the owner may strike agreements for the use of the required business assets owned by one or more other companies. A fourth form of conversion mechanism is the strategic alliance. Strategic alliances are developed when a firm with an innovation and the required business assets does not have access to an adequate market. When this is the case a firm may establish an alliance with a company that has market access or positioning but not give it any rights to the innovation.

Licensing is only one of the ways in which innovators can convert their product or service ideas into cash. In the past, when the courts did not provide the support for ownership rights that they currently do, licensing was not necessarily a key component of a commercialization strategy. Now, however, with the increase in the value of innovation due to the increasing strength the courts have placed on ownership rights, firms are becoming more interested in developing stronger and more innovative licenses as well as strategies for using the licenses to achieve the firm's strategic objectives.

FACTORS AFFECTING LICENSING AND ROYALTY TERMS

A wide range of factors affect the setting of licensing terms as well as the amount of royalties required by the license. Indeed, the list of potential licensing terms is almost as long as there are people to contribute to it. But a relatively small number of factors are of primary importance.

Major Factors. Two factors dominate discussions of licensing and royalties: competitive strategy and duration.

1. *Competitive Strategy.* The first and by far the most basic consideration is whether and how the potential license could be structured to the competitive advantage of the out-licensing firm. This anti-competitive view of licensing is strongly held by most firms involved in competitive businesses. For knowledge-based firms, the use of licenses as part of a competitive strategy is of the utmost importance. Firms that survive by selling the products of their intellectual capital must ensure that the licensing of their intellectual assets or know-how will be done only if it either enriches the owning firm at the expense of the competition or if the licensor puts the competing licensee at a strategic disadvantage position.

   The first question firms tend to ask when approaching a license discussion with another is: is this company a current or potential competitor? If the answer is yes, then the firm must create a set of terms and conditions that will either improve its own strategic position or in some way worsen the tactical or strategic position of the competitor.

2. *Duration.* The second major factor affecting licensing terms and royalty amounts is the length of time the license is to be in force. Licensors that believe their technology may be short-lived will press for long-term duration while licensees will take the opposite view. Similarly, licensees that believe a currently low-royalty technology is likely to become a hot market property will want to lock in a long-term license at favorable terms.

   License duration thus is in some ways a surrogate for, or a result of, a number of other factors that affect both terms and rates. For example, it may be an indicator of the commercial success of the technology, its current or potential level of refinement, its acceptability in the marketplace, or its immunity (or lack of immunity) from substitute technologies. Duration, for all of the foregoing reasons, is a principal topic of every license discussion.

Other Factors. Six other factors often affect the final licensing terms, royalty rates, or both. These factors are:

1. *Protection:* The nature and amount of protection that a licensor offers to the licensee is a major consideration. The licensee must be assured not only that adequate legal protection is in place, but also

that the licensor is prepared to enforce and capable of enforcing this protection against infringers.

2. *Exclusivity:* The nature and degree of exclusivity offered is another frequent consideration. Exclusivity exists in both specific areas and degrees. An area of exclusivity might be a territory or market. A license might be completely exclusive or exclusive under specified terms. Licenses that offer absolute exclusivity with no conditions are worth more than licenses that offer only area or conditionally exclusive arrangements.

3. *Utility/Advantage:* The usefulness or amount of advantage the technology confers upon the licensee is also of concern. Technologies offering a marketplace head start on the competition are more valuable than those that merely provide opportunities for keeping up. Technological capabilities that will enrich the licensee firm and allow it to develop capabilities to significantly enhance its strategic position are the most valuable.

4. *Commercial Success:* Technologies that are proven to have marketplace appeal and that significant increase sales are more valuable than technologies that are untested in the marketplace or whose commercial success is not an issue.

5. *Refinement:* The maturity or immediate applicability of a technology often affects the terms and royalty rates of a license. Technologies that require development or refinement before they can be commercially applied are less valuable than are technologies that can be immediately used in the design or manufacture of products for the marketplace.

6. *License Commitment:* Negotiators look at the degree to which the licensor is committed to ongoing support of the license. Licensors unwilling to actively pursue infringers, to continue seeking barriers to infringement, to provide ongoing training and support, or to continue development of the technology will find licensees unwilling to pay high royalty rates for their technology.

COMPANY STANCE

We have all observed that a person's perspective can color judgment about the thing that is viewed. A roaring surf, viewed from the beach, is a powerful and beautiful scene. A roaring surf, viewed from the small boat whose crew wants to land on the beach, is awesome and quite terrifying. Differing perspectives greatly affect the view of licensing, licensing negotiation, and even the desirability of selected terms in a license agreement. In the case of licensing, we call the different perspectives of the participants their stance or posture.

A firm's stance or posture is not only a major determinant of how it views the terms and conditions of a potential license, but may also be a major predictor of the outcome of the license negotiations. For both out-licensing and in-licensing, there are active and passive participants. Each side naturally assumes distinct roles and positions.

Out-Licensing Firms

Strategic out-licensors are firms actively seeking to generate income from their strategic intellectual property, either through product sales or through the licensing of their technologies. Energetic firms are willing to invest in harvesting their portfolio of intellectual properties.

Opportunistic out-licensors are firms interested in receiving income on nonstrategic intellectual property, but not ready to invest substantially in an active harvesting of the firm's intellectual property portfolio.

In-Licensing Firms

Seekers of technology are companies actively interested in obtaining already-developed technology rather than bearing the cost of creating it. They are willing to pay for technology, but not to overpay.

Infringers are companies found to be infringing upon the patent rights held by another person or firm.

The Effect of Company Stance on Licensing Objectives

Although the details of a firm's licensing objectives are unique to its technological, business, and legal situation, the firm's stance also is a major determinant of its licensing objectives:

Strategic out-licensors are interested in developing income from their licenses. To do so they are willing to invest in the creation of an income-generating licensing office. Typically such firms usually press for early cash flow.

Opportunistic out-licensors are relatively passive in their approach to the market. By definition, such companies either license only their nonstrategic intellectual properties or they do not make the internal investments necessary to obtaining a stream of licensing income. Opportunistic out-licensors seek terms and royalty rates that are consistent with common industry licensing and royalty practice.

Technology seekers are individuals or firms looking for rapid closure on a technology license so they may implement the technology quickly. Firms in this position seek royalty rates that are low enough to provide what they consider to be a good profit.

Infringers are individuals or firms that, for whatever reason, are already using the intellectual property of someone else. They are usually already in the marketplace, and for this reason the finances of their production activities are established and their costs and profit margins are known. They know that any new costs, such as royalty payments, will cut into their existing margins and profits. Therefore, the strategies of firms in this position tend to focus on seeking ways to pay the lowest possible royalty as well as on ways to delay payment as long as possible.

The Effect of Company Stance on Licensing Strategies

In addition to its effect on licensing objectives, company stance also has an effect on general licensing strategies. Strategic out-licensors, for example, tend to follow a three-step strategy. First, they identify potential licensees, both seekers and infringers. Second, they target companies that are financially capable of paying royalties, such as firms that sell final assemblies or end products rather than those that sell components or subassemblies. Third, they attempt to minimize the administrative costs of generating licensing income through procedures such as license or patent packaging.

Opportunistic out-licensors tend to follow a different strategy. They do not actively seek out potential licensees but wait until they are approached or until an infringer's presence becomes known to them. Their licensing strategy tends to have two components. First, they seek terms and royalty rates that are consistent with industry norms. Second, they too work to keep down the administrative costs of licensing and, like their more energetic cousins, seek administrative mechanisms to minimize the costs of obtaining or overseeing their licenses.

On the in-licensing side, technology seekers have an active two-pronged strategy. First, technology seekers identify the practical range of alternative sources of the technology they seek. As part of this strategy component, they learn in some detail the costs associated with each alternative. After examining the costs, if licensing is the best cost alternative, these firms seek out the owners of the technology and press for rapid closure on a license. The second component of their strategy concerns the price (royalty) they are willing to pay. Because they already know what their cost alternatives are, firms in this position are able to determine how much they are willing to pay to the licensor in order to realize their own profit objectives. Licensors unwilling to agree to the acceptable cost to the technology seeker will find that companies in this position would rather leave the table and pursue their other alternatives than pay more than the technology is worth to them.

Infringers pursue licensing strategies that are very different from those already discussed. They already know both the costs and the value of the technology to their operation. They also know that any royalty payments they are forced to make cut into their profits. Infringers' strategies usually involve minimizing the amount of royalty to be paid as well as delaying the payment itself for as long as possible. Following this strategy, infringers, on learning that they are being asked to take out a license, will immediately begin to gather cost information, usually identifying alternative sources of the technology, and for each alternative learning what it will cost to obtain. In addition, infringers will identify the amounts probably owed to the owner of the technology and calculate whether it would be cheaper to pay the royalties or to delay and litigate in anticipation of arguing the royalty costs downward.

The Effect of Company Stance on Licensing Negotiations and Outcomes

The respective positions of the negotiating parties can often be a major determinant of the success of negotiations. Exhibit 2.1 shows how the positioning of firms can affect negotiations.

The Effect of Company Stance on Licensing Terms

A firm's position is also a major factor in the view it holds of any of the factors identified above. Exhibit 2.2 provides some examples of the differing views a firm may hold on any factor, depending upon its positioning. Strategic and opportunistic licensors have more in common with each other in their views on each potential license term than does either kind of license

	Seeker	**Infringers**
Strategic	• Both sides interested in exchange • Negotiations likely to be smooth	• Significant differences likely Licensor: maximum royalty Licensee: minimum royalty • Negotiations likely to be difficult
Opportunistic	• Licensor likely to seek royalty and terms at industry norm • Licensee likely to agree	• Licensor at industry norm • Licensee will try to reduce • Negotiations serious but not contentious

Exhibit 2.1.   Position and Affect on Negotations

Factor	Licensors		Licensees	
	Aggressive	Passive	Seekers	Infringers
Protection	• Have protection, are willing to exchange for financial consideration		• Want guaranteed protection, particularly if protection is a competitive issue	• Want protection for as long as possible in order to reduce any future payments
Exclusivity	• Prefer not to offer exclusive license as this precludes other income from the patent		•Wants exclusive	
Utility/Advantage			• See cost advantage of not having to recreate the technology	• See cost advantage of minimizing costs by obtaining license
Commercial Success	• Unable to guarantee commercialization success unless other licensees or patent-holders have already commercialized		• Want some guarantee of commercialization success	• Already know about commercialization success, wants to minimize cost outlay
Refinement	• Probably see little refinement required		• See more need for refinement, which lowers potential profits	• Further refinements unnecessary, by definition
Competition Where Licensor & Licensee are Competitors	• Seek cross-licensing terms			
License Duration	• Minimize duration in order to be able to renegotiate periodically	•Offer license for life of patent	• Seek license for life of the patent	•Seek maximum terms - e.g. license for life of patent
Royalty Amount	• Seek maximum	•Seek standard	• For new technology seek running rate, for known technology seek one-time payment	• Seek one-time payment
Support/Train	• Offer after-sale training and support		• Seek after-sale training and support	• No training sought, to minimize cost
License Commitment	• De facto commitment to license because it is a source of strategic revenue	• Commitment to license must be requested of passive licensors	• Very interested in commitment to license	• Commitment to license not an issue
Enforcement Burden	• Already interested in enforcement	• Enforcement interest unsure; licensee may need to press for guarantees	• Does not want to have to enforce, will seek guarantees of enforcement	• Enforcement already demonstrated
Foreign vs. Domestic	•No preference		•No preference	
Crossover Sales	• Cross-over sales may be possible		• Allow crossover sales if terms are advantageous	• Minimize crossover sales to reduce costs
Advice of Expert				

Exhibit 2.2. Perspectives on Factors Affecting Licensing

have with the other. Licensors are fundamentally businesses with an intellectual asset they wish to convert into dollars through the mechanism of a license. They differ only in the amount of money they seek to obtain for the use of their intellectual property. The two kinds of licensees, on the other hand, differ from each other significantly in their views on potential licensing terms. Infringers want to minimize any cost outlay they make to a licensor. After all, they reason, every dollar we give away in a royalty payment is one less dollar of profit for us. Seekers of technology, in contrast, view licensing as an opportunity to save money. Typically, they have done their homework and know both the cost and the flowtime it would take for them to create the technology on their own. For the seekers, licensing expenditures are part of the cost of obtaining a technology. But for a licensing opportunity, seekers might have to select a more costly solution to their technology acquisition problem.

LICENSING AND BUSINESS STRATEGY

Most firms tend to think of out-licensing as a method for generating cash and in-licensing as a way of obtaining needed technology. There is much more to the technology licensing story than these simple and relatively narrow views. Licensing is a key part of the business strategy of most well-managed firms.

Many well-managed companies have well-articulated visions of what the owners expect the firm to become. The existence of such a vision makes the work of an executive easier than its absence. With a vision, one can ask whether the next business decision has any implications for the firm's ability to actualize the vision.

In the strategic sense, licensing is one of the company's activities that move it toward the realization of the vision. With this in mind, it is possible to think of a range of ways in which licensing contributes. In the case of some firms, licensing is a method for generating the cash needed for other activities that will lead the company toward its desired future. For firms in this category, cash may be generated by leasing of one or more of their *strategic* intellectual assets (patents from the firm's portfolio). Other firms in this category generate cash by licensing *non*strategic technologies from the portfolio. Another strategic use of licensing is as an anticompetitive activity—licensing may be used as a two-pronged anticompetitive effort. First, licensing a firm's technology to business competitors can be a way of harvesting cash from its markets. Second, licensing key technologies to competitors keeps them from developing their own technological capabilities. Yet another strategic use of licensing is as a way of minimizing the chance of infringement litigation. Where litigation is a concern, firms have found that using cross-licensing with technological competitors is an excellent method for minimizing the probability of an infringement lawsuit.

Licensing can have a range of strategic as well as tactical uses. The rationale for licensing has a strong bearing on the manner and kind of licenses a company may produce. Similarly, the firm's posture in licensing negotiations has much to do with the final form a license agreement will take as well as with its contents.

The positioning of out-licensing as well as in-licensing firms also influences how they approach a license negotiation. This positioning affects their perspective on key license terms and how they will be written. Finally, the wording and content of the non-dollar terms of the license have a major effect on the dollar terms. The more clearly firms understand the effect of positioning on themselves and on their negotiating partners the better they will be able to develop licenses that meet their needs.

BIBLIOGRAPHY

Cases: Patent Damages

Del Mar Avionics, Inc. v. Quinton Instrument Co., 836 F.2d 1320 (1987)

Fromson v. Western Litho Plate and Supply Co., 853 F.2d 1568 (1988)

Georgia-Pacific Corporation v. U.S. Plywood Corporation, 318 F. Supp. 1116 (1970)

Georgia-Pacific Corporation v. U.S. Plywood Champion Papers, 575 F.2d 205 (1971)

Kearns v. Ford Motor Co., 726 F. Supp. 159 (1989)

King Instrument Corp. v. Otari Corp., 767 F.2d 853 (1985)

Lindemann Mashinefabrik v. American Hoist & Derrick Co., 895 F.2d 1403 (1990)

Panduit Corp. v. Stahlin Bros. Fibre Works Inc., 575 F.2d 1152 (1978)

Polaroid Corp. v. Eastman Kodak Co.

TWM Manufacturing Co. v. Dura Corp., 107 S. Ct. 183, 789 F.2d 895 (1986)

Books:

Smith, G. and Parr, R. L. (1989). *Valuation of Intangible Assets*. New York: John Wiley & Sons, Inc.

Articles:

Andonion, Joseph K., "New Method to Determine Royalty Rates," *Les Nouvelles*, June 1991, pp. 58–59

Ansell, Ed, "Assessing the Value of Technology," *Law and Business of Licensing*, 1980, pp. 734.7–734.11

"Apple-IBM agreement networks old systems, creates new ones," *Information Access Company*, November 21, 1991, vol. 63, no. 23, p. 13

"Attention IBM PS/2 Clone Makers-Buy Patent Rights Now," *Elsevier Advanced Technology Publications*, March 1988, vol. 4, no. 1

Burke, Steven, Robert L. Scheier, Jimmy Guterman, Richard March, "IBM Intensifies the Campaign," *PC Week*, July 4, 1988, vol. 5, no. 27, p. 1

Chisum, Donald S., "Remedies for Patent Infringement," *AIPLA Quarterly Journal*, 1985, vol. 13, no. 4, p. 380, 386–89

Coale, Kristi, "EFI, Kodak agreement raises patent issues; Agreement increases validity of EFI's claim," *IDG Communications, Inc.*, February 11, 1991, p. 44

Doler, Kathleen, "MicroAge Franchisees want Lowered Royalty Schedules; Company Focuses on Large Sales Accounts," *PC Week*, Ziff-Davis Co., February 13, 1989, vol. 6, no. 6, p. 51

Enlow, Paul M., "Future Changes in Computer Licensing Practices," *The Law and Business of Licensing*, vol. 1 1980 Revision, pp. 506.109–506.112

Finnegan, Marcus B., and Herbert H. Mintz, "Determination of a Reasonable Royalty in Negotiating a License Agreement: Practical Pricing for Successful Technology Transfer," *The Law and Business of Licensing*, Clark Boardman Co, Ltd., N.Y., 1985, vol. 3, Chap. 3, pp. 3D-3–3D–28

Francis, Robert, "Clone Makers Get Warning on Patents," *Datamation*, August 1, 1988, vol. 34, no. 15, p. 28

Goldscheider, Robert, "An Economic Analysis of Royalty Terms in Patent Licenses," *Minnesota Law Review*, April 1983, vol. 67, pp. 1198–1234

Goldscheider, Robert, "Expert Witnessing: The Licensing Process and Intellectual Property Litigation," *Technology Management Handbook*, Clark Boardman Co., Ltd., N.Y., 1984, chap. 23, pp. 191–207

Harbert, Tammi, "Patent Portfolios Emerge as Corporate Money Makers," *Electronic Business Information Access*, Cahners Pub. Co., April 16, 1990, vol. 15, no. 7, p. 53

Jereski, Laura, "Patent Profit," *Forbes*, May 2, 1988, p. 104

Kessler, Edward J., and Robert W. Sacoff, "Products of the Mind," *Trial*, July 1984, vol. 20, no. 7, p. 40(5)

King, F., S. Labrum and G. Franck, "Valuing Intellectual Property," *Les Nouvelles*, December 1991, vol. XXVI, no. 4

Locke, Dennis H., "A Systematic Approach to Patent Valuation," *Idea*, 1986, vol. 27, pp. 1–5

Main, Jeremy, "Business Goes to College for a Brain Drain," *Fortune*, March 16, 1987, p. 80

Manners, David, "Korea; catching up with the best," *Electronics Weekly*, June 26, 1991, no. 1559, p. 17(2)

Marshall, Martin, "IBM Demands License Fees for RISC," *InfoWorld*, July 4, 1988, sec. news, p. 5

Matsunaga, Yoshio, "Determining Reasonable Royalty Rates," *Les Nouvelles*, December 1983, vol. 18, no. 4, pp. 216–19

Matsunaga, Yoshio, "Determining Reasonable Royalty Rates," *The Law and Business of Licensing*, Clark Boardman Co, Ltd., 1985, vol. 3, chp. 3, pp. 3D117–3D125

McGavock, Daniel; Haas, David A.; Patin, Michael P., "Licensing Practices, Business Strategy, and Factors Affecting Royalty Rates: Results of Survey," *Licensing Law and Business Report*, March–April 1991, vol. 13, no. 6

McGavock, Daniel M.; Haas, David A., "Licensing in the Real World: A Survey of Those Who Know," *Licensing Law and Business Report*, May–June 1990, vol. 13, no. 1, pp. 146–56

McGavock, Daniel; Haas, David A.; Patin, Michael P., "Factors Affecting Royalty Rates," *Les Nouvelles*, June 1992, vol. XXVII, no. 2, p. 107

Morais, Richard, "What is Perfume but Water and a Bit of Essence," *Forbes*, May 2, 1988, p. 90

Palmer, Archie M.; Behrens, Meredith W.; Davis, Albert S. Jr., "The Making and Application of Royalty Rates," *Patent Licensing*, Practicing Law Institute, 1958, pp. 56–73

Parr, Russell, "Insights into Royalty Rate Economics," *Les Nouvelles*, June 1990, vol. XXV, no. 2

Powers, N. Richard, "At the End of the Second Rainbow; Calculation of Damages in Patent Cases," *Delaware Lawyer*, March 1989, vol. 7, no. 3, pp. 18–26

Preston, John T., "The Role of the University Licensing Office in Transferring Intellectual Property to Industry," M.I.T.

Reed, Sandra R., "See you in court; Intellectual Property Lawsuits and Computer Crime View From the Valley," *Information Access Company*, Hayden Publishing Co., August, 1989, vol. 13, no. 8, p. 179

Ristelhueber, Robert, "IBM Enters OEM Market for PCs and Subsystems," *Electronic News*, June 29, 1992

Ryan, Alan J., "IBM Hikes PC Royalty Rates," *Computerworld*, April 11, 1988, p. 105

"Sharp and Standard Microsystems Sign Comprehensive Worldwide Royalty-Bearing Semiconductor Patent CR," *PR Newswire Association, Inc.*, September 6, 1989

"Standard Microsystems: Will Commence Legal Proceedings Against Texas Instruments," *PR Newswire Association*, January 19, 1990

"Technology & Licensing Agreements; Toshiba, TI in Royalty-Bearing Cross-Licensing Agreement," *HTE Research, Inc.*, December 24, 1990, vol. 90, no. 18

Teece, David J., "Profiting from Technological Innovation: Implications for Integration, Collaboration Licensing and Public Policy," Elsevier Science Publishers, June 1986

Teece, David J., "The Dynamics of Industrial Capitalism," Haas School of Business, UC Berkeley, May 1992

"The History of the invention and development of the integrated circuit at Texas Instruments," Texas Instruments 1988

Weil, Ulric, "Some vendors use litigation as a profit center," *Information Access Company*, July 20, 1992, vol. 11, no. 15, p. 27

Wilson, Sonsini, Goodrich & Rosati, *Licensing & Intellectual Property Law Bulletin*, June 1991, vol. IV, issue 2

"Unix Files Antitrust Suit Against Microsoft," *Newsbytes News Network*, November 8, 1990

Journal: Licensing Economics Review:

Parr, Russell L., AUS Inc., N.J.

"Infringement Cases," September 1991, p. 6

"Insights from the Experts," December 1991, pp. 7, 19

Notes on Kearns v. Ford, September 1990, pp. 4–5

"Reasonable Royalties: An Analysis of the Damages Award in the Kearns v. Ford Motor Company Patent Infringement Case," November 1991, p. 11–16

"Recent Licensing Transactions," November 1990, pp. 2–3

"Recent Licensing Transactions, Taiwanese Firms," February 1991, p. 3

"Recent Licensing Transactions, Japanese Firms," February 1991, p. 3

"Recent Licensing Transactions," July 1991, pp. 4–5

"Royalties," January 1992, pp. 9–10

"Royalty Rates For Proven Pharmaceuticals," March 1991, pp. 7–8

"Techniques for Comparing and Analyzing License Agreements," September 1991, pp. 14–18

3

Intellectual Property Portfolios in Business Strategy

Patrick H. Sullivan

The ICM Group

J. J. Daniele

Xerox Corporation

Companies obtain patents with at least four corporate objectives in mind: near-term competitive protection, design freedom, litigation avoidance, and the creation of a basis for establishing alliances and joint ventures. At its simplest, a patent portfolio is a collection of innovative ideas for whose use the company has been granted a legal monopoly. In most cases, individual patents protect a product or process innovation so that it may be commercialized without fear of imitation; commercialization patents are obtained to generate and protect near-term income. As companies grow and produce improved and new technologies they often build a significant portfolio of patents and other intellectual properties. Some companies use the portfolio only on a patent-by-patent basis, devising a strategy for each one. Other companies have clear uses for the entire collection, and employ *portfolio strategies* and tactics as a key part of their corporate business strategy.

In this chapter we address a number of questions: what are the different kinds of patent portfolios, and what makes them different? Are the differences focused on the content of the portfolio, its uses, or both? Are there really different portfolio strategies? Are differences in portfolio strategies really significant or are they merely differences in the degree to which some elements of a generic strategy are implemented? Is it possible to obtain more

27

or different value from a broad collection of patents than from single patents? Is a portfolio of patents (a large group of patents managed collectively) of greater value to the firm than the same set of patents managed individually or in small groups? What constitutes a "successful" portfolio? In short, we discuss the content of patent portfolios, the intent that guides their development, and the relationship between a company's patent portfolio and its business strategy.

To address these questions in a broad and practical context, we conducted more than a dozen interviews with portfolio managers in companies that have a portfolio of intellectual properties and a portfolio manager. Using the results of these interviews, we developed a model and portfolio dimensions, structure, and uses. The relationship of these elements to the underlying structure and strategic intent of the firm constitutes its portfolio strategy.

Companies that derive profits from the ideas of their employees are often referred to as *knowledge companies*. In such companies, ideas are generated, codified, and protected. Protected ideas are known by the legal term *intellectual property* (IP), and patents are a major class of intellectual property. A collection of patents, like a collection of any liquid assets, is called a portfolio. Intellectual property portfolios may be actively managed or stored and maintained for future use. Viewed from the long-term perspective, IP portfolios represent the firm's investment in ensuring the freedom to develop new designs and to do business using those designs. Portfolios of intellectual properties are the result of a very significant investment of human capital, intellectual assets, and money.

The companies we interviewed were both large and small and represented a range of industries: aerospace, biotechnology, pharmaceuticals, chemicals, business machines, systems and communications, and telecommunications. Their portfolios ranged in size from a dozen patents to several thousand. Some of the portfolios contained a small number of patents and a large number of trademarks and copyrights—we focused on the patent portion of these portfolios. The patent composition of the portfolios varied considerably— some contained patents only to protect specific products and applications for immediate use, others contained patents on technologies for potential future development and application. Some portfolios were tightly constructed around narrowly focused product strategies, others contained patents on technologies for which the company had no commercial application.

As we carried out these interviews, we sought to address a number of specific questions:

- How are the portfolios structured and why?
- How does this structure relate to the underlying corporate structure, the company's strategic intent, and the product related use?
- How is the portfolio generated, limited by budget, and maintained?
- How are the portfolios used?

THE DIMENSIONS OF THE PORTFOLIO

Portfolio managers, in considering their portfolio's content, use, relation to the business strategy, and importance within the firm, describe them in similar terms. To better understand this view, we asked the managers to describe the picture they have in their mind's eye of the company's portfolio. We have broken that description down into what we call the dimensions of the portfolio. Patent portfolios have at least five primary dimensions:

The Technologies. Technologies in the portfolio, either singly or in groups, have degrees of strength and weakness. Measures of the technological dimension are the breadth (range of technology types in the portfolio) and depth (number of patents in each technology area). A gap or gaps in a company's technology coverage may be seen as a weakness in its technological dimension. (See Exhibit 3.1.) Portfolio breadth and depth may be plotted graphically. A visual display of the portfolio's contents is an effective method for describing the technology dimension.

    Also relevant to the technology dimension are the relationship of technologies to current or future products, the degree to which technologies match the company's technology plan and strategic intent, and the degree of technological focus.

Strategic Objectives and Intent. This dimension of the portfolio involves the four primary objectives of the portfolio: competitive protection, design freedom, litigation avoidance, and the creation of a basis for establishing alliances and joint ventures. Each firm ranks these objectives in accordance with their fit with the strategy.

Strategic Use. This dimension involves the fundamental offensive, defensive, and negotiation uses of the IP portfolio as required in carrying out the firm's strategic objectives and intent.

Value. This dimension is concerned with how the portfolio brings value to the firm. A patent has at least two sources of value. The first is the degree to which the patent can exclude others. This is a measure of its strength or effectiveness. The second way a patent brings value concerns its importance in product-specific commercialization. Some patents are so central to a business opportunity that they represent a sufficient basis for creating a business. Others are less central and may require other complementary technologies as well as other business assets before they can form the basis for a business.

Income and Cost. Financial considerations cover two general areas: cost and income. For the small company any cost is significant and must be minimized. Small companies become aware at an early stage of the costs of patent generation and filing as well as the ongoing costs of patent maintenance. In larger companies for whom

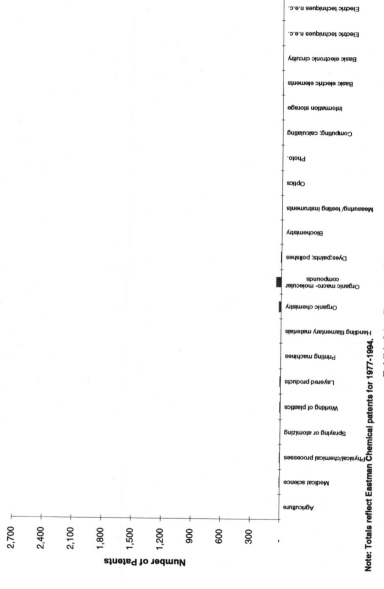

**Eastman Chemical
Corporate Patent Portfolio by Technology**

Number of Patents

2,700
2,400
2,100
1,800
1,500
1,200
900
600
300

Agriculture
Medical science
Physical/chemical processes
Spraying or atomizing
Working of plastics
Layered products
Printing machines
Handling filamentary materials
Organic chemistry
Organic macro- molecular compounds
Dyes;paints; polishes
Biochemistry
Measuring/ testing instruments
Optics
Photo.
Computing; calculating
Information storage
Basic electric elements
Basic electronic circuitry
Electric techniques n.e.c.
Electric techniques n.e.c.

Note: Totals reflect Eastman Chemical patents for 1977-1994.

Exhibit 3.1.   Example of Technology Profile

30

the patent portfolio is a significant strategic element, portfolio costs may be unknown—these costs are often bundled with the general legal costs, are not often reviewed outside of the legal context, and are not a source of financial concern. In others, the costs of creating and maintaining it are well known and are one of the portfolio manager's primary responsibilities. In virtually every company where the portfolio has strategic importance there are systems in place for monitoring and reporting costs as well as company procedures for routinely reviewing and managing costs.

For most companies in this study, income from out-licensing and from cross-licenses with royalty provisions is a secondary financial consideration. However, some of the most forward-looking companies have established out-licensing programs (and organizations) and are actively managing and increasing out-licensing income. Some companies have been able to extract a significant amount of out-licensing value from their portfolio of intellectual properties, such as Texas Instruments, IBM, and Motorola.

The portfolio dimensions are useful in discussing similarities and differences across portfolios. They provide a common language and framework for comparison. But primarily they reflect the portfolio managers' view of the important elements of the portfolio from both the planning (future) and management (current) perspectives.

FACTORS AFFECTING PORTFOLIO CONTENT AND STRUCTURE

Portfolio content, structure, and subsequently strategy are determined by a number of factors, which range across a wide spectrum from general factors such as the company's philosophical view of the function of a portfolio, to such specific uses of the portfolio as tools in negotiations. Nevertheless, for the companies studied, we have found that the following elements have an impact on the shape and use of the portfolio.

Philosophy of Portfolio Function. There are at least two widely held and different philosophical views on the function of IP portfolios, and these philosophies fundamentally shape the ways in which companies use their portfolio of patents. One view is that the portfolio's best and highest use is to protect the firm's innovations from competitive attack. Other uses of the portfolio, proponents argue, might direct energies away from the firm's main business—commercializing innovation. The contrasting view is that the portfolio is a great source of corporate value for firms willing to exploit it. Companies holding this latter view believe that the portfolio has the potential to significantly enhance the value of the firm.

Companies holding the first (largely defensive) view oppose the idea that the IP portfolio should be used for any strategic purpose other than protecting their innovations. They believe that the portfolio's use should be restricted to achieving the four primary objectives for patenting. Their over-arching goal is to exclude others from using their patented innovations. These companies are often decentralized and structured around Strategic Business Units (SBUs). Their profits are created in the near term through the sales of the products and services of the SBUs. For the most part, the business units in these firms own the technologies, deciding what is to be patented and how their patents will be used. For these companies patenting is primarily a legal and a local business issue and is often managed or coordinated by the SBUs and the firm's office of general counsel.

Companies that take a more aggressive view use their portfolios to create superior value. These companies believe that extracting value from their protected innovations is not limited to bringing a better mousetrap to market. For example, a company may decide to license its mousetrap technology to others for manufacturing and distribution because it does not have the required capabilities itself. Similarly it may enter into a joint venture with another company, set up a strategic alliance with a partner that can give it access to markets it might otherwise be unable to reach, or simply sell a technology in which it no longer has a strategic interest. Such companies take a broad view of their patent portfolios. They seek to extract value from the portfolio by treating it as a collective corporate asset rather than as a collection of individual patents. The collective weight of the portfolio can be a significant bargaining tool in business negotiations with companies that lack such a strong asset.

Companies holding this second view are generally centralized. If they are organizationally decentralized, they have centralized the ownership and management of the firm's patents. Furthermore, because these firms wish to extract superior corporate value from the portfolio, they see this as a corporate business activity. The people assigned to this activity tend to have a business orientation and call upon the legal staff for support rather than for direction. Because of the strategic business orientation of this function, the organizational locus of the value-extracting activity for companies in this category is outside of the office of general counsel.

Companies holding the narrow view of portfolio function limit their ability to extract value from their portfolios, while companies holding the broader perspective have at least an option to pursue extra value, and usually expect to extract superior value from the portfolio.

Business Strategy Focus. Companies with a broadly focused business strategy tend to have portfolios that are larger and more diverse than those of companies of equal size with a narrowly focused business strategy.

Broadly focused business strategy—Technologies are developed and patented in anticipation of some future use. The portfolio is created with an expectation that it can contribute to the creation of some future market demand. The corollary of this is that often a technology is patented in order to stake out an early claim to future design freedom. Companies with a broadly focused business strategy tend to be strategically opportunistic.

Narrowly focused business strategy—Technologies tend to be the results of targeted R&D and are often developed to meet a known or narrowly defined current (or potential) market demand. Their time horizon for commercialization typically is short. Companies in this group tend to cull their portfolios routinely to ensure that the portfolio's contents continue to be tightly arranged around the focused business strategy.

In most firms we interviewed the patent portfolio is an outgrowth of the firm's business strategy and merits the attention from senior managers that one would expect for a valued corporate asset. However, in a few firms the patent portfolio has no apparent relation to the firm's business strategy. This group of companies treats its portfolio differently.

First, portfolio management in such firms is assigned to the legal department instead of being given an operational or business function. Second, the person assigned the role as portfolio manager in these companies tends to be relatively junior and often has the position as a collateral duty. The portfolio manager in these companies has little internal status and sees the position as a maintenance activity. We also noted that the portfolio manager's role is poorly defined and he or she receives little guidance from the firm. These companies have several distinctive characteristics.

- Their strategic intent focuses on litigation avoidance, and they tend to use their portfolios defensively.
- They are unable to describe the contents of the portfolio (in terms of specific patents) and have no written patent policy.
- Although there is anecdotal information within the firm, there is little specific knowledge of the real costs of patent obtention or of maintaining the portfolio. Instead, this information is scattered across the entire spectrum of business activity.

Strategic Objectives and Intent. All companies with patent portfolios create them with an expectation of how they will be used in the near term and in future technology-based business opportunities.

Protection from Competition—The holder of a patent is granted a fundamental monopoly right that prohibits others from commercializing the patented technology without the express permission of the patent holder. The protection aspect of patents has several complementary elements:

Exclusivity—The degree to which a patent may be able to effectively exclude others from infringing on a commercial opportunity is a measure of its strength. Particularly strong foundation patents are able to exclude others from a commercial field entirely. Other patents, perhaps not quite as strong, may be able to exclude infringers from a portion of a business area and require complementary patents to extend their range of exclusion.

Blocking—Sometimes patents are designed to block a competitor from achieving its own key technology position. They are part of a strategy to build a thicket of patents around a key commercial patent in order to ensure that the commercial patent can be fully utilized. It is often possible for a company to identify improvement patents to block a competitor's technology thrust. Blocking may be strategic—a long-term denial of access in order to amortize large R&D expenses (such as in the drug and chemical industries)—or it may be tactical, a short-term bargaining chip to be used in business negotiation.

Complementary Protection—Some patents are developed with no view toward direct commercialization. They provide complementary protection for a similar innovation but are created using different materials or processes. Complementary groups of patents formed around a key patent afford it a higher degree of protection and guard against thicket formation by competitors.

Design Freedom and Litigation Avoidance—A portfolio often contains patents on future technologies, created in order to ensure that the firm has a prior claim to a specific area of technology. It signals that the firm is seriously in business in this area and can be expected to defend its intellectual property position forcefully. These prior claims are made to ensure the ability to commercialize new technologies over an extended period of time without threat of infringement.

Basis for Alliances—An alliance is any business relationship formed with another party to meet a critical business need. Such needs include market access, product line expansion, technology transfer, and manufacturing competency. As customer demands become more complex, so do the technologies and services required to create solutions that will sell in the marketplace. Since no single company is likely to have expertise in the ever-widening span of technology, putting together a winning market solution often requires putting together a partnership or an alliance.

A large and strong portfolio and the means to continue generating large numbers of quality patents is a measure of the technological and commercial strength of a technology-based firm. This can be a major advantage when seeking alliance partners who themselves are looking for a company with strengths to complement their own.

Strategic Use. While strategic intent focuses on what the firm wants to happen in the future, strategic use focuses on portfolio activity in the present. Strategic use may be thought of in terms of business opportunities, either those currently being pursued or those to be pursued in the near future. Portfolios are structured mainly for offensive and defensive strategic uses, but often are put to other uses such as establishing strong negotiating positions and enhancing the technological stature of the firm.

Offensive Use of the Portfolio—Offensive use includes both direct commercialization and tactical blocking. Direct commercialization can be achieved by clustering groups of patents together in *estates* around planned or future products, to the core competencies of the firm, or both. These estates are aimed at producing a proprietary position in specific product areas. Offensive estates can also be clusters of improvements formed in a picket fence or thicket around the foundation patents of a competitor or a potential licensor. Offensive use usually involves excluding competitors from using the technology or business application for the life of the patent. Through careful use of licensing to excluded competitors, a firm may use the portfolio offensively to gain partial access to markets not otherwise within its reach. Similarly, a firm might develop alliances to gain access to needed technologies or markets.

Defensive Use of the Portfolio—Defensive uses of the portfolio tend to require a broad array of patents covering potential future uses of technology, processes, and materials that broadly cover as-yet-undefined products. In addition to ensuring exclusive use of a technology, defensive use of the portfolio usually means ensuring design freedom for the future. Successful defensive use also avoids litigation resulting from cross-licensing and other related strategic moves.

Negotiation—Another factor in determining the content of a patent portfolio is the firm's interest in using the portfolio as a bargaining tool. For the most part, firms interested in using the portfolio in negotiations have developed it in one of two ways. A portfolio may contain a set of patents focused around a specific technology or business area. Firms negotiating a cross-licensing agreement or a business arrangement can be aided by the mere existence of a highly focused portfolio with strengths in the area of interest of both firms in the negotiation. Alternatively, the creation of a large brood portfolio including both existing and potential technologies can itself be intimidating to a negotiating firm.

Frequently one firm or the other wishes to obtain low-cost access to a specific technology, and the negotiation is around the field(s) in which the technology is to be licensed. When low-cost access is desired, cross-licensing is often the mechanism that is used. The firm with the greatest strength at the table usually gets to decide the field exclusions and compromises that become a part of the final agreement.

In some cases the existence of a powerful portfolio and the means and will to regenerate it precludes the need for any negotiating at all. For example, a firm may find that its patents are being infringed by the technology of another firm. If neither firm wants to initiate litigation and both firms hold powerful portfolios, they may engage in a standoff—neither will take action lest the other might reciprocate. Both may agree, without conducting formal discussions, not to litigate as long as the potential infringement remains within some reasonable limits. These standoffs are possible only when each side has a powerful enough portfolio to be a significant threat to the other.

Enhancing the Technological Image of the Firm—A large and strong portfolio and the means and will to continue to generate large numbers of quality patents is a measure and indication of the technological and commercial stature of the firm. This is a factor in seeking joint venture partners, and in the silent effect a strong portfolio (and the ability to continuously regenerate it) has on potentially infringing competition.

Patent-Generating Policies and Procedures.   Most firms that use their patent portfolios to extract value for the firm have formal patenting policies. In well-managed firms the patenting policy complements the overall business strategy. Since each patent can have direct legal and maintenance costs in the tens of thousands of dollars, and can have value in the millions, especially when it is filed globally, the patent decision is an important one.

Most of the companies we surveyed have committees that review new invention proposals to determine whether to invest in obtaining a patent. These committees are either centralized or decentralized, and can be either standing or ad hoc. They generally consist of a patent attorney and technical and product development employees of the firm. They are usually chaired by a senior administrator or technical person. In most cases, the committees base their patent decisions on a combination of technical, business, and legal merits.

Companies that rely on a small number of significant technologies may have a policy of patenting only exceptional discoveries. Other firms seeking to stake out design freedom for a range of potentially significant technologies might have a broader patenting policy that encourages the patenting of any technology with a reasonable chance of technical and commercial success. Individual company patent policies span a wide range. A company may decide to:

- Patent discoveries that have a clear and immediate application to the firm's products or processes.
- Patent most things that have a chance of technical and commercial success.
- Patent discoveries that have a strong chance of technical and commercial success whether exploited by the firm or by a potential licensee.
- Develop groups of patents around key product or competency areas to establish future proprietary positions.
- Patent in a thicket around key patents held by competitors.
- Patent discoveries that might block use of similar discoveries in competitors' products.
- Patent in order to have a portfolio with which to negotiate licensing agreements with other companies.
- Patent only the occasional discovery of exceptional business and technical importance.
- Patent nothing.
- Publish most of what it chooses not to patent to ensure design freedom.

Company Size. Company size has implications for a company's need to build assets or to harvest them. Small firms are usually interested in building a core set of intellectual assets, not only for current commercialization but also for near future uses. Future uses include commercialization, business negotiations, cross-licensing, and increasing the value of the firm's portfolio and proprietary competitive position with an eye toward a potential initial public offering (IPO), a merger, or acquisition of the firm.

Large and mature firms often use their intellectual assets more fully than new and small firms. The large firms, perhaps because of the wider range of business activities their larger size allows and requires, are interested in asset utilization in addition to asset building. Asset utilization usually includes the direct commercialization of some technologies in the portfolio, using some patents for blocking competitive activity, building an estate of protection patents around one or more strategically critical patents in the portfolio, using the patent portfolio in licensing negotiations or to establish a bargaining position in business arrangements.

Budget. Some firms determine in advance how much to invest in portfolio development, and that budget drives decisions about additions or deletions to the portfolio. Thus the portfolio's contribution to the business strategy is strictly limited by the constraints of the budget. Companies in this position must be aware of all of the life-of-the-patent costs associated with patent generation, filing, and maintenance, both in the U.S. and in the countries of competitive interest to the firm and its licensees.

FOUR REPRESENTATIVE PORTFOLIOS

A company's use of its patent portfolio depends on its business strategy, the degree to which the portfolio is an element of achieving the goals outlined in the strategy, and who owns and manages the portfolio within the firm. Four of the major companies we interviewed have representative portfolio structures and management approaches.

Hewlett-Packard and Eastman Chemical, while in different industries, are both managed on an SBU basis, and their portfolio ownership, structure, and uses reflect the relatively short-term specific product focus that results. In contrast, Xerox and Merck, also in different industries, have portfolios that are centrally owned and managed and take a broader, long-term approach to portfolio management. Accordingly, their portfolios are larger and broader and support a wider variety of long-term defensive as well as near-term product-related offensive uses. The following are four examples of company portfolio and portfolio strategies:

Hewlett-Packard is a technology-based company that specializes in producing technological solutions to customer problems. HP designs and manufactures computers, medical instruments, information systems, and printers. Its portfolio of patents reflects several unique aspects of the corporation, which, in turn reflect the company's basic strategy:

Business Strategy—The firm strives to develop new products that focus on the solutions to the problems of current customers in the near term. HP takes pride in the fact that 70 percent of its annual profits are generated from products less than two years old.

Portfolio Ownership and Management—The technologies in the portfolio are developed in HP's SBUs with some central research contributions.

Hewlett Packard
Corporate Patent Portfolio by Technology

Number of Patents

Exhibit 3.2. Profile of the Hewlett-Packard Portfolio

Technology and Portfolio Focus—The portfolio is narrowly focused around near-term products and product lines in predetermined business areas. It is based on SBU-funded research, and its future-oriented technologies are provided from central research.

Technology and Portfolio Profile—HP has approximately 3,000 U.S. patents covering a range of technology areas, including electronics, computer systems, instruments, and electronic printing. It was issued 429 U.S. patents in 1994 with more than one-fifth of them (88) in patent class 395: Information Processing System Organization.

Portfolio Uses—Hewlett-Packard uses its portfolio defensively as well as offensively. Defensively, the portfolio provides protection for the company's commercializable technologies and ensures the exclusivity of its patent monopoly; HP research into future technologies produces a series of "design freedom" patents intended to ensure HP's freedom to develop and sell products in these areas and the weight of the HP portfolio minimizes the risk of litigation against valid infringing patents of others. Offensively, HP uses its portfolio to ensure protection and exclusivity in each new technology-based business area it enters; it uses the portfolio to attract potential alliances where the company wishes to obtain access to outside technologies and to do so at a low cost.

Xerox is a technology-based company that sees itself as defining the document market through the development of technologies that will generate demand for new document creation and management. Xerox's portfolio of patents reflects this unique vision.

Business Strategy—The firm strives to exploit current technologies in the marketplace and to develop new technologies that will create future demand for applications in the document business.

Portfolio Ownership and Management—The technologies in the portfolio are developed in Xerox's central research facilities and are considered to be corporate assets. The corporate strategic intent and direction is the final consideration in discussions about the use and disposition of Xerox patents.

Technology and Portfolio Focus—Using an internal procedure and a long term technology road map keyed to corporate strategic intent for identifying interesting and potentially valuable applications and technologies, Xerox targets research on technologies that it believes will create future demand. These technologies, once developed, are patented and become part of the portfolio.

Technology Profile—Xerox has approximately 6,000 U.S. patents covering a wide range of technologies including electronics and computer systems, graphic user interfaces, chemistry, and mechanical and

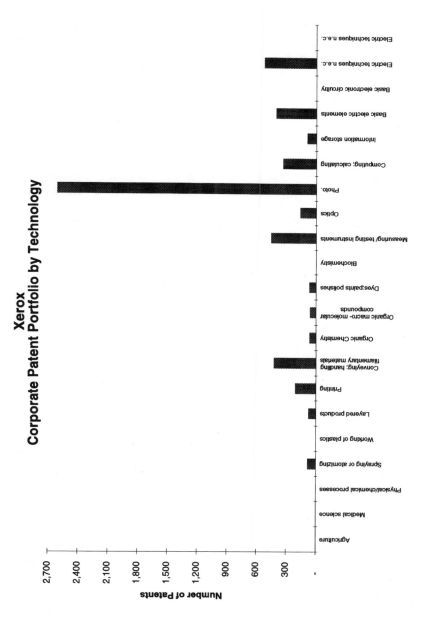

Exhibit 3.3. Profile of the Xerox Portfolio

electrical control systems. Xerox and its Japanese venture Fuji Xerox were issued 774 U.S. patents 1994 (613 for Xerox and 161 for Fuji Xerox); these patents were distributed across 70 U.S. patent department classes. Nearly half, or 300 patents, were in the two patent classes 355 and 430: Photocopying (where Xerox had the highest number worldwide) and Radiation Imagery Chemistry (where Xerox was third following Fuji Photo and Eastman Kodak).

Portfolio Uses—Xerox uses its portfolio defensively as well as offensively. Defensively, the portfolio protects the company's current and future commercializable technologies; future technology patents ensure Xerox's freedom to conduct commercialization in selected area of interest, and its breadth and depth of coverage of current technologies minimizes the risk of litigation by others and provides a basis for a wide range of alliances and business arrangements. Offensively, Xerox uses its portfolio to ensure protection and exclusivity in each new technology-based business area it enters. Xerox also actively out-licenses its byproducts and its primary technologies for by-product uses.

Merck & Co. is a $15 billion science-driven pharmaceutical company that has a presence in every major category of disease therapeutics ranging from cardiovascular to diabetics and bone biology. Its portfolio reflects the nature of the pharmaceutical business and the major R&D expenditures required across a broad array of research areas. Less than one in a thousand chemical or biological discoveries results in a product.

Business Strategy—Merck's strategy is to develop highly proprietary pharmaceutical solutions in major disease areas using both internal R&D and licensing-in as needed to create patent estates around a few key discoveries. Merck then enlarges and enhances these estates as a product launch becomes more and more likely, to ensure as many years as possible of proprietary product line and sufficiently broad patent coverage to delay duplication and substitution by competitors.

Portfolio Ownership and Management—Portfolio generation and ownership is corporate-based and directed by a long-term technology road map that broadly covers every major disease category. The company takes a long-term view and its R&D is directed by strategic intent. The focus is on development of future product lines—patents are developed around product estates, which grow larger and more powerful as the product line develops and the probability of a product launch increases. General background R&D and patenting are done in genetic materials and processes to ensure basic design freedom for future products.

Exhibit 3.4. Profile of the Merck Portfolio

Patent attorneys and project teams direct and manage the development of these estates.

Technology and Portfolio Focus—Merck focuses on long-term product development and on creating a few winning products with patent estates strong and broad enough to ensure at least a few years of proprietary protection. Active licensing-in is a major part of portfolio generation, and about 20 percent of the portfolio is licensed-in from universities and other sources. This technology search and screening and the formation of joint ventures are important management functions.

Technology and Portfolio Profile—Merck has several thousand patents generally formed into product estates with a broad background of patents in genetic materials and processes to ensure design freedom. Merck & Co. was issued 164 U.S. patents in 1994 in 20 patent classes with half (82) in class 514: Drug, Bio—Affecting Body Treating Compositions. In this class they were issued more U.S. patents than any other company in the world.

Portfolio Uses—Merck uses its portfolio mainly to ensure a few years of proprietary market position on its mainline products to enable sufficient margin and the return on the long-term R & D required in this business. The portfolio also ensures design freedom and is the basis for establishing joint ventures and conducting license negotiations.

Eastman Chemical is a $4.3 billion dollar company specializing in performance and industrial chemicals. Its products range from performance plastics and coatings to filter products and fibers.

Business Strategy—Eastman Chemical's strategy is to generate new technology with real commercial benefit and to build a patent portfolio of compositions, uses, and processes to support it. The company's technology is based on core competencies, including polyester, industrial intermediates, and cellulose chemistry. Its portfolio is generated and clustered in these areas.

Portfolio Ownership and Management—While the technologies are developed in Central Research, the contents of the patent portfolio are owned and managed by the Strategic Business Units. The SBUs pay all patent filing and maintenance costs and make all filing decisions through fifteen intellectual property teams. Each IP team consists of representatives from the SBUs and the Research and Legal Departments, and each is headed by a senior technology manager reporting to an SBU president. These teams decide what will be patented and where, which SBU will pay for and own the patent, and what will be done with it. Patents are generally exclusively

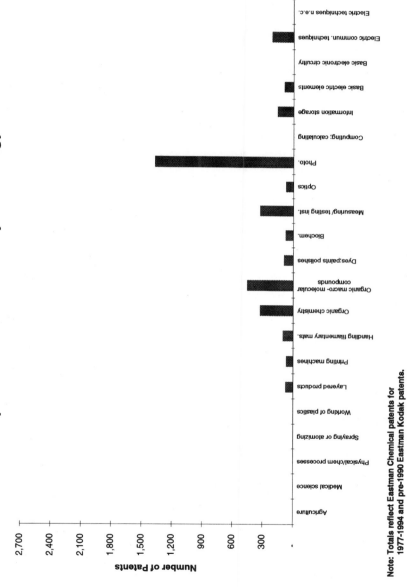

Eastman Kodak
Corporate Patent Portfolio by Technology

Number of Patents

2,700 | 2,400 | 2,100 | 1,800 | 1,500 | 1,200 | 900 | 600 | 300

Electric techniques n.e.c.
Electric commun. techniques
Basic electronic circuitry
Basic electric elements
Information storage
Computing; calculating
Photo.
Optics
Measuring/ testing inst.
Biochem.
Dyes;paints polishes
Organic macro- molecular compounds
Organic chemistry
Handling filamentary mats.
Printing machines
Layered products
Working of plastics
Spraying or atomizing
Physical/chem processes
Medical science
Agriculture

Note: Totals reflect Eastman Chemical patents for
1977-1994 and pre-1990 Eastman Kodak patents.

Exhibit 3.5. Profile of the Eastman Chemical Portfolio

owned and controlled by a specific SBU but joint ownership can be negotiated up-front. Any income from the patent goes back to the SBU holding it.

Technology and Portfolio Focus—Technology is focused in the core competencies of the firm and the portfolio is structured accordingly. As products are developed, patent estates are formed around them and patent costs are taxed back to the product manager.

Technology and Portfolio Profile—Eastman Chemical has a portfolio of approximately 1,300 U.S. patents and was issued 64 patents in 1994. Approximately half of these patents (31) were in three patent classes. The portfolio is focused around the company's core competencies with specific patent estates centered on current product lines. There is some background technology in manufacturing process improvements to provide a basis for design freedom.

Portfolio Uses—Eastman Chemical uses its portfolio both offensively and definitively. It uses the portfolio defensively to obtain freedom to practice in its product areas, to establish a basis for cross-licenses, and to settle and avoid litigation. It makes offensive use of its patent estates to establish proprietary positions in specialty products, preserve market share, and enhance and maintain margins. The company uses its overall portfolio to support technology transfer through out-licensing, joint ventures, and licensing of international subsidiaries. And finally, it looks to its portfolio to enhance the technological stature of the firm in specific commercial sectors and with potential partners.

The foregoing examples, summarized in Exhibit 3.6, show a range of similarities and differences. The companies profiled have distinctly different business strategies. Both the Hewlett-Packard and Eastman Chemical strategies focus on the products of specific business units, whereas the Xerox and Merck strategies are based on products that arise out of the firm's core competencies. Accordingly, their portfolio ownership and management strategies also differ. Both Xerox and Merck have a strong corporate ownership and management of the portfolio; Hewlett-Packard has strong SBU ownership but corporate management, while Eastman Chemical has strong SBU ownership that shares portfolio management with their corporate function. As a result of these corporate structural differences, the technology and portfolio focuses are different. The technology focus of Hewlett-Packard and Eastman Chemical is on technologies and products for near-term use in the marketplace. Xerox and Merck focus on developing technologies and applications that will define future products and markets. The differences in the technology profiles of the companies are in both the breadth and the depth of patents in areas of technological strength.

Exhibit 3.6.   Contrasts and Similarities Between the Two Dominant Portfolio Management Structures and Approaches

Company Interviewed	Portfolio Focus and Objectives	Portfolio Ownership and Management	Structure of Portfolio
Eastman Chemical	Used defensively and offensively	SBU-based with some central research contribution, but in transition	Structured around product lines: some background patents provided by central R&D
Hewlett-Packard	Used defensively, offensively, and in negotiations research	Primarily SBU-based with some central contribution	Structured primarily around near-term products: some background/future patents provided by central research
Merck	Used offensively, defensively, in based technology, and in negotiations	Corporate research	Structured around long-term product estates, some background patents in basic processes. A significant fraction of the portfolio is licensed-in
Xerox	Used defensively, offensively, in based technology, and in negotiations	Corporate research	A very large, broad portfolio structured around the technical competencies of the firm. Generation is based on the strategic intent of the firm and a resulting technology road map.

The similarities of the companies are as revealing as the differences. Most important, the companies have similar philosophical views of the function of the portfolio. All four companies believe the portfolio can create value for the corporation through more than just the protection it offers for the patented technologies. Like all holders of patent portfolios all four companies use their portfolios defensively. In addition, all four act offensively by actively seeking out methods for extracting additional value from the portfolio through cross-licensing, joint ventures, and alliances in new business areas.

SUMMARY AND CONCLUSIONS

In this exploration of IP portfolios and portfolio strategies, we established that a company's long-term goals and strategy are the major determinants of portfolio content, structure, strategy, and success. We have shown that portfolios have dimensions portfolio managers themselves use in talking about their portfolios. The dimensions are technology, strategic objectives and intent, strategic use, value, and income/cost. Although we do not attempt to develop a set of measurement tools to further refine the concept of dimensionality, the authors believe this is possible to accomplish and that such tools could be useful for portfolio managers.

Differences in portfolio content are attributable to the company's perspective on portfolio function, technology focus, strategic objectives and intent, strategic use, and breadth of business strategy focus. Portfolio strategies also differ from company to another, largely for the same reasons that define the differences in content.

We know that some companies are able to extract more value from their IP portfolios than others. Perhaps the most important element in extracting value from a portfolio is the company's own perspective on portfolio function. Companies with a narrow view, that see the portfolio as a defensive tool, limit their ability to extract the most value. Companies with a broader view provide themselves with an opportunity to extract superior value. In addition, value is affected by the full dimensionality of the portfolio, including technology content and structure, as well as by the firm's business strategy. Finally, alignment of the portfolio strategic intent and use with the firm's business strategy is the most important element in determining how a company develops and uses its portfolio.

Success for a portfolio should now be definable. Firms should be able to define success for their portfolios in terms of company long-term goals and business strategy. A successful patent portfolio is one that helps its company achieve its strategic goals. Companies with well-articulated goals and well-executed strategies should be able to predict with some accuracy how much an IP portfolio will contribute to achieving those goals. For most firms this is the starting point for building a successful portfolio and portfolio strategy.

BIBLIOGRAPHY

Ashton, W. B. and R. K. Sen. "Using Patent Information in Technology Business Planning—I," *Research—Technology Management*, Nov.–Dec. 1988, pp. 42–46.

Ashton, W. B. and R. K. Sen. "Using Patent Information in Technology Business Planning—II," *Research—Technology Management*, Jan.–Feb. 1989, pp. 31–41.

Berkowitz, L. "Getting the Most from Your Patents." *Research—Technology Management*, March–April 1993, pp. 26–31.

de Pury, "'Innovate or Die' is the First Rule of International Industrial Competition." *Research Technology Management*, Sept.–Oct. 1994, pp. 9–12.

Hamel, G. and C. K. Prahalad. "Strategic Intent." *Harvard Business Review*, May–June 1989, pp. 67–78.

IFI/Plenum Data Corporation, *Patent Intelligence and Technology Report 1994*.

Prahalad, C. K., and G. Hamel. "The Core Competence of the Corporation." *Harvard Business Review*, May–June 1990, pp. 79–91.

4

TQM for IPM™: Applying the TQM Model to Intellectual Property Management

Edward Kahn

EKMS, Inc.

In spite of the current buzz in the business press about the recognized value of intellectual property, it's not easy to see how improvements to an organization's intellectual property management practices benefit the bottom line. Do such improvements generate revenue? Maybe, at distant point in the future. Will they enable the company to save money? Not necessarily.

Nonetheless, organizations that examine their intellectual property practices honestly and manage to place them at the heart of the corporation will prosper. And one touchstone of this belief is the lessons we have learned from the movement toward quality. The current struggle to get a handle on intellectual property management closely resembles the efforts of a previous generation to control and direct the corporation using quality management as a guiding principle.

Whether systematically or not, in every enterprise, ideas and their associated intellectual property (IP) are acquired, traded, and developed. As ideas evolve, the know-how and skills that grow up along with them also undergo an evolution; eventually ideas and IP play a role in the process of commercialization. If a product or service is successful, the IP associated with it can be said to generate a return via sales, either directly or by means of a licensee.

The set of capabilities we'll call "IP management" center around the organization's ability to recognize and plan a business around a new idea.

Superb management of intellectual property is associated with continuous innovation and desirable outcomes such as increased market share and faster product development. For manufacturing companies, the holy grail of excellent intellectual property management (IPM) is the chance to create an entirely new category and market for a truly innovative product, as Sony did with the personal music system. For all companies, however, IP management aims to spur innovation and growth.

MANAGING INTELLECTUAL PROPERTY: BETWEEN HYPE AND REALITY

Of Drumbeats and Bandwagons

Michael Odza, publisher of Technology Access, a newsletter that tracks licensing and collaborative ventures, reports that technology transfer activities have sharply increased in the past five years. The number of licenses issued to universities is up, and the annual survey by the Association of University Technology Managers (AUTM) reported that royalty income from licenses granted to industry topped $242 million in fiscal 1993. Cooperative research and development agreements (CRADAs) have significantly increased the number of collaborative projects between federal agencies and commercial companies and raised the visibility of these efforts. Company-to-company activity, although harder to track, has unquestionably heated up.

In the ten years we've been in business as a consultancy specializing in technology transfer, we've seen an enormous change in the vocabulary and consciousness of business leaders and the press. Business, universities, government agencies, hospitals, nonprofits—all are looking for new ways to develop and use their IP. A front-page story by Thomas A. Stewart in *Fortune* last year trumpeted intellectual capital as a company's most valuable asset. Joint ventures, out- and in-licensing arrangements, collaborative efforts, virtual corporation arrangements, and all kinds of fluid partnering agreements are now established ways that business entities interact with one another. This is evidence that the boundaries between organizations have grown more porous. Meanwhile, the traditional relationships that businesses have always engaged in, sometimes for centuries—the roles described with such words as vendor, supplier, client, customer, and contractor—have also been altered by an understanding that a more explicit or deeper exchange of IP within the customary transfer of products and services can enrich the transaction and add value to it.

We are at the point in the Information Revolution when an organization's intangible assets—whether embodied in software, know-how, or within the brains of company employees—are understood to be worth a lot, as witness the $3.5 billion IBM paid recently for Lotus Development Corporation. It's no longer far-out thinking to believe that knowledge and information are at the heart of how companies operate, communicate, ensure customer satisfaction, and improve the quality of their goods. The management theorist Ikujiro Nonaka has identified lasting competitive advantages for knowledge-creating companies. A crude measure of the value placed on intellectual assets is the spending on systems to process and manipulate information, which has topped $1 trillion dollars in the United States according to the U.S. Department of Commerce. Such expenditures reflect the historic shift away from traditional equipment resources and raw materials and towards intangible sources of value, especially information transformed by company efforts into knowledge.

But the billions poured into information systems have not directly boosted the bottom line, according to Erik Brynjolfsson, professor at MIT's Sloan School, and others who study the payoff from technology. And the returns from good IP management are similarly hard to pin down. While the press is full of reports of collaborative relationships, consortia, joint ventures, and so on—entities formed to leverage the value of IP—these arrangements have seldom resulted in money being made overnight. Indeed, the reports about tech transfer frequently have dwelt on such flawed efforts as the Microelectronics & Computer Technology Corporation (MCC), which spent years and millions of dollars pooled from some of the ablest players in the electronics and semiconductor industries without producing a major product hit. And the success of biotech companies like Biogen and Amgen, which hit home runs by building on discoveries made in university settings, may be so unique that they will never be replicated.

Indeed, while the market value of a company's intellectual assets is momentarily clear when a knowledge-based company like Lotus changes hands, the challenge for most companies is not in accounting for intellectual assets but in deploying the assets appropriately to fuel product development and business growth. That's because the failure rate for new technology—no matter its origin—is so high that it will be years before we know if the methods evolving now are working better than the more traditional processes.

Seeking a Balance

A shift in thinking about IP has taken hold, but companies are struggling to strike a balance in their practices—between ignoring (and perhaps squandering!) intellectual assets on the one hand, and rendering intellectual assets useless (sterile) by hoarding them in a miserly way.

In Europe and Asia, companies are prepared to pay the extraordinarily high cost of maintaining all their patents—seemingly for life. A lot of sweat goes into carefully tracking such payments. But, surprisingly, almost no energy is devoted to recycling IP via licensing or containing costs by pruning worthless patents.

At U.S.-based companies, until the mid-1980s licensing activity was largely confined to cross-licensing between large competitors to prevent infringement suits and to the licensing of foreign affiliated entities. As *de novo* licensing activities (both out- and in-) intensified into the mid-1990s, driven by increasingly rapid product cycles and down-sizing in R&D, we have witnessed several philosophical swings.

A corporation, driven by the example of Texas Instruments or Honeywell infringement successes, will sometimes think like this: "We have so many unused patents, surely there is money to be made there. Let's hire an out-licensing staff of six." Two years later, disappointed by short-term results, the pendulum will swing back to one of two more traditional positions—the first, the classic "crown jewels" approach, is marked by a belief that *no* company technology should belong to anyone else under any circumstances. The second attitude was expressed to us by a patent counsel at a very large computer maker who explained that a patent would be dropped automatically unless it defended a company product or was out-licensed by three years from issuance. Several companies we know of have undergone mood swings—from treating all their technology as crown jewels to hastily establishing a licensing function in-house, dissolving such an office, outsourcing licensing functions to broker-consultants, and going back to dropping patents fairly thoughtlessly or regarding technology once again as crown jewels.

Should declining margins be accepted as inevitable signs of a mature commodity business? Companies resign themselves to this outlook at their peril. Instead, they must recognize the impact innovative technology can have on product mix and on higher margin and share. They can intensify their efforts to leverage IP. Companies thus motivated will find that there is a power in communicating through the full loop, from customer to sales to marketing to manufacturing to patent office to R&D.

WHAT WE CAN LEARN FROM THE TQM MODEL

TQM Defined

Our thesis is that the movement to elevate intellectual property will turn out to be as unpredictable and far-reaching in its effects as the movement toward quality was in the manufacturing sector. The link between intellectual property management and corporate well-being is still tenuous because companies have not yet entirely organized themselves around the value of intellectual property. However, in the beginning of the Quality Movement, too, it was difficult to be certain where to apply the interventions where they would do the most good.

Total quality management, or TQM, is defined by F. D. (Derm) Barrett of York University as a mode of management formulated for the purpose of achieving excellence through constant improvement. The TQM movement focuses on what the customer wants when he or she buys a service or product. Quality is defined by the customer, not by the company. The word total is important too; it denotes that the company/organization is striving toward quality in every aspect of its business. Further, quality is understood to add value. All processes are aimed at preventing errors and defects before they occur and doing it right the first time.

Quality management rewards risk-taking, enterprise, and innovation. It flourishes best in an environment of permanent change, implying a dynamic corporate culture characterized by ceaseless learning. In an organization where quality management is taken seriously, employees are empowered to make many decisions without consulting their supervisors. Teamwork is stressed because process improvements must cross departmental boundaries. This is a change from the standard practice about a generation ago, when quality was not widely understood to be a critical business goal. Compared to the cost of labor and raw materials, quality seemed like a soft concern. Sensible commercial companies aimed for the minimum acceptable standard of quality, since quality was assumed to mean raised costs and/or lower margins.

But wait. Some companies, led by the Japanese automotive giants, turned this paradigm on its head and saw a way to drive down costs—and slash product development time—by improving the processes that ensured quality.

Whose Job is IPM?

Through the early 1970s and early 1980s, it was far from obvious that something so humble as making car doors close without gaps was related to industry survival. And further, American companies attempting to eliminate defects were wedded to a traditional reliance on inspection–rejection–waste. Honda and Toyota steadily gained customer loyalty by offering products with fewer defects. Combining higher quality and lower costs proved to be an irresistible formula in several industries and American manufacturers surrendered market share. But finally, in Detroit and throughout the land, it was understood that the best way to get doors to close with no gaps was not by inspecting–rejecting the doors that didn't close properly but by revamping upstream processes to prevent defects. Slowly and painfully, quality became everyone's job.

Companies that succeed in making IPM everyone's job will enjoy similar benefits. IP management can't be confined to the patent lawyers, licensing office, R&D, corporate planners, or any single corporate department. Later in this chapter we will discuss some ideal IPM practices. For now, let us just register the thought that requiring patent lawyers to file claims more broadly does not qualify as a holistic IPM change. Applying better practices way downstream in the patent office may be compared to an industrial com-

pany striving to raise product quality by sorting and rejecting defects efficiently. It's not TQM for IPM! Rather, responsibility for and understanding
of IP has to become a basic biological condition of being that permeates the
corporation. Firms that elevate the importance of IP activity companywide
are taking the critical first step in embracing IPM.

TQM for IPM Goes Beyond Patent Management

There are companies today searching for a quick, easy way to generate a return from intellectual property management. Deriving value from infringers
is sound policy. As companies are inspired by the success of Texas Instruments, which has reaped considerable rewards from its integrated circuit
patent portfolio, it's tempting to lodge the responsibility for IPM with the
patent department. But unless a company knows it is sitting on top of a gold
field—and how many companies are there like TI that own pioneering
patents that served as the foundation for a major new industry?—it's magi-
cal thinking to believe you're doing IPM when you are essentially com-
mencing a search for nuggets buried in the backyard.

Companies must develop a greater awareness of their technology assets
and deficits. Awareness and communication are precursors to the recognition
of even more critical early identification of technology weaknesses, trigger-
ing plans to acquire outside technology via in-licensing. Such awareness is
also a necessary precondition to improving and exploiting prodictized IP assets via internal product line extension, secondary field of use license, first
time license, intrapreneurial new product launches, spin-off companies, or
joint ventures.

Companies should certainly use a rational process to decide which inventions to acquire and/or patent. They should sort the weeds from the desirable plants in their patent garden by looking at the company's overall
business strategy. This will not only reduce patent maintenance fees and enable them to discover unexpected opportunities, but it may also enhance
their long term technological (and thus, marketplace) competitiveness.

Companies must also create an integrated methodology for managing innovation that goes well beyond patent management. Tools and methods that
succeed in bringing the right technology to market in a timely way will differentiate companies that prosper from those that fail. To be effective, such
activities must occupy the entire corporation and add value to IP at every
point in the chain.

A paradigm shift in IPM will be several orders of magnitude more challenging—and rewarding—than simply stepping up infringement policing.
Companies like General Electric, which have been working to tie R&D
closely with business units, are on the right track. Developing a robust method
for originating new products is more important than worrying about how to
sell the technology rejects and patent detritus. Indeed, a deep company-wide

commitment to change on the IPM front may be seen as part of the battle for global competitiveness.

WHY ORGANIZATIONS ARE EXAMINING THEIR PRACTICES NOW

Rocks and shoals are invisible when they are covered by water. If the water were to evaporate over time, or suddenly disappear, the rocks would emerge and your craft would run aground. The practical disconnects in regard to intellectual property are appearing now, just at the moment when people are starting to take IPM seriously, because the factors that tended to conceal the rocks—protected markets, comfortable margins, generous R&D funding— are gone. Customers demand high quality. Low cost production, often made possible by low paid overseas labor, is driving even high-end businesses. New product cycles are now so rapid that companies seldom enjoy a lengthy phase when they can sit alone on top of a market.

With mature products generating ever-diminishing returns, companies are searching for a process able to perpetuate new, unique value-added products by means of continuous innovation. In sum, the competitive pressures on companies today are so intense that even quite risk-averse organizations are willing to look at cheaper or surer ways to develop and market products.

Large pharmaceutical companies have all come around to taking equity positions in small biotech start-ups and/or licensing technology from smaller players because the risk and expense of in-house R&D is simply crushing. Universities and small start-ups offer a product pipeline. In some industries, it's routine for companies to interact in complex ways. In the computer industry, for example, it's not unusual to be simultaneously a vendor, customer, licensee, licensor, OEM, and competitor. For example, Canon licenses its bubble jet technology to Hewlett Packard and Digital, but also competes against these players in some other segments of the computer printer market. We're encouraged by such shifting roles because ideas travel readily across permeable borders, opening up possibilities for the optimal application of IP.

The traditional reluctance to adopt technology "not invented here" has abated in many (although not all) industries. Corporations typically begin to intensify out-licensing and in-licensing as they grow to understand the limits on even the best internal R&D—the slogan "anything invented anywhere" replacing "not invented here!" The trend toward farming out R, and even D, continues, although the infrastructure and standards that would support entirely virtual R&D are not yet in evidence. But it has never been more important to thoroughly understand a company's core mission. Companies are crafting their R&D strategy to reflect that mission. And while a company must stick close to its core knitting, there is a corollary to this principle: a company must also have an intelligent process for spinning off functions that don't further long-term company goals. The irony for those companies trying to sort through their technology priorities is that as product life gets shorter, the likelihood of licensing leftovers goes down too!

IDEAL INTELLECTUAL PROPERTY MANAGEMENT

What Does The Promised Land Look Like?

Is there a proper way to "do" IPM? Except for quite general principles, we do not believe that a one-size-fits-all approach will be helpful to most organizations. But while we're not there yet, let us now gaze into the promised land and offer our observations.

It will come as no surprise, for example, that a corporate culture that encourages creative thinking, cross-functional communication, and teamwork will be more successful at IPM. Further, we have observed in our own practice with companies both large and small that companies open to new ideas, no matter their origin—companies prepared to trade, sell, and buy technology assets from others and to others as needed in a fluid way—are in a better position to take advantage of the changing weather and circumstances in their IP gardens.

It has become clear that the *process* by which internal technologies are identified, cleared for approval, and marketed for out-licensing reveals a lot about—and may even influence—IPM practices in the wider corporate arena. Successful out-licensing intrapreneurs in the corporation can inspire IPM changes in other arenas, but they need help and support. Long before a technology asset arrives at the corporate patent office, product developers, marketing staff, and others should be thinking in terms of how to use ideas to generate new revenues.

For example, at Grumman Corporation (now Northrop–Grumman), Charles Pieroth, head of licensing from 1991 to 1994, made an early decision to pursue only projects that had the support of the business units responsible for the innovation. He spent much of his time exhorting Grumman researchers working on narrow, defense-related products to think about where their technology could have additional, noncompeting uses. Bennet X-Ray, a Long Island maker of mammography equipment, is paying royalties to Grumman for use of an algorithm (developed under the U.S. Space Surveillance Program) to enhance its medical images. In another licensing deal—a deal that came about because Grumman's small commercial aircraft business recognized that its researchers had a solution that would satisfy a design constraint in Boeing's 777 program—Boeing licensed from Grumman a method of assembling control rods for an aircraft's flap control systems.

Licensing these and other undeveloped technologies generated profits from Grumman's licensing department after just two years.

At another Fortune 250 manufacturer, the licensing office looked first for releases and approvals to out-license secondary applications of core technology. Important chemical processes, materials, and electronics that could be utilized in non-competing fields, were readily approved for significant licensing efforts. The technical scale-up and patent protection efforts were robust, since business and R&D managers understood that the technologies were important to company products as well as to outside licensees.

On the other hand, when a technology is fragmentary and not in some way part of an active business unit effort, deal-making becomes unlikely. Our company was once asked to find a licensee for an orphan technology for a Fortune 500 industrial company. There were prototypes built, samples readily available, and good patents filed. Moreover, the inventor of the device was still employed by the company and early market data had been developed that suggested that there was licensing potential, although insufficient to make the product launch. We found one prospective licensee who willingly signed secrecy agreements and studied the opportunity. Shortly after this party declined to license, support for our effort ended. The R&D manager who had identified this out-licensing opportunity was—correctly— preoccupied with the next reduction-to-practice of a company winner. The patent department did not have the enthusiasm, the skills, or the budget to extend the process. The company was amiable to the process of IPM, but not committed to significant change.

Connecting Technology with Markets

In a 1993 speech to the annual meeting of the Licensing Executives Society (LES), we borrowed the concurrent engineering concept to describe an ideal model for placing IP at the heart of the corporate enterprise. (See Exhibit 4.1)

Concurrent engineering, also called simultaneous engineering, is the practice whereby product developers from different disciplines work together in teams to come up with product specifications that meet the constraints of design, engineering, manufacturing, marketing, distribution, and sales. Ideally, customer focus groups and outside parts suppliers should also have early input into product design. The methodology, widely adopted in the automotive and aerospace industry in recent years, is credited with taking years off new product development cycles and helping to inspire such hit products as the Ford Taurus.

The concurrent engineering metaphor works because it creates an attitude throughout the company that encourage employees to work toward matching internal corporate technology capabilities (or deficits) with the future strategic direction of the enterprise. Our co-speaker, Joe Daniele, principal and

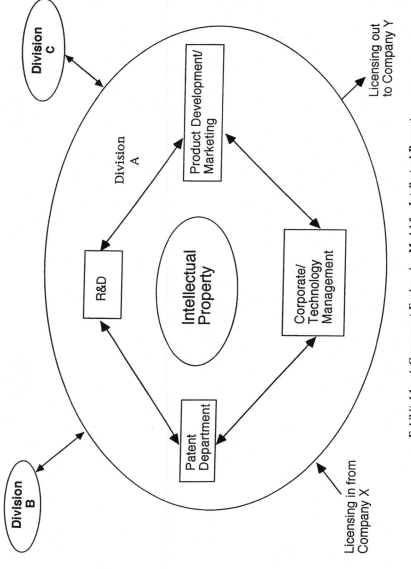

Exhibit 4.1. A Concurrent Engineering Model for Intellectual Property
©EKMS, Inc. 1993

58

manager of Xerox Corporate Licensing, voiced this theme succinctly by stating that "IPM is the direct connection of R&D to the markets."

Exhibit 4.1, A Concurrent Engineering Model for Intellectual Property, shows IP at the center of an organization, with two-way communication going on between product development and marketing, R&D, corporate technology management, and the patent department. Throughout the corporation, there is an ongoing conversation about the value and cost of IP and its applications and market potential. Decisions about how to handle IP—for example, to spin off a new product, develop it internally, or license it to another business entity—are made with the timely input and awareness of all functions and departments. Corporate groups are in regular touch with other company divisions and outside companies that may have a role in developing, licensing, selling, or using the IP. The same ongoing conversation goes on throughout the corporation about outside properties that could be licensed in or acquired to enhance the company's IP portfolio.

Every decision about IP should be made while other decisions are being formed—that is, concurrently. If IP is handled sequentially—that is, thrown over the wall from R&D to patent department and then thrown over the next wall to marketing and so on—the result may be a product idea that has a weak relationship with the market, encumbrances that prevent it being licensed to outsiders, an R&D department whose mission does not reflect the corporation's future, a murky understanding of the needs for in-licensing, costly administrative processes to correct early wrong decisions, and ultimately, properties that are slow to come to market and expensive to build as specified. The concurrent engineering model also presupposes that people within departments are empowered to take more responsibility and are aware of the big corporate picture as they do so.

By enhancing internal communication of technology status across functional and divisional lines, an organization will identify:

- strategic needs that could be filled by in-licensing,
- commercial opportunities for valuable out-licensing, and
- cost savings from patents that can be pruned.

The first step we recommend, aimed at shifting the corporate attitude, is not complex. Identify any structural barriers to communication among the R&D, product development, marketing, and legal department, corporate strategists, and top management. Then use the customary tools—internal databases, roundtables, and technology fairs are common at companies like 3M and DuPont—to foster intracorporate communication about IP. Regular meetings about patent filing activity are helpful. Companies should also be constantly trolling for useful external technology by searching technology transfer databases and employing technology scouts.

Naturally, the usefulness of such tools will depend on corporate culture and the rewards management puts into place to implement changes. As David Garvin notes in his discussion of the learning organization: "Knowledge is more likely to be transferred effectively when the right incentives are in place. If employees know their plans will be evaluated and implemented—in other words, that their learning will be applied—progress is far more likely. At most companies, the status quo is well entrenched; only if managers and employees see new ideas as being in their own best interest will they accept them gracefully." (*Harvard Business Review*, July–August 1993, p. 88)

Tolstoy's maxim about families seems to apply to intellectual property management: All successful approaches are happy in the same way, but the unsuccessful efforts are each unique in their unhappiness. We have observed at Grumman and other exemplar companies that the following three factors, in combination, lead to improved IPM processes:

1. Top management support
2. Intradepartmental communication
3. Strong focus on technologies with internal core value

JUST DO IT!

IPM consciousness can't be confined to a top-down approach, and the overall movement need not wait for optimal conditions to exist. Rank and file people, if they're empowered to make things happen, can identify the problem areas in their worlds. The individual manager can begin by highlighting the missing pieces, seizing responsibility, and bringing deficits to the attention of others. Identify the opportunities that may come from overcoming the barriers.

Quality improvement programs, now so firmly entrenched that the term TQM is out of fashion, established themselves after much trial and error over a couple of decades. Today, schools and governments have adopted the language and tools of the quality movement to reinvent themselves. Companies far from business's cutting edge operate with the understanding that quality is a never-ending process.

Manufacturers had to embrace TQM throughout the enterprise. So, too, does the company need to embrace IPM company-wide. However, the leading companies now working to place IPM at the heart of the corporate enterprise cannot expect to have decades to refine their thinking and practice. They must realize that any practice that confers a business advantage will spread fast in our speeded-up environment of global communication, competition, and technology.

BIBLIOGRAPHY

Barret, Derm. *Fast Focus on TQM*. Portland, OR: Productivity Press. 1994.

Brynjolfsson, Erik. "Technology's True Payoff." *Information Week*, October 10, 1994.

Brynjolfsson, Erik, and Loren Hitt. "Paradox Lost? Firm-level Evidence on the Returns to Information Systems Spending." Unpublished paper. November, 1994.

Garvin, David A. "Building a Learning Organization." *Harvard Business Review*, July–August 1993.

Kahn, Edward. "A Concurrent Engineering Model for Intellectual Property: Placing IP at the Heart of the Corporate Enterprise." Licensing Executives Society 1993 Annual Meeting, San Francisco, CA. Workshop presentation, October 18, 1993.

Larson, Bruce A., & Margot Anderson. "Technology Transfer, Licensing Contracts, and Incentives for Further Innovation." *American Journal of Agricultural Economics*, August 1994.

Nonaka, Ikujiro. "The Knowledge-Creating Company." *Harvard Business Review*, November–December 1991.

Stewart, Thomas A. "Your Company's Most Valuable Asset: Intellectual Capital." *Fortune*, October 3, 1994.

5

Strategic Objectives Supported by Licensing

*Jack A. Nickerson**

John M. Olin School of Business
Washington University in St. Louis

INTRODUCTION

Licensing can no longer be thought of as a nonstrategic activity. The pace of technological change and increasing competitive intensity in today's global economy has more rapid commercialization critical to short-term as well as long-term financial success in many if not most product markets. Crowded technology fields are weakening the advantages held by one-time intellectual property fortresses. Technology development and commercialization costs are rapidly escalating. Furthermore, product and technology standards are playing a greater role in many markets, thereby increasing the importance of strategies that encourage customer adoption. These are just a few of the changes that are placing licensing at the nexus of business, technology, and intellectual property strategy and at the forefront of strategic management. The strategic importance of licensing to this nexus of decisions can be recognized by the range of choices available to a firm in today's global economy.

Historically, most commercialization decisions about new technology and associated intellectual property were bipolar—firms would choose either to commercialize through vertical integration, with all activities undertaken by the firm, or they would store the intellectual property in case it might be valuable for commercialization or defensive purposes at some later date. Licensing typically was an afterthought, a reaction to inquiries made by

*The concepts developed in this chapter have benefited greatly from discussions with Peter Grindley. Nonetheless, the author is solely responsible for the opinions expressed.

63

other firms, and often it was thought of as counterproductive to creating a protected competitive position.

No more. Today, capturing full value from new technology and intellectual property may require any of a wide array of commercialization strategies. While integration is still a vital strategy, licensing by itself or in conjunction with new organizational forms such as joint ventures, partnerships, and co-development agreements are opening up new possibilities for maximizing the value of a given technology. These new strategies, as this chapter discusses, can generate a number of competitive advantages that, among other things, reduce commercialization time and costs, improving both short-term return on investment as well as long-term profits. In other words, strategic licensing can yield comparative advantage.

Unlocking the opportunities provided by licensing activities can and should be an integral part of a firm's competitive arsenal. Using licensing to support business and technology strategies, however, first requires an appreciation of all of the possible strategic advantages to licensing. When can licensing provide commercialization benefits? How can it be used to gain competitive advantage? Unfortunately, very few articles about licensing and intellectual property strategy have provided an appreciation for the richness of strategies supported by licensing. Licensing strategy, when discussed, tends to focus on a single objective or strategy instead of the instrument itself, a license, and the different ways in which the license can be used to gain competitive advantage. Before a detailed and consistent decision logic for licensing can be laid out, all the strategic objectives for licensing must be revealed. This chapter attempts to fill this gap by identifying and describing a full range of strategic objectives for licensing. Its intent is to synthesize the different types of strategies for which in-licensing and, in particular, out-licensing play a critical role. Creating a taxonomy of licensing's strategic objectives will provide licensing executives and corporate strategists with the full range of strategies licensing can support. This may help them capture greater value and gain competitive advantage by enabling them to make the most effective use of their technology and intellectual property portfolios. The synthesis developed herein relies on academic research on licensing found in the economics and innovation literatures, on observations of industry practices, and on interviews with licensing executives. It is meant to provide an overview of the strategic objectives for licensing rather than a detailed assessment of the precise conditions for which licensing is an optimal strategy.

The chapter introduces a taxonomy that places licensing activities into four basic categories of strategic objectives: efficient commercialization, technology and intellectual property access through cross-licensing, strategic interactions, and opportunistic licensing of strategic misfits. *Efficient commercialization* describes a broad range of situations in which both in-licensing and out-licensing offer an innovator the most profitable commercialization path by providing access to low-cost complementary assets or to assets that the innovator does not possess and would find purchasing or creating extremely costly and/or time consuming, if not impossible. *Technology and intellectual property access through cross-licensing* is a set of strategic objectives for gaining access to other firms' intellectual property and innovations through cross-licensing. Cross-licensing can neutralize potential blocking patents, eliminate the need for design-around costs and delays, and enable access to critical technology (and sometimes raw materials) at low cost. The third category encompasses the broader theme of *strategic interaction*, whereby an innovator's decision to out-license influences decisions made by customers, competitors, and suppliers. This includes risk reduction, standard competition, and strategic deterrence. The final category, *opportunistic licensing of strategic misfits*, refers to nonstrategic licensing of innovations and related services that are not central to business strategy but nonetheless valuable to other firms.

Each strategic objective is described in greater detail in the sections below. Examples of many of these strategies are provided to suggest how out-licensing can be used as part of a firm's strategic arsenal to increase profitability and influence competitor, customer, and supplier decisions. The chapter concludes by placing strategic objectives of licensing in the broader context of business, technology, and intellectual property strategy.

EFFICIENT COMMERCIALIZATION STRATEGIES

Perhaps the most common objective for licensing is its usefulness for commercializing technology. The value of an innovation is maximized by linking it with other enabling technologies and employing the most efficient set of assets and capabilities for its commercialization in the least amount of time. While simple in concept, efficient commercialization spans a wide variety of alternative organizational forms and can involve the stitching together of an even wider array of technology, assets, and organizational capabilities. For example, between the historical modes of integration and patent storage alternative commercialization vehicles have emerged, and most of them rely on licensing agreements as their foundation. Joint ventures, partnering, co-development agreements, spin-offs, and franchising are some of the more complex organizational structures firms use to commercialize technology. At the core of all of these organizational forms is licensing's ability to provide access to complementary assets.

Indeed, gaining access to complementary assets is one of the strategic cornerstones of intellectual property licensing. Complementary assets are those assets and capabilities used to transform technology or innovations into revenue generating products. First described by Teece (1986), complementary assets include tangible assets and capabilities such as design, high-quality manufacturing, marketing, distribution, support services, and capital, as well as intangible assets such as brand names and reputations. Complementary enabling technologies are also included in this list. In fact, each step in the commercialization value chain may employ one or several complementary assets and capabilities that contribute to the value delivered to the end-customer. Accessing complementary assets through organizational forms other than vertical integration can, under the right circumstances, dramatically increase profits by speeding time to market, lowering commercialization costs, or expanding commercialization opportunities that would be otherwise unavailable through vertical integration or buyer–supplier relations.

Complementary assets can be distinguished as either critical or generic. Critical complementary assets are, to some degree, unique and difficult to imitate or develop. Specialized production equipment, consumer recognition of a brand name, and distribution channels for which long-term relationships are required are all examples of critical complementary assets. Generic complementary assets, as the name suggests, are not unique and easily imitated or developed. Standard production equipment, generic product names, and distribution that is easily accessed by any firm are all examples of generic complementary assets. Licensing may be used to gain access to generic complementary assets so that the innovating firm's commercialization resources can be deployed for higher-valued projects. The general conditions under which licensing gains access to each type of complementary asset and enhances value are reviewed below.

Critical Complementary Assets

Licensing to gain access to critical complementary assets is often an economic necessity. Increasingly, global competition makes accessing complementary assets in a timely and low-cost way critical to profitable commercialization. This may be especially true for enabling technologies where today it is unlikely that any one firm will possess all relevant intellectual property rights and technology. Today, firms *from* all areas of the world are competing *in* all areas of the world. Indeed, reductions in trade barriers and the ease with which technology diffuses internationally promises a future of greater not lesser competitive intensity as time-to-market becomes the hallmark of success. Survival in the new global economy has forced many firms to focus on core capabilities and jettison complementary assets and capabilities that are not competitive or that otherwise sap resources or blur strategic focus. Alternatively, small and medium-sized firms in many instances simply do not have and never have had the requisite capabilities and assets needed to commercialize all of their innovations. As a result, firms may not possess all of the critical complementary assets they need to commercialize a new technology or may simply possess complementary assets that are high cost.

Licensing, whether out-licensing or in-licensing, provides one strategy for splicing together the most efficient complementary assets even if they are owned by different firms. In order to understand when out-licensing might be an appropriate strategy, we compare licensing to vertical integration and outsourcing.

Integration is generally favored when a firm possesses relevant complementary assets. Teece (1986), for example, describes a decision logic that predicts when a firm should integrate and when it should contract for complementary assets. Integration, he argues, is the best commercialization strategy when an innovation requires access to complementary assets for commercial success, the firm has needed complementary assets, the technology and intellectual property protection is strong, specialized assets are critical for commercial success, the innovator's cash position can support integration, and imitators and competitors are not better positioned. If any of these conditions are not met then integration could lead to high commercialization costs, long delays, low return on investment, or commercialization failure. Contracting for access to complementary assets may yield a higher value commercialization strategy when any of these conditions are not met.[1] As Teece describes it, contracting could involve licensing, other organizational forms such as joint ventures, or buyer–supplier agreements.

Buyer–supplier agreements are mostly used when raw materials, components, intermediate products, or services are relatively generic or are based on another firm's technology, core capabilities, or intellectual property rights. Supply agreements may prove to be an inefficient arrangement when suppliers have to make nontrivial investments that are specific to the buyer (for example, redeploying the specific investment would yield much lower returns) or when technology and know-how appropriation is a risk. Buyer–supplier codevelopment of a technology provides an example. Once resources are expended for developing the technology, the buyer may act opportunistically to manipulate prices, leaving the supplier with depressed returns. Alternatively, a supplier may attempt to appropriate the buyer's technology and know-how if it is not strongly protected. Additionally, other technologies might leak out to the supplier if close cooperation for commercialization is needed. Avoiding these problems may require either incentive alignment features or contractual and organizational safeguards not easily supported by typical buyer–supplier relationships.

With the limitations of buyer–supplier relationships on one extreme and the expense an opportunity cost of integration on the other extreme, there may be a wide range of technologies and circumstances for which out-licensing may be a profit-maximizing commercialization strategy. Out-licensing agreements

---

[1] Teece (1986) also acknowledges that in some instances, storing the technology might be optimal.

offer advantages over integration and buyer–supplier relationships in several ways. First, through licensing, firms can access complementary assets quickly so long as other firms already possess them (if not, integration may be the only alternative). Second, leveraging another firm's specific investments in complementary assets avoids costly development or duplication and can lead to economies of scale in the complementary asset(s) of relevance. Third, licensing agreements facilitate the use of two-part pricing schemes (fixed fees and royalty rates) that can be useful for optimally aligning incentives based on the commercialization risks each firm faces. Fourth, licensing agreements can include clauses that provide legal protections against misuse and misappropriation of technology (for example, field-of-use restrictions) as well as specify grantbacks when complementary innovations might be expected that may not be easily implemented in buyer–supplier contracts.

Consider, for example, a licensing agreement where the innovator licenses a technology to a foreign firm for the purposes of commercialization in the licensee's home country. Assume that commercialization requires expenditures specific to the product. A field-of-use restriction safeguards the foreign firm's specific investment by providing a legal recourse should the innovator try to free-ride on the foreign firm's investments by out-licensing, once initial success has been obtained, to other firms selling in that country. It also safeguards the innovator's investment (or licensee's investments) in neighboring countries. Without a field-of-use restriction, the licensee would not have made the investments necessary for commercial success for fear of not earning a sufficient return. Indeed, as Chapter 7 discusses, many licensing agreement restrictions provide a comparatively efficient contract-based solution for accessing complementary assets.

It should be noted, however, that because of the aforementioned contractual difficulties (such as specific investments for commercialization and weak appropriability) licensing to access critical complementary assets sometimes requires more protective and complex governance structures. Technology codevelopment agreements, partnerships, joint ventures, and strategic alliances are organizational structures that, although adding complexity and cost to licensing activities, provide additional safeguards and incentive alignment mechanisms unavailable through licensing agreements alone. These more complex governance structures are beneficial because they can align incentives, provide safeguards, and maintain relationship continuity by providing an organizational structure where firms share investments, monitor each others' investments and activities, and make adjustments to problems not anticipated *ex ante*.

Accessing Generic Complementary Assets

Commercializing technology does not always require the use of critical complementary assets. For some technologies, generic complementary assets are all that is needed for profitable commercialization. The fact that only generic complementary assets are needed has important implications for a firm's commercialization strategy. With generic assets, a firm gains no competitive advantage over rivals by integrating into all assets and capabilities needed for commercialization. In other words, all profits, should they exist, accrue to the technology and its associated intellectual property (so long as it is not easily appropriated by others).

Out-licensing to access generic complimentary assets is relevant for two situations. First, out-licensing may be an optimal strategy when commercializing a new technology that requires only generic complementary assets so long as its intellectual property rights are strong. Strong property rights can support just about any commercialization strategy. For example, the innovator could reveal the technology and product idea in licensing discussions and extract all supraprofits through licensing without fear of appropriation. Out-licensing to gain access to generic complementary assets can be superior to integration when a firm's resources are constrained or when they can be redeployed to pursue more valuable commercialization opportunities. Out-licensing under these conditions maximizes return on investment because the innovator is not employing its own capital.

Licensing when technology is weakly protected is more problematic. A firm's commercialization strategy when intellectual property protection is weak will depend on a number of factors. For example, if appropriation is likely, the innovator may want to commercialize the technology without licensing so long as the market potential is large and some first-mover advantage is attainable. Alternatively, the innovator may out-license the technology to a firm where a long-term relationship or contractual ties from other transactions creates interdependencies between the firms. Such interdependencies will greatly attenuate the likelihood of appropriation. Another alternative is to bundle a specific technology with other desirable technologies so that the innovator can threaten dissolution of the contract by withholding more desirable technologies if the weakly protected technology is appropriated.[2] If the market and first mover advantages are not sufficiently large or if no additional safeguards are available, out-licensing a single weakly protected technology is the strategy of last resort.

Second, out-licensing can be an optimal strategy for a product that is already commercialized and produced by the innovator but where competition has changed so that the complementary assets needed to support commercial success are no longer critical. In other words, once the requisite complementary assets become generic, firms might consider out-licensing so that

---

[2]Of course, care should be taken in bundling technologies so as not to create an illegal tying arrangement. One way of avoiding such an arrangement is to develop know-how or complementary technology needed for commercialization for which strong intellectual property rights can be developed.

they can redeploy their complementary assets to more specific and higher-value activities. Viewed more generally, out-licensing of this type is a strategy of vertical disintegration. Firms should integrate into and develop assets and capabilities along the value chain if they provide a competitive advantage and *only* as long as they provide a competitive advantage. Complementary assets often need continual investment and updating. However, if incremental investment is done based on generic rather than specific needs, then the firm may invest unwisely and diminish a competitive advantage. Maximizing profits or return on investment may require that specific complementary assets be used only for new products and technologies. Old products and technologies that are still commercially successful but no longer need access to costly and critical complementary assets can be out-licensed. Hence, out-licensing provides an efficient and profitable strategy for firms to redeploy their critical assets to higher-valued use, thereby sustaining and possibly enhancing value.

The idea of vertical disintegration, or shifting the use of complementary assets from old products to new, touches on the idea of learning economies. Whether critical or generic complementary assets are needed for commercializing technology, innovators need to evaluate out-licensing with regard to learning opportunities. The chance to learn from commercializing technology may give greater or lesser impetus to out-licensing depending on the type of learning available and the complementary asset that benefits from it. Two types of learning are relevant.

First, learning-by-doing is an important consideration whenever there is significant opportunity to improve production processes (that is, to lower cost or improve quality), come up with new innovations, or develop critical capabilities and skills where learning can be applied to other present and future products or processes. Process industries, such as chemicals and semiconductors, are well known for the steepness of their learning curves and the ability to transfer learning from one process to another. Learning-by-doing economies, however, are not limited to production; they are found in all segments of the commercialization value chain. Building capabilities, know-how, and complementary assets and the chance of discovering new innovations may be important considerations that diminish the attractiveness of out-licensing as a commercialization strategy. Nonetheless, out-licensing is the optimal commercialization path for many technologies. Although learning is an important factor, executives should scrutinize the degree of the benefits of learning from an integration strategy as well as from other organizational structures including licensing.

Second, learning from licensees is an important consideration when licensees exploring different commercialization venues might provide new information about the technology and incremental innovations that innovator might not otherwise discover. Receiving feedback and information from several licensees can increase the likelihood of refining a technology quickly and developing a broader variety of incremental innovations. Integrated commercialization by a single firm can severely limit the number of experimental trials, range of experiments, and sources of new information compared to those available when several firms are experimenting and trying to improve a technology. Take the situation where out-licensing provides access to customer segments that otherwise might not be reached. These customers may use products in ways that might not be considered by the innovator. Out-licensing to reach these customer segments could provide new sources of ideas for technology refinements. Innovators can use out-licensing and grantbacks as an efficient way to enhance technology development that otherwise might not have occurred. The potential for learning from licensees increases the incentive to out-license.

TECHNOLOGY AND INTELLECTUAL PROPERTY ACCESS THROUGH CROSS-LICENSING

The second strategic objective for licensing is to access technology or intellectual property through exchange. Rather than viewing technology and intellectual property strictly as a source of revenue, the strategic objective of technology access through exchange views technology and intellectual property as a currency, a bargaining chip, or a type of leverage that can be used in a negotiation process to achieve one of several objectives. Exchanging technology and intellectual property rights can serve four overlapping purposes: design freedom, technology acquisition, litigation resolution, and leverage.

Design Freedom

Design freedom is a term applied to the practice of cross-licensing intellectual property portfolios to expand design options, avoid costly design-around efforts, and avoid patent infringement-related monitoring and litigation. Cross-licensing for the purpose of design freedom is essentially an exchange of intellectual property rights—a firm grants the right to use its intellectual property but only in exchange for intellectual property rights. In some industries, like electronics, computers, and semiconductors, the number and density of patents in some technological fields are high and patent ownership diffuse. Indeed, the number of related patents is so extensive and ownership so diffuse that some products could never be commercialized unless licenses could be obtained from perhaps several competitors. It is in these industries where cross-licensing to gain design freedom is an important precursor to competition.

Cross-licensing to gain design freedom typically involves the exchange of rights for entire patent portfolios. Cross-licensing patent portfolios for the purpose of gaining design freedom is not a new idea; the practice has existed for many years, although the particulars of the agreements have changed over time. For example, open-ended agreements with survivorship rights used 20 years ago in the semiconductor industry have evolved into agreements with comparatively short durations and no survivorship rights.[3] Negotiating portfolio cross-licensing agreements can be problematic because portfolios may differ in size, quality, and value. Some large firms in the electronics, computer, and semiconductor industries have resolved this problem by evaluating differences in aggregate quality and value of property rights in the exchanged portfolios. Differences in portfolio value are compensated by a one-time up-front payment sufficient for the duration of the cross-licensing agreement. Payments are based on negotiations between the cross-licensees. Royalty rates typically are not a component of these agreements. At the end of the agreement's term, portfolios are revalued and payments renegotiated if the cross-licensees wish to continue the agreement.

Cross-licensing patent portfolios economizes on a number of costs. Negotiations are undertaken only at the beginning of the licensing period rather than each time a license is needed. Cross-licensing portfolios for fixed duration greatly reduces the high transaction costs that would characterize the repeated nature of an as-needed cross-licensing approach. Further, monitoring products for potential intellectual property violations and litigation are obviated.

The opportunity to cross-license patent portfolios to gain design freedom can have important implications for a firm's R&D investment strategy. Firms with large patent portfolios and overlapping markets are the ones most likely to engage in portfolio cross-licensing. Firms with small portfolios may not have patents of sufficient number, quality, and value to act as exchange currency with firms with larger portfolios, thereby making cross-licensing a potentially expensive proposition if a negotiated exchange is feasible at all. This difficulty might be counteracted by an R&D policy that emphasizes either the patenting of all innovations even if they are outside of the strategic focus of the firm in order to increase the portfolio's size and value or directed research to patent technologies that are valuable complements to other firms' patent portfolios. Patenting for the express purpose of developing currency for cross-licensing may be one way of not only gaining design freedom but doing so inexpensively.

Technology Acquisition

A second objective for cross-licensing is to use technology and intellectual property to acquire other firms' technologies and intellectual property rights by exchanging one set of technology and property rights for another. Tech-

---

[3]A five-year duration is common.

nology acquisition is an objective similar to design freedom except that the former may include the exchange of know-how and ongoing support while the latter is concerned solely with the exchange of intellectual property rights. Technology acquisition also tends to focus on a small number of technologies rather than on entire portfolios.

A distinguishing feature of cross-licensing for technology acquisition is that it is done on an as-needed basis. That is, firms attempt to enter into a cross-licensing agreement when they need the right to use another firm's technology and intellectual property rights. The agreement is predicated on the contemporaneous need by two firms of each other's technology and patent rights. The absence of contemporaneous needs makes the use of cross-licensing agreements to access technology problematic.

As-needed cross-licensing agreements may pose special problems because of their discrete nature as compared to portfolio cross-licenses. Examples of cross-licensing difficulties can be found in large firms where divisional structures and dispersed divisional ownership of patents may constrain licensing negotiations. One intellectual property executive for a large diversified chemical company explained that cross-licensing negotiations can easily break down if one operating division supplies a patent for cross-licensing and another division within the same firm receives the exchanged technology and intellectual property. Differences in opinion over an intellectual property's value and difficulties associated with setting internal transfer prices makes cross-licensing in these situations problematic. The executive explained that when these situations occur, technology exchange is best organized through individual licensing agreements whose independent value can be determined without the added burden of intradivisional politics. The exchange would proceed only if each individual license makes sense.

Litigation Resolution

It is not uncommon to find competitors with overlapping intellectual property right claims. Whether a matter of happenstance or strategic maneuver, legal disputes that arise from conflicting intellectual property right claims are often lengthy and costly. Claims and counterclaims attempt to invalidate the other's patents while invoking antitrust laws. Although no statistical data is available, personal observation suggests that many of these disputes end in cross-licensing agreements either because such agreements are forced upon the parties by the court or because they stop spiraling litigation costs.

Litigation concerning conflicting intellectual property right claims has several strategic implications. First, realizing that granting cross-licenses may be a likely litigation outcome, firms could negotiate a cross-license to avoid costly litigation and the detrimental impact that litigation risks can have on financing activities. Second, a firm attempting to access a particular technology might attempt to develop technology patents, similar technology, or conflicting intellectual property right claims with the intent of entering a litigious dispute.[4] Third, realizing that competitors might attempt to gain access to a firm's patents through litigation, a firm might attempt to secure its intellectual property position through a thicket of patents.

Leverage

Another use of intellectual property as an exchange medium involves exchanging intellectual property for tangible goods or preferential pricing. For example, one chemical manufacturer decided to cease production of an intermediate commodity and purchase it from an outside supplier instead. The supplier was the largest producer of the commodity and the manufacturer quickly became its largest customer. Such a buyer–supplier relationship can be problematic as each side attempts to use its power to influence pricing. Rather than disbanding the research team that supported the manufacturer's production of the intermediate good, it continued investing in research and developed a technology protected by intellectual property that was of great value to the supplier. A license for the intellectual property was used as leverage to acquire and safeguard a low price from the supplier. This case suggests that intellectual property can be used as leverage to gain preferred pricing or perhaps an exchange for other tangible assets. R&D can be an inexpensive strategy to earn handsome returns by using its output, intellectual property, as an exchange medium of partial payment for purchases. Although included as part of the section looking at the strategic objective for licensing as part of an exchange vehicle, as shown in the next section, leverage also can be thought of in terms of strategic interactions.

STRATEGIC INTERACTIONS

Out-licensing can be used to interact strategically with investment and purchasing decisions by customers, suppliers, and competitors to expand, and in some instances to create demand for a new technology. Out-licensing to influence decisions made by other actors has three main objectives: risk reduction, standards creation, and strategic deterrence. While they are discussed separately here, the objectives are not mutually exclusive; a successful licensing strategy sometimes encompasses several, if not all, of the objectives.

---

[4]The timing of such a strategy is likely to be critical. Obtaining an overlapping patent several years after the first one is granted may not succeed. In general, the tactic may be inherently limited.

Risk Reduction

Out-licensing can expand and create demand for a new technology by reducing customer and supplier adoption risk. Three types of adoption risks are relevant: price gouging, quality gouging, and supply disturbances. Price gouging can occur when a customer or supplier is locked into a particular product because switching costs would be prohibitive. Although promises might be given (even through contracts), once they are locked in suppliers may find ways to circumvent their promises and opportunistically increase price. Only the magnitude of the switching costs buyers must absorb to change suppliers constrains such opportunistic actions.[5] Customers, realizing the potential of opportunism, might not adopt the product unless producers find a credible way of keeping their promises. Farrell and Gallini (1988) have pointed out that out-licensing a technology provides a credible commitment by an innovator to abstain from price gouging, because licensees provide market discipline against *ex post* opportunistic price increases.

Quality gouging is a hazard similar to price gouging and again is problematic when customer and supplier switching costs are nontrivial. While contracts might be relatively complete for safeguarding against price gouging, they often are relatively incomplete when specifying quality. Consider an innovator that creates a new widget for which a patent has been obtained. A customer who designs and produces a product containing the widget is locked into the widget supplier to the extent that designing around the widget and altering its manufacturing is costly. A long-term contract might protect the customer against price increases but not against the supplier lowering quality and saving on production costs. Shepard (1987) has argued that customers recognize the risk of quality gouging and will reduce demand or forgo purchasing the product altogether to avoid being gouged on quality. Shepard has shown that like the aforementioned commitment to abstain from price gouging, out-licensing is one mechanism an innovator can employ to credibly commit to abstaining from *ex post* opportunistic quality gouging. Out-licensing reduces the risk of opportunism and thus can increase demand for a technology.

Supply disturbances are a third source of risk for customers and suppliers that must confront nontrivial switching costs once a technology is adopted. Relying on a single supplier for a product can be disastrous for an assembler or intermediate goods producer when there is a discontinuity in supply. Especially during the past decade when many firms have implemented just-in-time production systems with little or no inventory, unanticipated production line shutdowns can impose excessive costs on an

---

[5]Opportunism can occur in both directions. For instance, a buyer may act opportunistically once a supplier has made specific investments. In this case, a supplier's switching costs rather than a buyer's switching costs are critical for constraining opportunism.

assembler, and its production and distribution can grind to a halt if critical components are unexpectedly unavailable. Out-licensing provides a safeguard against supply disturbances by offering lower probabilities that all suppliers would experience supply disruption simultaneously. Unless a safeguard such as out-licensing a second source is offered by the innovator, customers may choose a different, potentially less advanced technology in order to avoid possible supply disruption risks.

In general, out-licensing can be used as a strategy to increase, and in some instances create, demand for new technologies. Out-sourcing can be viewed as a credible commitment mechanism that forces the licenser to abstain from *ex post* price and quality gouging and to provide insurance against supply disruptions. Commitment and risk reduction also play important roles in establishing technology and products as standards, as is next described.

Standards Creation

For many products and technologies creating a standard is vital for commercial success, and out-licensing is a pivotal instrument for creating a standard (Grindley, 1995). Standards are particularly important in markets that display what economists call network externalities. Network externalities occur when a product is more valuable to a consumer when more consumers adopt the same or compatible products. Benefits can be both direct and indirect. Take the Internet as an example. The more people who have access to the Internet the greater the direct benefit to individuals using it. For instance, I get more benefit from communicating via the Internet if my friends also are connected. Also, the greater the number of users the greater the indirect benefit from more offerings of complementary products with greater variety (prices may also become lower as the market expands).[6]

Creating a standard is a coordination problem that requires (sometimes simultaneously) adoption by customers, suppliers, complementary product suppliers, and, occasionally, competitors. Out-licensing can solve the coordination problem in several ways. Out-licensing can influence customer expectations. Given two or more equal alternatives, customers will gravitate towards products with the lowest appropriate risks (as described in the section on risk reduction). Even when a proprietary product has clear superiority advantages over a rival out-licensed or open standard product, the inferior product may win.[7] Suppliers of complementary products are similarly swayed. For example, as Microsoft's Windows clearly became the dominant personal computer interface, Apple Computer began having difficulty con-

---

[6]In the short run, a tidal wave of new Internet users may impose costs on existing users because of slow response times, the equivalent of Internet traffic jams. In the long supply of services should catch up to customer demand.

[7]See Grindley (1995) for a more detailed discussion.

vincing independent software vendors to write or update software products for its computers.[8] Out-licensing also can limit some commercialization risks by shifting investments a firm might otherwise have to make alone to competitors (licensees) who share the risks.

The creation of a standard does not require out-licensing as an integral part of a firm's strategy to get its products adopted as a standard. IBM's introduction of the 360 mainframe offers the classic example of a firm that created a de facto standard without the use of out-licensing. IBM developed the computer, the software, and all the peripherals, and it provided service as well. Without integration, it would have been far more difficult for IBM to have coordinated the simultaneous introduction of the full complement of products that contributed to the 360's success. The market dominance of Microsoft's Windows offers a more recent example of a product that has become a de facto standard without out-licensing its technology to other competitors.[9] Nonetheless, out-licensing is often a critical strategic instrument. Even though Microsoft is the celebrated victor of the PC desktop interface wars, many industry observers argue that even as late as 1991, Apple could have been the heir apparent if it had out-licensed its operating system. With competitors attempting to make their products and technology a standard, the timing of market entry and the speed at which an installed base is built up is critical.[10] Out-licensing can greatly hasten the adoption of a standard and could combat the growing dominance of a competitor. As typified by Apple, choosing not to out-license could be a serious strategic miscalculation.

Several out-licensing tactics that are integral to reducing risk also could be employed to encourage standards adoption. Three key tactics include out-licensing to key suppliers, open licensing, and assignment of a licensing program to a standards-setting body. Sun Microsystems (SMI), for example, implemented a highly publicized strategy employing all three tactics. It out-licensed its microprocessor (MPU) designs, which encouraged several semiconductor manufacturing firms to adopt and proliferate its MPU designs, thereby allowing it to use its capital for other purposes while insuring low manufacturing prices for its MPUs. It out-licensed information exchange protocols, which helped to place SMI at the center of today's move towards networked computing. Finally, it has participated in standard-setting bodies

---

[8]One might argue that Apple's partnership with Motorola and IBM and its shift to the Power PC microprocessor was an attempt to counteract problems it has been having with independent software vendors by expanding the market.

[9]This is not precisely true. Microsoft licenses Windows to personal computer manufacturers so that PCs are sold with Windows installed. However, licensing of this nature has more to do with copyright protection than patent protection.

[10]Many researchers have investigated standards competition. For reviews of the theoretical literature see Bensen and Johnson (1986) and Bensen and Saloner (1987). For an applied discussion see Grindley (1995).

to get the industry to adopt some elements of its technology. These strategies were critical to SMI's rapid growth and financial success in a highly competitive business segment.

Firms profit in several ways from out-licensing to create a standard. Should a firm succeed in creating a standard the market would greatly expand, allowing the innovator to operate profitably even when it has rivals and to profit from licensing fees. In markets where technological change and innovation is ongoing, the innovator might be able to use its first-mover position to advantage by providing new innovations and thereby retaining a large market share. An innovator that fails to get its technology accepted as a standard when network externalities are present will be relegated to the periphery of the market if it survives at all.

Strategic Deterrence

Several researchers (Gallini, 1984; Gallini & Winter, 1985) have studied the use of out-licensing as a strategic mechanism to deter competitors from investing in innovative activities that might lead to superior technology. Gallini (1984), for example, argues that an incumbent firm, when confronted by a small number of potential entrants, might license its production technology to reduce the incentive of potential entrants to develop their own, possibly better, technology. In other words, situations might arise whereby deterrence is achieved by inducing entry.

While out-licensing for the purpose of strategic deterrence and the maintenance of a dominant market position may draw antitrust scrutiny, Gallini's model predicts that wasteful research and development from simultaneous work by rivals may be lessened by out-licensing, because a firm has an increased incentive to wait for a possible offer to share a technology discovered by its rival. Gallini and Winter (1985) developed a model that shows that deterrence depends on the cost differences between firms. They claim that out-licensing encourages research when firms have similar costs and discourages research when firms have costs that are far apart. Thus, the ability for out-licensing to strategically deter competitors will depend upon relative cost positions. It is important to note that using out-licensing for strategic deterrence may invite antitrust scrutiny but should not be per se illegal from an economic standpoint, because in some instances social welfare is enhanced.

STRATEGIC MISFITS

The moniker of strategic misfits is given to the fourth and last licensing objective. As the name implies, it refers to those technologies and intellectual properties that are inconsistent with a firm's product market focus. Strategic misfits are the byproduct of the innovation process. Even the most targeted research and development efforts have spillovers that lead to unintended innovations. Also, R&D is not the only source of innovations. Customer feedback, learning-by-doing, and serendipity can lead to innovations that are inconsistent with a firm's strategic focus.

An important question for a firm is what to do with these strategic misfits. Should these innovations be ignored, not patented, or put in the public domain to preempt competitor patenting? Or should these innovations be pursued at least to the stage of generating strong-enough intellectual property rights so that they can be out-licensed?

Examples of firms following either strategy can be found. Firms that follow the first focus all of their intellectual capital on generating only those innovations that fit with their existing business plans. These firms tend to be in fast-paced technology industries such as electronics, computers, and semiconductors. Although leaving fallow innovations or potential innovations outside of a firm's strategic focus forgoes income opportunities, it also reduces the additional expenditures needed to acquire and maintain intellectual property rights and eliminates losses from research efforts that defocus the firm's strategic technology direction.

Firms that follow the second strategy use out-licensing as a means of capturing value from technological spillovers. Many industries require R&D efforts that are broad in scope. Broad research programs lead to a broad set of possible innovations even though only a few may lead to commercialization. Indeed, one large U.S. chemical company claims to rely on only 3 to 5 percent of its patent portfolio to support its current businesses.

Unfortunately, the jury on determining which strategy is best is still out. It is likely that the optimal strategy for handling misfit technology will differ by industry and perhaps by company depending on the nexus of business, technology, and intellectual property strategies it employs. Consider the differences found between the electronics and chemical industries. Electronics manufacturers such as Hewlett Packard operate in markets with very short product life cycles. A technology must be developed and brought to market quickly or it will become outmoded sometimes as quickly as 18 months after it is first conceived. The nature of the technology is such that research and development can and must be focused on specific technology trajectories. Undertaking significant efforts to develop, protect, and out-license strategic misfits may be misguided, because there may be few of them and the resulting reallocation of research efforts may ultimately slow innovation in strategic areas. Chemical manufacturers such as Dow Chemical Company face the opposite conditions. Broad R&D activities often are needed to identify new chemical compounds, making technological spillovers a frequent occurrence. Product life cycles are much longer than in the electronics industry and expending effort and resources to protect a broad set of technologies may have little defocusing effect while, at the same time, generating new opportunities for income. Undertaking significant efforts to develop, protect, and out-license strategic misfits may be an optimal strategy for maximizing profits in this industry. Indeed, in some instances the profit-maximizing strategy may be to link technology strategy with intellectual property strategy with the purpose of generating technology that can be out-licensed.

DISCUSSION AND SUMMARY

This chapter synthesized licensing activities into a four-part taxonomy of strategic objectives. The taxonomy encompasses efficient commercialization, technology and intellectual property access through cross-licensing, strategic interactions, and opportunistic licensing of strategic misfits. Under efficient commercialization, in-licensing as well as out-licensing may provide the most efficient commercialization path by providing access to low-cost complementary assets or to assets that the innovator does not possess and would find purchasing or creating extremely costly and/or time consuming. With technology and intellectual property access through cross-licensing, licensing is used to neutralize potential blocking patents, to eliminate the need for design-around costs and delays, and to gain access to critical technology (and sometimes raw materials) for low cost. Licensing with the objective of influencing decisions made by customers, competitors, and suppliers as a means of creating a standard or expanding demand represents a strategic interaction. Finally, opportunistic licensing of technology and intellectual property that is not strategic to an innovator but valuable to other firms can be used to increase returns on R&D investment. This taxonomy spans the range of strategic objectives that can be served by licensing activities.

Historically, it was not uncommon for firms to pay little attention to licensing. Licenses, when they were granted, often were the result of the innovator reacting to an inquiry from another firm. Firms simply did not consider licensing a tool in their strategy toolbox. Thus, many valuable and strategic licensing opportunities were laid fallow and lost as technology became outdated or intellectual property rights expired.

The fundamental message of this chapter is that licensing can no longer be thought of as a peripheral activity. It maintains that the strategic use of licensing greatly expands the alternatives firms have for profiting from their technological innovations and intellectual property. Not only does licensing open up new profit making opportunities, but remaining competitive in today's global marketplace may demand that firms adopt strategic objectives only achievable through licensing. Indeed, those firms that do not fully exploit their technology, intellectual property portfolios, and innovation capabilities may not only limit their profitability but also decrease their chances for long-term survival.

This is not to say that firms should license out all technologies or that licensing should be the focal point of a firm's business, technology, and intellectual property strategies. Taken to an extreme, licensing may limit a firm to the role of a contract research center, ultimately destroying the value of its complementary assets and narrowing its set of core competencies. While a small number of firms can operate in this niche profitably, it is not the optimal strategy for most firms. Indeed, developing complementary assets and core capabilities and using them to commercialize innovations is likely to remain the most profitable strategy for many firms. Nonetheless, licensing can play an integral role in creating and capturing value.

In today's competitive environment it would be unwise for firms not to consider the strategic options made available to them through licensing. Licensing clearly intersects the nexus of business, technology, and intellectual property strategy. Firms that consider licensing proactively expand the range of commercialization strategies and can lower commercialization costs or expand market demand. Licensing thus broadens the business strategy alternatives available to a firm. Recognizing that technology can be licensed in or out can influence a firm's investment decisions. Why expend scarce resources re-inventing or inventing around a technology available through a license or cross-license when those resources might be better spent on developing technologies that are key and strategic? Thus, the identification of licensing alternatives and cross-licensing opportunities is an important factor to be considered in a firm's technology decisions. Furthermore, intellectual property strategy used to be a binary choice—patent every innovation or patent only those innovations with large expected values. Competitive analysis of a firm's patent portfolio vis-à-vis competitors and potential competitors for the most part was unimportant. By considering licensing, intellectual property strategy becomes multidimensional, requiring ongoing competitive analysis in order to inform both business and technology strategy. Firms must continually monitor competitor technology trajectories to identify changes in its patent position, provide input into the commercialization process about organizational options and other advantages gained through licensing, and recognize opportunities to lower costs or capture value by culling or licensing unnecessary intellectual property.

It is likely that the high-performing firms in the year 2000 and beyond will tightly link business, technology, and intellectual property strategies. Licensing is a tool that provides greater alternatives, opportunities, and flexibility to firms for gaining competitive advantage and capturing the full value of their innovations and intellectual property. The challenge for management is to make the transition from reactive licensing to proactive licensing by modifying its internal management and planning processes so that licensing can take its appropriate place in their firm's strategy toolbox.

BIBLIOGRAPHY

Bensen, S., and L. Johnson. 1986. *Compatibility Standards, Competition, and Innovation in the Broadcasting Industry*. Santa Monica, CA: RAND Corporation.

Bensen, S., and G. Saloner, 1987. "The Economics of Telecommunications Standards." In R. Crandall and K. Framm (Eds.), *Changing the Rules: Technological Change, International Competition and Regulation in Telecommunications*. Washington DC: Brookings Institution, pp. 177–220.

Farrell, Joseph, and Nancy Gallini. 1988. "Second Sourcing as a Means of Commitment: Monopoly Incentives to Attract Competition." *Quarterly Journal of Economics*, 108, pp. 673–694.

Gallini, Nancy. 1984. "Deterrence by Market Sharing: A Strategic Incentive for Licensing." *American Economic Review*, 74, pp. 931–41.

Gallini, Nancy, and R. Winter. 1985. "Licensing in the Theory of Innovation," *RAND Journal of Economics*, 16, pp. 237–252.

Grindley, Peter. 1995. *Standards Strategy and Policy: Cases and Stories*. New York: Oxford University Press.

Shepard, Andrea. 1987. "Licensing to Enhance Demand for New Technologies." *RAND Journal of Economics*, 18, pp. 360–68.

Teece, David J. 1986. "Profiting from Technological Innovation: Implications for Integration, Collaboration, and Licensing and Public Policy." *Research Policy*, 15, pp. 285–305.

6

Establishing an Out-Licensing Activity

Patrick H. Sullivan

The ICM Group

Stephen P. Fox

Hewlett-Packard Company

Extracting value from intellectual property is a popular discussion topic. Articles appear regularly in the media announcing major licensing deals and large damage awards in patent law suits. Major corporations such as Texas Instruments and IBM are reported to be collecting hundreds of millions of dollars a year in licensing royalties. Seminars and conferences on how to value and benefit from intellectual property are legion. In this environment, it is not surprising that an increasing number of companies are actively considering ways to turn their intellectual property assets into cash generators. One way to do this is by establishing some type of corporate office to out-license patents and technology.

Companies contemplating the creation of an out-licensing office struggle with the basics: How big an organization is required? Will the investment be cost effective? What is the likely return on investment and how long will it take? Does the income prospect outweigh potential business risks inherent in licensing programs such as licensee retaliation, protracted litigation, or a compromise of competitive position?

Many companies seem to be considering whether to invest in out-licensing. While there is great interest in the topic, very little appears to be known about what the actual experience has been for companies that have already implemented out-licensing offices. Most of what is known is anecdotal rather than codified. We have decided to collect anecdotal information about out-licensing offices to see if any insights emerged. We drew upon our own knowledge as well as on the knowledge of eight licensing executives or corporate counsels of technology-based firms that have developed profits from their intellectual assets. While we freely admit that ours was less than a scientific sample of the business community, we also believe that the information resulting from this exploration describes current corporate practice around this growing activity.

This chapter explores some of the historical reasons why many companies in the past did not find out-licensing to be attractive and what motivated those that did, as well as the reasons why out-licensing may be more attractive now. We examine the conditions under which an out-licensing office is considered, the decision rules companies apply in its creation, the patterns companies follow in developing these offices, and the characteristics of companies that decide to set up such offices or decide not to do so.

PERSPECTIVES ON OUT-LICENSING

In any discussion of out-licensing, there are three kinds of companies to be examined. The first includes those companies (a relatively small number) already extracting large profits from their out-licensing activities. These companies believe in and are already practicing the extraction of extra value from their portfolio of patents. The second set of companies are those that believe that there may be significant profits available if they choose to extract them from their portfolio, but they have not yet done so. The third set of companies are those with no intention of investing in the development of an out-licensing activity. They believe that a patent portfolio is to be used largely to defend the technologies and markets created by the company and that other uses are considerably less significant.

Companies most likely to be interested in this chapter are in the second group—they believe that there are significant profit opportunities available to them from their portfolios but they have not yet been successful in obtaining them. However, other companies, those already successfully extracting extra value or those with no intention of doing so, may also find this chapter to be of some interest.

BACKGROUND AND HISTORY

In earlier decades, voluntary, systematic out-licensing programs for patents generally had little appeal unless they were closely coupled to central business strategies. Most efforts were directed to licensing patent and know-how combinations, or to cross-licensing packages of patents to assure that the parties had freedom to compete in the marketplace. Outside of these scenarios, prospective licensees were reluctant to pay for a bare patent license. The political and economic climate did not generally recognize value in patents, and the patent laws were not conducive to enforcement.

The value of patents was perceived to be low, commensurate with the degree of judicial recognition. The U.S. Supreme Court was generally antimonopoly and antipatent during the so-called Black/Douglas era (1946–1965). The low point for patent enforcement probably came in the mid-1970s. The chances of a patent being held valid, infringed, and enforceable in litigation were only about one out of three. Hence many companies found that it was more cost effective to avoid taking patent licenses, and instead spend their time in a defense posture, fighting the infringement allegations of patent owners where the odds were more favorable. Given the low chances of success in litigation, patent owners were reluctant to spend a lot of time and money in lawsuits. Moreover, the U.S. Department of Justice subscribed to the view that patents were bad monopolies that stifled competition in the marketplace by preventing companies from copying each others' products. The DOJ adopted its "Nine No-Nos" of patent licensing, which greatly restricted patent owners from exploiting their inventions on an exclusive basis. Companies that attempted to use their patent and technology prowess in an aggressive manner sometimes found themselves the subject of governmentally enforced consent decrees that required low or no royalty patent licenses to competitors. Overall, patents were viewed by many as a stagnant or even a counterproductive asset.

This state of affairs made an about-face in just three short years—1983 to 1985—the convergence of events. The President's Commission on Industrial Competitiveness was formed and two years later produced a report that addressed Intellectual Property (IP) as one of four areas critical in achieving and maintaining competitiveness in American industry. Protecting technology through IP laws was considered a priority item. At the same time, the new Court of Appeals for the Federal Circuit became active and began to unify legal precedent in patent cases that previously had been fragmented among the eleven Circuit Courts of Appeal. Antitrust restrictions were relaxed, as evidenced by the National Cooperative Research Act (1984), which permitted competitors to do joint research more freely. Also, the DOJ decided that the incentive of a patent is pro- rather than anticompetitive, and that patents served a positive purpose in discouraging free riders who copied technology originated by others, sold it more cheaply, and thus discouraged innovators. All of this had a tendency to reduce the number of competitors, and thus cause new products to be limited and prices to increase.

Over time, the events in the early 1980s led to a paradigm shift. The number of patents held valid in litigation more than doubled. Damage awards in patent cases grew larger. Courts were more willing to grant injunctions against infringers an often denied a stay of injunction while the case was appealed, thereby precluding the infringer from buying time during the appeal process. Prejudgement interest on the infringer's liability was condoned by the courts and sometimes was higher than the actual damage award, thus penalizing the infringer for extending the litigation. Treble damages were assessed for willful infringement. The scope of what was protectable by patents continued to broaden. Lastly, the international importance of patents in global economies became highly visible, due to efforts around the world in conforming to the precepts of the North American Free Trade Agreement (NAFTA) and the General Agreement of Tariffs and Trade (GATT).

Stated simply, a patent is now a more powerful asset than it ever was before. One claim in one patent has the power to put a competitor out of business. The chances that patent owner will be successful in litigation are high. Under a typical risk/reward analysis, companies are now often led to the conclusion that it is better to be a licensee than an alleged infringer. Licensing as a viable solution to risk management is a more justifiable alternative than it had been in the past.

In some industries, the increasing complexity of customer needs and the recognition that one company cannot do it all has led to a proliferation of strategic alliances and technology joint ventures. This allows the participating companies to leverage their core competencies more cost effectively in markets where customer demands are greater than any one company can meet. The rise of standards within some technology areas has increased the need for compatibility among competitive products and at the same time has made it easier for companies to work together to create solutions to complex problems. At the formation of an alliance or joint venture, one of the first action items is to define the value that each party brings to the table. Patents are one of the more convenient indicators of such value. They can be licensed out to coventurers in creative and tailor-made ways to achieve specific business objectives. As the alliance relationship progresses over time, the patents newly acquired by each party serve as a way to keep score, giving recognition to a party for its technical innovations as well as giving the other party freedom to use those innovations under appropriate licensing provisions.

In the continuing stream of technological advancement, often new developments are patented but not used significantly by the originating company, perhaps because the developments fall outside a shifting strategic business path or perhaps because of rapid technology advances. As a result, many companies have large portions of their patent portfolios lying fallow. These dormant patents may have value because others perceive a need for the protected innovations or because they sell infringing products. In these cases, the challenge is to convert dormant patents into realizable income by licensing them out to others.

THE GROWING AWARENESS

Companies considering whether to develop an out-licensing activity rarely find that a specific circumstance or event prods them to act. Usually there is a growing awareness of circumstances that leads to a collective acceptance of the concept of extracting portfolio value corporately as contrasted with simply extracting value from patents individually. This acceptance typically includes the concept of developing an out-licensing activity to capture the extra value, but it does not necessarily include agreement on the kind of activity that should be established.

The awareness and acceptance of a company's need or at least willingness to out-license may itself be triggered from outside the corporation—for example, by observing that other companies are obtaining profits from their portfolios, or by noticing new opportunities on the business landscape. Alternatively, the awareness can arise from within the corporation when companies become aware of the existence of many nonstrategic technologies in their portfolio that could be turned into profits with relative ease. But regardless of the stimulus, awareness (and eventually acceptance) are necessary conditions for any decision to create an out-licensing office or activity.

The awareness usually comes from one or more of the following situations:

High Anticipation of Revenue or Profits. Some companies develop a belief that they can emulate the success of others in extracting extra value. They *anticipate* additional revenue or profits from the portfolio. This anticipation of results fuels their interest in developing a serious out-licensing activity. There are no hard and fast numbers associated with the general anticipation of revenues and profits, but some companies that have been successful in out-licensing find that it produces roughly one percent of the firm's total revenues and over five percent of its profits.

Noncore technologies. Many companies find they have what they believe to be a surplus of technologies in their portfolio that are current, interesting, and useful, but not a part of the company's strategic thrust. For this reason they are not counted in the company's core of strategic technologies. Although not core, these technologies are marketable, and companies with significant amounts of such noncore technologies in their portfolio begin to think of ways to harvest the R&D investment that produced these technologies.

Core technologies. Still other companies are willing, even eager, to out-license their core technologies. This is particularly true of companies that have learned that they cannot achieve the full market penetration level their technology makes available. To reach all potential customers would require more resources than the company is able to afford. For this reason, many companies out-license their core technology into other geographic regions or into markets available to competitors but not themselves.

Take advantage of non-strategic markets. Still others out-license core or non-core technology into markets that are not strategic to their long-term goals. For these companies, their technology has application in markets beyond those for which it was created. Such companies can out-license the technology into other industries or areas of business and without putting themselves at strategic jeopardy.

Inevitability. There are companies that realize that regardless of the coreness of their technology, someone is going to license it or similar technology into their marketplace. Companies in this situation often find that if they don't out-license their core technology someone else will. Under those circumstances, core technology quickly finds itself on the out-license list.

Design Freedom. Companies with a focus on the design freedom issue will often determine that it is in their best interest frequently to cross-license with business and technology competitors in order to ensure a continuation of their freedom to do business with a certain area of technology.

Create or perpetuate standards. A subset of companies license their core technology because its widespread use creates a standard. Often the creation of such standards cause competitors to seek a license in order to produce products or services consistent with the newly established standard.

Strategic Alliances. Many companies have learned that the market's demand for new and more complex products requires a range of competencies and technologies far beyond what any one company can provide. Such an awareness leads to the desire to create strategic alliances with firms that have the capabilities needed. Successful negotiations with such firms are often enabled by cross-licensing of specific technologies or competencies.

These situations are usually transformed, through the company's internal discussion and decision process, into purposes for which out-licensing offices are created. With their roots in stimuli and debate, specific company purposes are a key determinant of an out-licensing office's focus, size, and constituency.

PROFILES

Eight companies have provided descriptions of both their expectations and their experience with out-licensing. These companies' situations demonstrate how companies see their out-licensing situation.

Motorola

There is a licensing group that comprises a small staff of attorneys, who in turn call on in-house IP counsel for assistance when needed. The licensing group reports into the Patent and Licensing Department which reports to the Chief Corporate Staff Officer. Licensing is responsive to the Company's businesses, some of which have an objective of design freedom and/or income. Generally, core technologies are not licensed except in some cases where the perpetuation of standards is involved. Licensing income is returned to the businesses. Income from licensing substantially exceeds the Patent and Licensing Department budget.

3M

There is no formal licensing office at 3M. Licensing-out is not commonly done, however it does occur in some situations to meet specific business objectives. The various business sectors operate independently, each with decision-making authority on whether to license. However, a corporate committee must review and approve all licenses. Core technology generally is not licensed out.

DuPont

The corporation is the owner of all intellectual property; however each business unit is responsible for the cost and management, including licensing, of the intellectual property relevant to its operations. Licensing of patents and know-how which are generated by the corporate R&D function, unconnected with any business unit and funded at a corporate level, is handled by the Corporate Technology Transfer Group. Licensing revenues, in general, flow back to the business responsible for the intellectual property being licensed. There is no central licensing department responsible for activities across the company; however, an informal licensing communications network is maintained by the Corporate Technology Transfer Group which has as part of its role the responsibility to be a resource of licensing information and options. Such know-how is made available to any business unit upon request. The same network is a useful conduit for effectively receiving and processing licensing inquiries from parties outside the company. All license agreements must be approved by a central patent board prior to execution. Historically, licensing at DuPont has been either (1) strategic, e.g., intended as part of a global manufacturing strategy, or (2) reactive, that is, granted to outside parties upon their request. The latter largely relates to nonstrategic technology in the forms of patents and know-how, which if licensed, don't involve unreasonable licensing costs or don't negatively impact the company's business. To capture more value from past R&D investment, corporate attention is now focused on leveraging idle portfolios through licensing or other means. Most business units carry out periodic patent reviews where licensable portfolios are identified. Licensing as a business priority varies across the company, but in general, with respect to non-strategic or idle technologies, it is viewed as a low yield and low income effort. Depending on market orientation, product lines and culture, licensing is a natural for some business units, whereas for others the costs are viewed as outweighing the gains. Cross-licenses are typically entered into as a means to (1) enable developments with industrial partners, (2) obtain necessary freedom to operate, or (3) resolve a dispute and avoid litigation.

Xerox

Xerox has a three person centralized Licensing Office that relies on Corporate patent and licensing attorneys, contract personnel, specialist consultants and Xerox technical resources as needed. This office was newly established three years ago and reports into Xerox Technology and Market Development. The manager of the Licensing Office is also the manager of the Corporate Office Management of Intellectual Property Committee. All Xerox intellectual property transfers, worldwide are managed through this Committee as Corporate assets. The primary goal of the Licensing Office is to bring new technology to market through proactive out-licensing and through founding of specific licensing businesses or programs. Patents, copyrights, and know-how are licensed with a focus on by-product technology that the Company generally chooses not to market in its own products. Core technologies are primarily cross-licensed, but also may be licensed for byproduct use. Considerable effort within the Licensing Office is being made to establish new licensing programs for income generation in specific targeted technology areas. One new licensing business has been established and funded at the five person level. About half of the licensing income is retained at the Corporate level, and half returned to the originating groups, with a share for operation of the Licensing Office. There is a recognized delay in acquiring royalty income due to licensee product start-up time. Licensing income is expected to grow rapidly as new royalties come on line.

Eastman Chemical

A formal licensing office exists at the Corporate level staffed with people with business, technical, and legal backgrounds who also work on mergers, acquisitions, divestitures, and joint ventures. Established intellectual property teams throughout the company are responsible for identifying patents for licensing. The impetus for the program is to license patents that are no longer on the company's strategic path and that cover non-core technologies. Core competencies are not likely to be licensed except to strategic partners or for equity participation and there is little cross-licensing activity.

Phillips Petroleum

A large licensing office comprising several dozen business people and attorneys exists at the Corporate level and it is integrated with the Patent Legal Department. Most licensing is directed to technologies currently used by the Company. A goal of licensing is to help expand and maintain Company markets. Almost all company technology is available for license. One motivating factor in licensing is that much technology is deemed a commodity and that variations of it will be obtained by potential licenses from others if the need is not met by the Company. The general view is that if the Company does not license the technology, someone else will. Technology not actually used by the Company is rarely licensed. Both patents and know-how are licensed; however, profits have been found to be related to the strength of the patents. Royalty income is shared between the Corporate licensing office and the business units with appropriate accounting for costs in perfecting the licenses. Licensing income is on the order of 1% of total Company gross revenue.

IBM

A large licensing office with several dozen professionals is part of the Office of the General Counsel. The licensing office comprises both business people and attorneys and often relies on support teams in the business divisions. There are licensing programs directed to both technology transfers and patents. Licensing income is allocated to the operating business. The Company actively licenses out technology related to its products and will license competitors. Based on the continuing status of IBM as the largest issuer of U.S. Patents over the past few years, it is expected that licensing income will continue to be strong and grow.

Hewlett-Packard Company

There is no formal licensing office; however, licensing activities are handled on a centralized basis in the Corporate Legal Department. Attorneys work with business people in the product groups to do out-licensing of technology and patents. Licensing activities are directed primarily to strategic alliances, joint ventures and those who would otherwise infringe company patents. Core technologies are generally not licensed, except in some cases as part of broader cross-license agreements. Non-core technologies and older or unused technologies are licensed when there is appropriate patent coverage. One objective in licensing is to achieve design freedom for the creation of future products. Licensing income is secondary and generally passed back to the businesses when there is an identified technology owner. Licensing income fluctuates from year-to-year depending on the business drivers, programs underway, and opportunities discovered.

DIMENSIONS

Out-licensing activities can be differentiated along three primary dimensions—purpose, size, and skill mix. There are, of course, other descriptors that are occasionally used, but these three are most often heard in discussions between and among out-licensing firms to describe their offices.

The first of these, purpose, is the reason why the office was created and what it is expected to accomplish for the company. As already discussed, there are a wide range of purposes. The impact of purpose or rationale on the structure, focus, and size of an out-licensing office is perhaps one of the most fundamental findings of this investigation, and it is discussed in detail below.

The second major dimension that describes out-licensing activities is size. Size is defined as the number of professional staff associated with the office. The third major dimension is the mix of professional staff. Usually, professional staff are divided into two categories: attorneys and businesspeople. The fundamental orientations of these two kinds of professionals are very different. Attorneys tend to focus on the protection issues and on offensive and defensive postures. Businesspeople tend to focus on income-generating capability and on entrepreneurial matters. Most out-licensing offices characterize their skilled professionals as being either legal or business.

IMPORTANCE OF PURPOSE

One of the most striking (and least surprising) results of this investigation was to note that a company's specific purpose for mounting an out-licensing activity had a major impact on the nature and kind of office that was established. Purposes arise from situations, which in turn provide the reason why companies decide to move into out-licensing. The purpose for out-licensing can be expected to have a direct effect on office size, structure, and constituency. Moreover, there may be multiple purposes that overlap one another. In the following, for each purpose we briefly discuss the underlying rationale and the implications of that purpose for the kind of office established:

Core Technology. Companies interested in out-licensing their core technology are interested in obtaining the best possible measure of income and competitive advantage. They are active seekers of licensing partners. They describe the process of finding partners as very much like combing the sea floor for buried treasure. Just as it takes a lot of staff resource to find the treasure so too does it take a lot of staff to identify and pursue licensees who are both interested in the core technology and willing to pay a premium price.

  Implications: The office will require a relatively large number of staff, both legal and business professionals.

Non-Core Technology. Companies in this category see their technology as a byproduct of strategic activity. They are fundamentally interested in picking up income from the sale of technologies that are no longer key to their strategy. Companies in this position usually are interested in maximizing income but only if they can minimize their investment in obtaining the income. The analogy here is that they wish to wade into the river and shoot those fish that happen to come to the surface. This purpose usually means that the firm will invest a minimum amount into the out-licensing activity.

  Implications: Expect a small out-licensing office, although this does not mean that out-licensing noncore technology is an inexpensive enterprise. On the contrary, there will be significant expenditures of management and technical staff time in determining which of the firm's technologies are core and which aren't. The major expenditure for firms in this category is the cost of developing and maintaining an internal decision process that initially (and perhaps routinely) decides which technologies are to be classified as non-core. Offices developed for this purpose usually are staffed mostly with business professionals.

Anticipation of Becoming a Profit Center. Firms developing an out-licensing office for this reason tend to move slowly. They often are unsure of the amount of revenues or profits that might be expected from out-licensing their technologies. They usually create a very small activity at first, using a wait-and-see attitude. If the activity begins to generate income and profits, they consider increasing the investment. Firms with this purpose in mind tend to bootstrap their out-licensing offices, making them pay for themselves while they grow.

Implications: Firms with this purpose can expect to begin with a very small out-licensing activity and monitor its activities and progress closely. If it begins to produce revenues and income, the firm tends to respond favorably to requests for increased funding. If it develops revenues or profits slowly, the firm also responds slowly to requests for growth in funding. The skill mix for this purpose tends to be relatively balanced between legal and business professionals.

Non-Strategic Markets. Out-licensing technology for firms with this purpose in mind must develop a capability for identifying markets that are far afield from the firm's traditional ones. Usually this means finding entirely different businesses or industries that use the technology but for very different applications than the developers may have foreseen. In addition, once identification has been made, the firm must then identify target companies and initiate discussions leading to negotiations. Investing in an out-licensing office for this purpose is often seen as a risky venture. Most firms with this purpose will move slowly, investing in one person to see if the non-strategic market idea will be productive. When income begins to flow from successful licenses, the firm will add staff, and probably will do so at a slow pace.

Implications: A small staff, usually heavily weighted toward business rather than legal professionals.

Design Freedom. Companies with this purpose for their out-licensing find themselves developing large patent portfolios and entering into cross-licensing agreements with a range of partners. Cross-licensing agreements are often time consuming to develop, negotiate, and complete to the overall satisfaction of all parties.

Implications: This purpose requires a relatively large staff, many of whom can be expected to be attorneys.

Alliances. This purpose for out-licensing is similar in its affect on office structure to the Design Freedom purpose. It requires the use of cross-licenses as part of the mechanism for cementing alliances. For this reason, this purpose involves time-consuming work around preparing and negotiating cross-license packages.

Implications: Offices formed for this purpose will tend to have large staffs, balanced between business and legal professionals.

Infringer Policing. Companies with this purpose in mind find that they learn relatively easily about infringers. Their marketing people and their customers both keep them aware of new or potentially infringing products in the marketplace. Nevertheless, a major cost of pursuing infringers is in the preparation for and negotiation of licenses. Further, the parties may get involved in litigation proceedings before resolution and this, too, takes a considerable amount of staff time and money. A side benefit of this purpose is that where it is successfully pursued, the out-licensing activity becomes largely self-supporting through the income received from infringer licensing.

Implications: Offices formed for this purpose tend to grow to a significant size. The skill mix in these offices is weighted toward attorneys.

Standards Perpetuation. This purpose for out-licensing has no direct profit motive. Companies pursue this strategic policy with an anticipation of some future benefit from their current or downstream technology as well as future market position.

Implications: No general implications on office size or skill mix.

Inevitability. Companies considering establishing an out-licensing office because of the inevitability that someone will license a competing technology for the same application, recognize that this need for out-licensing arises on an as-required basis. Rarely would a company consider creating a formal out-licensing activity for this purpose alone. Usually there are other reasons in addition to this one for the establishment of a formal office.

Implications: No general implications on office size or skill mix.

The foregoing outlines the implications that purpose has on two of the primary dimensions of out-licensing offices, size and skill mix. The following table summarizes these implications.

COST EFFECTIVENESS

"What will it cost and is this the best use of our next investment dollar?" This is the question most asked by financial officers when companies are de-

Exhibit 6.1. Summary of Implications of Purpose on Office Size and Skill Mix

Purpose	Size of Staff	Mix of Staff	Notes
Core Technology	large	balanced	
Noncore Technology	small	mostly business	Possibly significant costs in identifying noncore technologies
Anticipation of Profit	small	balanced	Start small, build as necessary
Nonstrategic markets	small	mostly business	Develop slowly
Design Freedom	large	mostly attorneys	
Alliances	large	balanced	
Infringer Policing	large	mostly attorneys	
Standards Perpetuation	no implications	no implications	
Inevitability	no implications	no implications	

liberating whether to invest in an out-licensing activity. As might be expected, there is no one answer to these two questions. There are, however, some patterns of behavior to suggest that real answers may be emerging from actual practice. The returns expected from investing in out-licensing are additional revenue and new profits. One suspects there must be a threshold amount for revenue and another for profits which, if an internal champion of out-licensing could guarantee it, would be sufficient to persuade even the most penny-pinching financial officer of the economic desirability of out-licensing.

A word should be said here about the costs of creating an out-licensing office. The direct costs of an office typically are budgeted as the cost of the people and their direct expenses. Overhead charges may or may not be added depending upon each company's accounting protocols. Nevertheless, it is often the case that these direct costs are not the whole picture; indeed, experience shows that firms tend to underestimate the total cost associated with out-licensing. Additional costs are associated with internal technology reviews and decision-making processes to select and approve technologies for out-licensing. These cost-laden activities grow in importance and resources as the licensing activity grows. These costs are indirect; and often, they are hidden. They are difficult to forecast and for this reason usually they are not fully considered in profit center proposals.

We hypothesized that if a company could guarantee that out-licensing would generate significant financial results, then any proposal with such a financial forecast would be worth considering. The question of the definition of significance then becomes important. Companies successfully developing income from out-licensing produce an amount of income or profits sufficient to meet the offices' purposes. For example, companies out-licensing primarily to generate income will be successful at a higher level of income generation than will companies out-licensing for the purpose of creating standards.

For companies whose out-licensing purpose is income generation, our interviews suggest that producing approximately one percent of the firm's total annual revenues from out-licensing is achievable. In terms of profits, a single figure is much more variable and difficult to define. Nevertheless, we conclude from the interviews that if an income-generating firm were to achieve 5 to 10 percent of its profits from out-licensing, it could consider itself successful.

There are other levels of income production that may be considered in terms of the success of an out-licensing activity. Some firms wish to generate enough income to pay for the costs of their patent and out-licensing activities; essentially to provide these services to their firm at no cost. In this case, the financial criterion for success would be a level of income sufficient to meet the budget for the patent and licensing activities.

SUMMARY AND CONCLUSIONS

Companies considering creating an out-licensing office are faced with a series of questions whose answers determine whether they will invest in out-licensing. We have learned that companies come to the decision point after a period of rising awareness of some situation that the firm will use as its reason for out-licensing. In this chapter we interviewed eight companies and were able to identify nine reasons why out-licensing offices are created.

Companies debating whether to invest in a formal out-licensing office wrestle with the potential cost-effectiveness of such offices. The data we have been able to gather show that successful out-licensing companies should anticipate generating approximately one percent of their annual revenues from this enterprise.

We learned that the rationale that causes companies to decide to out-license is transformed into the purpose for their out-licensing activity. The purpose is the most powerful force affecting the size, structure, constituency, and focus of the out-licensing activity. Further, based upon the purpose it is possible to determine in advance what the size and constituency of the office is likely to be.

This brief study has only touched on a few major points of interest concerning the establishment of out-licensing offices. Further interviews to describe current practice, followed by ideation and conceptual work, should develop a set of metrics that will guide firms more fully through the difficult task of deciding whether to out-license, for what purpose, and how to focus office activity to the strategic benefit of the firm.

7

Licensing and Business Strategy in the Chemicals Industry

Peter C. Grindley
Law & Economics Consulting Group

Jack A. Nickerson

John M. Olin School of Business
Washington University in Saint Louis

INTRODUCTION

Licensing is playing an increasingly important role in the development and commercialization of innovation in many industries. Licensing has long been a component of business strategy, but in the past its use has often been restricted to areas away from the firm's core business. Out-licensing has been used to earn residual value from unused or mature technology, or to provide access to foreign markets or product markets the innovator has no plans to enter directly. While this remains a predominant approach to licensing, there has been a gradual increase in the volume and extent of licensing activity, especially over the past decade, making it more central to firms' strategies. Facing stronger innovation-based competition, often on a global scale, firms have become more aware of the value of licensing, and are more likely to include it as a component of their competitive strategy. Firms have broadened their licensing objectives with a greater variety of commercialization methods and partnership structures. They may also be more willing to license-in technology as an alternative to in-house development.

There are several different objectives for technology licensing, which reflect underlying business strategies. These in turn depend on the nature of the innovation, the competitive conditions in the industry, the relative strengths of the parties, the quality of intellectual property (IP) being transferred, the strength of IP protection, and other concerns. Based on the analysis of a number of case studies, including the current study of the chemicals industry, four basic objectives of technology licensing have been identified: efficient commercialization, technology exchange, strategic interaction, and strategic misfits. For each of these objectives there are various forms of licensing structures, according to what is included in the license, how the agreement is organized, and how the license is integrated into a broader strategic relationship, if any. Structures range from simple arms-length licenses for patent rights, to turnkey technologies combining IP rights and know-how, more complex structures involving licensing intermediaries, joint ventures for commercializing and/or developing technology, and finally to several forms of alliances and partnerships.

Categorizing licenses around strategic objectives serves at least three purposes. First, understanding the strategic objectives underlying the license can help licensing managers structure agreements in the most appropriate way. Objectives and structures are interrelated, and the form of the agreements is likely to be different in each case. Experience has shown that licensing attempts often fail because of the inability of the parties to resolve issues that are primarily strategic. Shifting the focus of licensing negotiations from, say, a unidimensional concern about royalty rates to a broader focus on the terms and conditions needed to make licensing agreements work greatly increases the chance of licensing success.

Second, this links licensing more securely to the overall innovation management of the firm as part of the development and commercialization process. Strategic choices may be needed to make licensing more effective (for example, through the development of in-house capabilities in technology transfer or the introduction of a focused patenting strategy), and, conversely, the inclusion of licensing options at an early stage in strategic decisions should enhance innovation performance (perhaps by deciding which products to develop or which markets to enter).

Third, from a legal and policy viewpoint, it is important to inform the debate about the impact of licensing on competition. Fuller understanding of licensing procedures, including the links between licensing and strategy, the efficiency rationale, and reasons for certain terms and conditions, may help allay antitrust concerns.

The purpose of this chapter is to review the different ways in which technology licensing is used as part of innovation strategy in the chemical process industry. We review the different objectives of firms for licensing in different segments of the industry, and we look more closely at the different structures of the licensing agreements, focusing primarily on the use of licensing in commercialization, the predominant motivation for licensing in the industry.

The chemicals industry has a number of attractions as a case study. The first is that licensing is a widespread and important feature of the industry.

Although technology is primarily developed in-house for use in manufacturing products, licensing is used extensively to acquire specific technologies and to access international markets.

A second attraction is that there is a broad range of types of licensing, including examples of each of the categories listed above. The main licensing activity is in the area of commercialization, where several strategic variations are evident. License agreements range from small to very large-scale complex projects, and may include alliances and joint ventures.

Third, licensing involves complex issues of IP protection and technology transfer. The emphasis in the industry is on process technology, and all but the simplest licenses involve a mixture of patents and know-how. Significant resources are needed to effect transfer, and there are special competitive concerns about the area of use of the technology and the ability to contain the leakage of know-how. These call for sophisticated valuation procedures and license negotiations with closely defined licensing conditions and restrictions.

Finally, there are currently a number of changes taking place in the industry's attitude to licensing as a source of revenues and of complementary technologies. Licensing in the past usually has been incidental to the firm's main goals. Firms are now more likely to use out-licensing and joint ventures as part of their commercialization strategies. They are also less able to develop all their own technology in-house and are turning to alliances and in-licensing of technology as a means of reducing innovation costs.

The case study bears on these issues by illustrating, for this particular industry, the range of licensing behavior in the different business divisions of the firms, as seen in the different objectives and structures of licensing agreements. It also shows the efficiency and strategic concerns guiding licensing behavior, and their impact on the structure of the agreements. This includes the role of license restrictions in enabling the firms to license out in ways that do no compromise the value of their IP or damage their competitive position. It illustrates some specific institutional arrangements that help overcome some of the problems facing a licensor. These include methods of negotiating licenses, valuing technology, alleviating the leakage of know-how, isolating legal and business risks, efficiently organizing the transfer of technology, and providing the resources and skills required. In particular this includes the use of specialist engineering firms as intermediaries in the licensing and construction of new process plants, which is an important feature of the industry.

More generally, the study illustrates some aspects of integration between a firm's licensing behavior and its innovation strategy, including the broad management of research and development, and the firm's intellectual capital. It shows current trends in an important, representative industry towards more active licensing policies and the closer management of the firm's IP portfolio.

The study is based on a series of interviews with licensing executives from a number of leading firms in the chemicals industry. We have also relied on a review of the relevant literature. We are most grateful to these executives for the time and effort they have devoted to this project. The study focuses on general licensing behavior in the industry, rather than the specific conditions facing a given firm. The analysis and opinions expressed here are those of the authors and should not be seen as necessarily reflecting the views of any of the companies involved.

LICENSING OBJECTIVES

Licensing is undertaken for a variety of reasons. The main strategic objectives that may be met through licensing are categorized as efficient commercialization, technology exchange and cross-licensing, strategic interaction, and licensing of strategic misfits. (These objectives are discussed in Chapter 5.) In this chapter, we report on licensing activities of several large firms in the chemicals industry and how their activities serve the strategic objectives. Although a given agreement tends to focus on a certain type of objective, there are many overlaps. All licenses are strategic in some sense, and all are ultimately involved in commercializing innovation. The categories reflect the main aim of the agreements, which in turn determine how they are negotiated and structured.

Efficient Commercialization

Innovation can lead to a range of commercialization options, from storage to integrated production. All the alternatives but the extremes, storage and fully integrated in-house commercialization, involve licensing. Efficient commercialization is the use of licensing to combine technology with the complementary assets, such as quality manufacturing, marketing, distribution, and continued product improvement, needed to succeed in the marketplace. The aim of this type of licensing is to supplement a company's own complementary assets by accessing those of other firms, whether they are production know-how, distribution, or capital. In the chemicals industry, complementary assets accessed by licensing are often in specific geographic or other markets that the innovator either cannot reach alone or can reach only at high cost. As described by several licensing professionals, licensing as a major component of technology commercialization has been steadily on the rise.

Up to 5 years ago, as claimed by several licensing professionals from a large diversified chemicals firm hereafter referred to as Firm A, licensing activity was mostly incidental to technology sales of mature processes and equipment. Licenses sometimes went along with these technology sales. Today, global competition is driving changes in the use of licensing. The increasingly rapid pace of technological change means that even if Firm A had the money to develop needed technology it could not afford to take the time to develop that technology internally. Competitive pressures extend to the entire commercialization process—developing new complementary assets such as distribution needed to commercialize a technology may require such large amounts of time and money that the choice of integration is an uncompetitive one. Indeed, time to access needed technology or complementary assets has become critical to profitable commercialization in a global economy.

Licensing is especially likely to serve strategic purposes when used as a means of entering foreign markets. Earlier studies in the literature have shown that the preferred method of international commercialization is often direct investment, because of the higher profits that can usually be earned by direct investment and the greater strategic control this gives the parent company. However, there are good reasons why a firm may prefer licensing to a noncontrolled foreign entity. Entering foreign markets can be a costly and long-term proposition, especially in terms of developing local production and distribution channels. Even a joint venture may involve too many risks (Contractor, 1985; Telesio, 1979).

Our study confirms many of these observations. Firm A's executives choose licensing when it is a more economical commercialization vehicle than internal development and commercialization would be. Licensing in this context may be a component of an interfirm relationship such as a joint venture, subsidiary, partnership, and so on, and it is seen as a necessary activity for meeting today's global competition by providing the most efficient way to commercialize technology rapidly. In response to this view, Firm A has been increasing its out-licensing activities to gain access to world markets.

Another large diversified chemical company, hereafter referred to as Firm B, has had a similar experience. It typically enters into commercial licenses to gain access to geographic markets that it does not and plans not to serve. Out-licensing technology is the only way that Firm B can profit from these geographic markets. Firm B also uses licensing to commercialize technologies that serve markets the firms considers to be too small to support its investment. Other firms, especially smaller ones, may be able profitably to address small markets, which would otherwise be too costly for Firm B to serve.

The strategic choice by Firms A and B to increase out-licensing is resonant with the objectives of two out-licensing programs that have received notable attention (Royse, 1993). Union Carbide and BP Chemical have actively licensed their production processes for polyolefins (hd/lldPE and PP) as a means of efficient commercialization since 1977 and 1983, respectively. With large capital expenditures needed for each plant, neither firm had the capital resources needed to commercialize the technology on a worldwide basis. Carefully timing the introduction of new processes was also important—there were advantages in being first to license extensively by preempting processes developed by competitors, and this also meant that intermediate products used in the process became more readily available earlier (*Business Week*, 1993; Evans, 1993). Today, licensees of the two firms combined account for more than 50 percent of the world's supply of these chemicals. The success of Union Carbide's licensing programs is emphasized by estimates of revenues from polyolefins in 1992 at $300 million (Royse, 1993, p. 4). In essence, out-licensing allowed Union Carbide and BP Chemical to commercialize their innovations efficiently worldwide by accessing other firms' capital and local capabilities.

Although many chemicals firms have a newfound interest in out-licensing, using out-licensing to commercialize a technology efficiently is not a new activity for BP Chemical. As a recent and small entrant into the chemicals industry in the late 1950s, BP America (then Sohio) was relatively unsophisticated and had no international experience (Evans, 1993). After commercializing a new low-cost process for acrylonitrile in the U.S., it engaged in an aggressive out-licensing program that continues today. With the licensing revenues it received, BP was able to invest heavily in research and development—an investment that has led to its position today as a leading chemical company.

Our examples thus far have focused on out-licensing activities, but in-licensing activities are also on the rise. Although licensing practices differ by business segment, Firm A has a corporate mandate in the chemicals area to acquire more outside technology through in-licensing rather than invent all technology internally. Firm A's agricultural products business provides an example. Licensing, it claims, is used primarily for the purpose of accessing technology to develop products or businesses. In-licensing is undertaken because it is often not profitable to develop technology internally. Internal development is not a timely development alternative when technology can be licensed in. Indeed, a recurring theme throughout our interviews was that accessing technology in a timely manner has become critical to commercialization success and that in-licensing is a way to save time.

Our interviews suggest that in the chemicals industry licensing activities for the purpose of efficient commercialization are on the rise. Firms A and B are exploiting in-licensing and out-licensing activities to achieve more efficient commercialization by getting to market faster, and by entering markets in which—for geographic or other reasons—they otherwise would not have participated or would have done so at high cost. Indeed, the success of Union Carbide and BP Chemical have shown the value of licensing activities. Changes in the global business environment have increased pressure to get to market quickly. Efficient commercialization has become an increasingly important strategic objective and may be the dominant motivation for increased licensing activity in the chemicals industry.

Technology Exchange

Technology exchange includes the cross-licensing of technology and intellectual property rights and the reciprocal exchange of complementary technologies. It can serve a number of specific objectives. The most widespread use of cross-licensing in other industries, especially electronics, is the mutual licensing of patent rights, within a field of use, to achieve freedom to operate by avoiding potential infringement litigation. Exchange is also used as a means of technology acquisition, as a resolution of litigation, and as technology leverage in licensing negotiations. Cross-licensing in general is used relatively sparingly in the chemical industry. This is primarily because the main technology content in the industry is in process technology, which tends to be specific to the individual firms and based on know-how and trade secrets. Nonetheless, exchanges of technology and intellectual property rights do occur, as highlighted by the following examples.

Freedom to Operate. Cross-licensing of patents is rare in the chemicals industry, and when it does occur it is much more focused than in the electronics industry. Cross-licensing typically is not undertaken in a proactive way. Whereas semiconductor firms, for example, enter into cross-licensing agreements prior to running into commercialization difficulties, firms in the chemical industry often wait until actual problems occur. Only then do they try to access bottleneck technologies or intellectual property rights through cross-licensing. Cross-licensing is the preferred mechanism for accessing technology and rights to patents because it requires neither cash expenditures nor running royalties.

Firm A provides an illustration. It prefers to exchange patents and technology for cross-licensing rather than to pay royalties, because such exchanges conserve cash. But cross-licensing depends on the particular business and circumstances. Firm A's bottom line is to avoid paying money up front for other firms' patents and technologies because cash payments are viewed as costly.

One circumstance that has lead to cross-licensing is when a firm becomes involved in new fields that are already crowded with patents. Firm A's medical products division, which is a relatively new line of business for the firm, A developed a new technology for detecting a type of bacteria. It was discovered that commercializing the technology required complementary technologies for which many patents already existed and designing around them was not economically feasible. In fact, it is not unusual that three of four in-licenses owned by other firms may be needed to commercialize products in Firm A's medical products business. Cross-licensing was the least costly way of gaining freedom to commercialize the innovation.

Technology Acquisition. The most evident form of cross-licensing in the chemicals industry in trading technology, or reciprocal licensing, in which a firm will give a license in order to receive one. In some cases this is an informal understanding that a future license is expected to balance a current license, in other cases there is a direct link between the licensing agreements.

Firms often choose to make a license agreement as an exchange of technologies. One reason, noted above, is a preference for noncash transfers, as the uncertainties surrounding a new project may make it difficult to justify a cash outlay at an early stage. Reciprocal licensing agreements are a feature of the chemicals industry, but these may be implicit rather than parts of a single agreement. Each is negotiated separately, with a cash value attached to it. Payments then may be netted out. The main problem is that it is very difficult to negotiate a double agreement, especially as separate business units may be involved on both sides.

The grain business offers one illustration from the current cases. A large diversified chemicals firm created a new biological product that requires a seed as a commercialization vehicle. Rather than enter the seed business, the firm has entered into a cross-licensing agreement with seed companies in a complex relationship that allows the seed companies to sell seeds containing the innovation to farmers who contemporaneously contract with the chemicals firm for growing the advanced grain or take out a license so they can sell the grain to end-customers. Without cross-licensing to gain access to seed technology, commercialization may have taken many years at much higher costs or, perhaps, might not have occurred at all.

More generally, reciprocal licenses include the exchange of unrelated technologies between firms that do not compete in the exchanged technology's particular market segment. Cashless cross-licensing agreements such as the one just described are more likely between firms that have an ongoing history of noncompetitive relations. Even when the exchange is between firms that are not competitors, reciprocal licenses face organizational obstacles. Firm B, for example, has been unable to complete any reciprocal licenses in the past four years. One executive suggested that the limited use of cross-licensing at his firm can be traced to two reasons. First, Firm B's reciprocal agreement opportunities are typically for the exchange of two technologies, not multiple technologies. He claims that both parties have the incentive to exchange patents of little value in an attempt to receive patents of high value, which makes valuation of intellectual property difficult. Second, negotiations and, in particular, agreement on a technology's value, are made difficult because of the organization structure and intellectual property management approach of most large chemicals firms. In most instances, a chemical company's intellectual property is managed by business units instead of at a corporate level. Cross-licensing agreements are likely to involve out-licensing technology from one division in exchange for in-licensing technology for another division. Each division's goal of profit maximization encourages them to overvalue out-licenses, undervalue in-licenses, and argue over internal transfer prices for splitting net gains from the cross-license.

As a result of these problems, licensing executives often will treat reciprocal licensing as two separate agreements where the monetary value of the technology in question is determined separately. Only when the monetary value of each technology is determined can they be exchanged on a cash equivalent basis without additional fees.

Litigation Resolution. It is not uncommon for intellectual property infringement issues to arise in the chemicals industry. Cross-licensing is one way for chemicals firms to resolve such litigation. In general, cross-licensing may take place at any point in the litigation process, either in the preliminary stage before the case has gone to trial, in the midst of a trial, or as part of the post-trial settlement. One company explained that once litigation has started, and costs escalate, it may resort to cross-licensing to end litigation, typically before trial or the completion of a trial. Executives from several firms with whom we spoke view cross-licensing as the most cost effective way to resolve litigation without the use of cash payments. However, cross-licensing is often viewed as a means of last resort for ending a dispute.

Leverage. Although it is perhaps the least frequently mentioned strategic use of licensing, cases of using licensing to gain leverage on competitors or suppliers were reported by our interviewees. A prototypical example that was offered by one firm described the use of licensing to solve what in the economics literature is called a bilateral monopoly problem. Firm A decided to exit from the market as a supplier of a certain intermediate product and to out-source its needs instead. It contracted with the largest remaining supplier and became that supplier's largest customer.

In this situation the risk is that Firm A may try to use its size to obtain a lower price from the supplier and the supplier may try to use its position as the only firm capable of supplying Firm A's needs to obtain a higher price. Partly to guard against these bargaining difficulties, Firm A, when it exited the intermediate product supply market, did not disband the associated research and development team. The team developed a technology of high value and importance to the supplier. Using its technology as leverage, Firm A was better able to negotiate a low-price long-term contract for the intermediate product in exchange for a license covering the new technology. Although such opportunities are rare, this example suggests that leverage opportunities in the chemical industry do exist and that at least some firms take advantage of them.

Strategic Interaction

Another use of out-licensing is to influence strategically the decisions made by customers, competitors, and suppliers. This can serve three specific objectives: to help establish a new product or process in the market by reducing the risk of adopting the innovation and building up the supply of intermediates, to help establish new product standards; and to deter other competitors from developing matching technologies. Important illustrations of these objectives can be found the strategic motivations of the licensing programs undertaken by Union Carbide and BP Chemicals.

In a recent article about Union Carbide's licensing activities, Richard Sol, director of licensing sales, explained how licensing was used to influence customers strategically as well as to provide for efficient commercialization. Customers, he states, might have been resistant to having only one supplier. So Union Carbide "had to invest in [its] own resin business to help stimulate the market" as well as simultaneously to license major US competitors such as Exxon and Mobil (Royse, 1993, p. 4). Reducing customers' perceptions of the risks involved in adopting the final product was clearly one of the strategic objectives that guided Union Carbide's decision to license in addition to commercializing through integration.

BP Chemical used licensing and the sequence of firms that it licensed as the means of getting its acrylonitrile technology adopted throughout the industry. After being rejected as a partner by one of the U.S. chemical giants in the early 1960s, BP began licensing Japanese manufacturers. Only then, a former director of BP America's Patent and License Division claims, did American manufactures recognize that BP Chemical (then Sohio) really had something, and that in order to compete with it and the Japanese, they must also take licenses. Over the next decade, companies in western Europe, eastern Europe, and, eventually, developing countries around the world took licenses. BP's process has become a de facto industry standard. Had the Japanese firms not been licensed when they were, the former director believes, they would have found a way to produce acrylonitrile without a license, and that would have made them a substantial competitor today. Furthermore, it is unlikely that U.S. firms would have taken licenses so quickly, and perhaps not at all, if the Japanese firms were not licensed.

The BP experience also provides insight into how licensing is used for strategic deterrence. Not licensing the technology would have encouraged other firms, in this case the Japanese firms, to invent around a technology. Licensing may keep potential competitors from investing in research and development to get around patents. Licensing for the purpose of strategic deterrence, however, is highly dependent on the license's royalty. Larry Evans, former Director, Patent & Licensing Division, BP America, Inc. argues, a royalty rate must be set "so that licensees will not be encouraged to expend significant effort to develop alternative processes that fall outside the license" (Evans, 1993, p. 77). Such strategic deterrence, while often considered anticompetitive, can have important social benefits if the licensee expends its resources improving the existing technology instead of designing around it.

In sum, licensing has been used in the chemicals industry for the purpose of strategic interaction. Reducing customer risks, creating standards, and strategically deterring competitors all provide important reasons for licensing. Licensing for the purpose of strategic interaction typically is only one of a set of objectives that also include efficient commercialization. Indeed, as is the case with many activities, a single license may serve multiple strategic objectives.

Strategic Misfits

Strategic misfits are those technologies that have no place in the firm's strategic plans. These nonstrategic technologies are either innovations developed to a certain point but not used, or generic competences with no particular strategic value that have been developed by the firm. At one level, the category of strategic misfits overlaps with the commercialization strategy for innovations that for various reasons a firm decides not to pursue, but from which it may earn some residual value by out-licensing. They may also be technologies in areas ancillary to the firm's main business, such as in information systems to support a service function within the firm.

All of our interviewees reported increases in their activities for out-licensing and nonstrategic technologies, but chemicals firms are proceeding with caution. For example, Firm A decided that it no longer relied on a set of paint-related patents so it attempted to out-license those nonstrategic technologies. One firm that wanted to license the technology also wanted the right to sublicense to one or more unnamed firms. For fear that the technology might be passed into competitors' hands, the licensing agreement was not executed.

Although this example suggests restraint in out-licensing strategic misfits, the opportunities from out-licensing misfits is large. Executives from Firm A believe that strategic businesses are supported by only 3 to 5 percent of the firm's patent portfolio, which consists of many thousands of patents. Even if only a small percentage of the remaining portfolio has commercial value for other firms, the opportunity for capturing value from these unused patents seems large. Still, so long as chemicals firms can recover their costs from attempting to license nonstrategic technology, it is likely that they will continue to pursue the out-licensing of strategic misfits.

STRUCTURING LICENSING AGREEMENTS

Definition of Licensing Structure

The strategic objectives that define major licensing categories depend on what the firms expect to achieve from the license, and consequently on the relationship between the parties. Thus a cross-license of patent rights is significantly different from a license for the transfer of know-how to build a new process plant. The aims, the information needs, and the relationship between the parties are different in each case. The licensing agreement itself is also likely to be different, with varying degrees of complexity and different requirements, restrictions, and guarantees built into the license.

Within these broad categories, there are specific characteristics of the organization of the license. We refer to these as the license structure, meaning the more detailed technical and legal content of the license agreements and the nature of the alliance between licensor and licensee. At one extreme the license may be a simple arms-length out-licensing of rights to use a patent in return for a fee. This is essentially a market transaction with few links between licensor and licensee, with the relevant terms of the agreement defined closely within the license itself. At the other extreme, the license may be part of a broad technology-sharing partnership. It may define the legal basis for technology exchange in the partnership, but necessarily it may be expressed in broad terms so that the true basis for the partnership lies in the informal relationship between the two firms. In between there are a number of alternatives with varying degrees of integration between licensor and licensee, including turnkey technology transfer agreements, licensing intermediaries, joint ventures, and strategic partnerships.

One of the aims of this chapter is to give a better understanding of the different licensing structures and how they are related to the nature of the agreements. In so doing we concentrate on commercialization licenses, which are the most prevalent and varied type of license in the chemicals industry.

Role of Licensing Department

The firms we are concerned with in this chapter are major chemicals producers. Their main objective is the manufacture and sale of products. Research is performed to obtain a proprietary position in the market, not to sell technology. For example, in the words of Robert Kline, chief patent counsel for DuPont, "[the firm] is not in the business of licensing technology. [It] does research to obtain a proprietary position" (Spalding, 1986, p. 31). The aim of licensing is to maximize commercial revenues from IP available for licensing. In our interviews, Firm B noted that licensing is undertaken as a cost center not a profit center; that is, it performs a service function for licensing technology developed for the primary goal of integrated production. This is mainly an opportunistic approach to licensing to extract value from existing IP.

However, it is also clear that today firms are using licensing as a more central part of their commercialization strategies, and that this is a continuing trend. This has gone further in some firms than in others. For example, the Union Carbide and BP Chemical licensing programs for major new production processes for polyolefins, discussed above, have placed licensing of particular technologies as a leading means of commercializing innovation. In Union Carbide's case a separate division has been set up to manage the transfer of technology. Interestingly, Union Carbide's strategy of out-licensing its Unipol polyethylene process was partly motivated by earnings pressure in the early 1980s (*Business Week*, 1993, p. 88). Licensing began in 1979, and in 1983 the company brought 4,000 of its engineers and technicians together into a new Engineering and Technology Services Group (ETS). This group licenses technology and provides catalysts, engineering services, process design, and project management to chemical and other process industry customers. In some cases Union Carbide markets the product as well.

Most of the corporations described in this chapter are taking a more active licensing and IP management stance. As a first step in this direction some firms have centralized licensing at a corporate level, which standardizes the licensing treatment across the corporation and enables a coordinated corporate strategy. It also facilitates a more proactive role in seeking licensing opportunities and in providing inputs into the broader problems of reducing the costs of maintaining the company's IP portfolio. This may take the form of reviewing the corporation's patent portfolio for licensing opportunities and weeding out unworked patents of no strategic value to the company. In some firms there is also interest in broader IP management, involving licensing and IP protection considerations in some way in technology development decisions. However, as yet there is little agreement on the best way to tackle this. The companies are primarily interested in developing and manufacturing product, and are cautious about letting licensing opportunities, often still seen as only of secondary importance in commercializing IP, influence development decisions.

A result is that the role of the licensing department differs between firms. In some firms it may have primarily an administrative or support role, whereas in others it may be more actively involved in seeking and negotiating licensing agreements. In Firm A, licensing decisions have in the past been primarily the responsibility of the business divisions, although a centralized licensing department is generally involved in formalizing agreements. There is limited uniformity in the structure of the agreements across divisions, and an opportunistic approach to licensing. In some cases conflicts of interest between divisions have been hard to resolve without an overseeing department, for example if one division wishes to license to a competitor of another. In Firm B, the licensing function is more centralized. Negotiations and agreements are more standardized, and the firm appears more likely to seek licensing opportunities on its own initiative. The firm has also instituted forms of communication channels across divisions to help coordinate IP management.

The sources of licensing opportunities vary, with many initiated by external inquiries but with some licensing departments taking more responsibility for finding business. This is most successful with targeted licensing—a rifle shot approach rather than scattershot mailings. The more successful licensors are those who are most active in seeking opportunities, who have an overview of the IP position of the firm, and who understand what the industry may need. The most advanced licensors have set up their own licensing subsidiaries to handle the effort needed to effect transfer. The less advanced are in response mode and have more limited activity.

Range of Licensing Structures

Commercialization of innovation may use a range of methods, from arms-length licensing to joint ventures and direct investment. The best mode depends on a balance of many factors. Some characteristics of potential markets, as noted in our survey, which favor licensing are that the market may be too small to justify investment, the market may be one in which the licensor does not normally compete, there may be strong established companies that might make entry difficult by opposing the entrant or by inventing around the innovation, or there might be an opportunity to get residual value from a mature technology, an unfavorable investment climate (one in which it is difficult to raise funds, or, in foreign markets, a liability to expropriation), and restrictions on foreign ownership. Reasons mitigating against licensing are the lack of strategic control over the use of the technology, the separation of the innovator from customers (and hence the inability to ensure high quality, or to invest in market development), potential exposure to litigation, and the fear of IP leakage.

At Firm B, commercialization licenses are seen as falling into three main types: nonstrategic (generic technology and capabilities), developmental, and commercial. This is a simplification of a range of licensing structures, as the innovation moves from the research stage up through development, prototype, pilot plant, and finally to commercialization. As the technology becomes more developed, what starts out in the research lab as a pure idea, and mainly protectable by patents, gradually becomes more complex and accumulates know-how, as knowledge about how to put the idea into practice is built up. For a process innovation, the final technology may be mostly know-how about how to build and operate the new plant, and there may be only a core of patents. This progression is accompanied by an increasing expenditure on the innovation, from the small amount in the initial laboratory stage, through the increasingly expensive development as it moves to pilot plant, to the even more expensive investment in plant and equipment as it moves into production. The progression also corresponds with the increasing value and strategic importance of the innovation. A critical point is where the new technology moves from an R&D cost center to a product profit center, when its development into production becomes much more expensive and it becomes a component of the firm's strategic business plans.

This progression is shown in Exhibit 7.1, which relates the development of an innovation to the combination of patent rights and know-how at the different stages. Embryonic technology in the research laboratory stage is

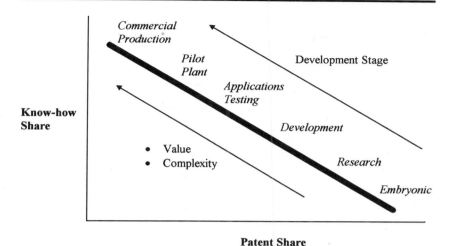

Patent Share

Exhibit 7.1.   Patent/Know-How Mixture and Development Stage
©Peter Grindley, Jack Nickerson, 1995

defined mainly in the patents surrounding it. As it moves up through development stages, in the sequence from research, process development, applications testing, pilot plant and finally to commercial production, the share of
know-how, shown by the thick center line, increases. It also becomes more
valuable and complex. In the end, process innovation, when it is fully commercialized in production, is mostly defined by the large amount of accumulated know-how. The importance of this relationship from the licensing point
of view is that development can be stopped at any time. This can happen for
any number of reasons. The firm may decide that the technology is not workable, or that though technically workable it is not commercially viable. Thus
the firm may have a number of unused technologies held at different stages
of development, with different combinations of patents and know-how.

Firm B is prepared to license incomplete technologies that it does not expect to pursue further. The purpose is mainly for residual revenue earning on
innovations that are not expected to have much strategic importance now or
in future, and have been abandoned. These may be at various stages of development. Some have not been taken beyond the research laboratory stage,
others have been developed towards production.

The firm may also license fully developed commercialized technologies
that have been put into production, although the strategic considerations are
more complex. It will license mature generic technologies that are in widespread use and are not a source of competitive advantage. It is unlikely to license innovations that could become a significant competitive threat in its
markets. Firm B, like the other firms mentioned in this chapter, including

Firm A, generally is unwilling to license fully developed technologies that are central to its business and in which it has a significant leadership position. There are few cases in which firms are willing to license out their core technologies, although this is occasionally used for major innovations too large for the firm to commercialize alone, and it is becoming less unusual to license leading-edge technology. In such cases, more elaborate relationships may be involved, such as joint ventures or partnerships, which reduce the strategic risks. The more central the technology is to a firm's strategy, the less likely it is to license it out, and if it does do so the terms for granting a license are likely to include restrictions on how the technology may be used.

The structure of a license agreement depends to a first approximation on the stage of development. An embryonic technology consists mainly of patent rights and is likely to be covered by a patents-only license. These are usually simple agreements, covered by a relatively standardized contract. However, there may be only a limited market for such licenses, as the licensee must have the technological competence to use the patent, and royalty earnings other than for the occasional key patent are likely to be modest. Licenses for developmental innovations tend to be simple boilerplate agreements for patent rights, although the terms of the grant are closely specified.

The bulk of licenses in this industry combine some level of know-how with the patent rights to enable the licensee to use the innovation without further development. The process technology tends to become quite firm-specific, so often a comprehensive package of know-how is needed for a turnkey license; which supplies all the necessary know-how and IP rights needed for a complete and ready to operate process. These combination licenses are more valuable to the licensor but are also more expensive to use, because rather than simply granting rights, they allow the transfer of technology. Transferring know-how is time-consuming and costly. The licensor usually must provide technical and management assistance and training and engineering support to complete the transfer. Although these licenses necessarily carry higher royalty and engineering fees, managing the transfer involves significant resources. These licenses also usually have greater strategic significance than pure patent licenses, because the agreements may essentially create competitors, supplying a licensee with all the capabilities needed to compete in the market with the licensor. Both these concerns may be enough to make out-licensing unattractive unless ways can be found to reduce their effect. These concerns contribute to the rationale for using licensing intermediaries, discussed below, and for restricting such transfers to those involved as part of more extensive agreements (for example, for joint product development or marketing).

Agreements typically are for a combination of patent and trade secrets. Protection of know-how by trade secrets is likely to be more complex than for patents, and contributes to the risks and greater resources needed. Patents, though sometimes covering only a small part of the technology being transferred, are extremely important in being able to protect the innovation. The value of the technology may lie mostly in the know-how, without which the patents cannot be worked effectively, but the patents provide the core for protecting the innovation from imitation, and preventing the licensee from licensing-on the technology to others.

Licensing is not the only way to obtain value from technology that the firm is not pursuing. As noted previously, Firm A estimates that as few as three to five percent of patents are actively involved in current products, but many more have strategic value to the firm. The firm may put technology into storage for possible future use, possibly for use as a bargaining chip or as support to future innovations. Because much of the IP is in fact know-how, storage often means keeping the knowledge as a trade secret within the firm.

Licensing Terms and Conditions

A license is the grant of positive rights to use proprietary IP. As such, both parties need to define the circumstances in which the IP can be used. The terms and conditions include restrictions on the use of the IP, as well as the definition of what is being transferred, the duration of the agreement, the fee structure, legal guarantees and warranties, and other information. Even in the simplest license there are a number of items needing close specification, such as the geographic and market areas for which the right is granted and if fees are to be paid as a lump sum or a running royalty.

The restrictions serve at least three main purposes. First, they help protect the IP, to ensure that the firm does not lose control over its technology as a result of licensing it out. Second, they enable the licensor to maximize the revenues from its technology, and ensure that licensing does not adversely affect the firm's competitive position. If these constraints were not included in the license a firm might not be able to license its innovation, and would be limited to commercializing it in-house. Restrictions are particularly important when the licensor is using a dual approach to commercialization, using the technology in-house to produce products for its home markets, and licensing it out for use elsewhere, either abroad or in other product markets. In such cases a firm is especially concerned about the competitive consequences of licensing. Third, the license contract is a legal document, and should attempt to limit the exposure of both parties in the event of litigation.

Firm B identifies the key terms and conditions to be negotiated as part of individual agreements to include the following: the definition of the license grant, exclusivity, field-of-use, territorial rights, duration of the license, patent coverage, payments and fees (royalties, know-how payments, service fees), technical assistance, definition, and improvements/grantbacks. There are also a number of more standardized terms and conditions, such as patent liability issues, guarantees and warranties, and other technical conditions.

The field-of-use and territorial restrictions define the market in which the IP can be used.

The terms are related to the firm's business interests for the technology. Thus a priority interest is in ensuring an aggressive licensee commitment to commercialize the technology. This is connected with the terms specifying an upfront fee and resource commitment by the licensee, which constitute an effective pledge of commitment. An exclusive license, for a given territorial market or field-of-use, may maximize licensee commitment and produce maximum returns—if this is the preferred commercialization strategy. Similarly, the scope of the grant depends on the nature of the global commercialization program. For example, if the aim is to maximize commercial activity—if one of the strategic interaction objectives is to establish a new process as broadly as possible in the market—than a nonexclusive license may be preferred.

In designing the license structure, the licensor is anxious to limit the resources it must devote to completing the transfer, which if not controlled could make the license uneconomic. This requires careful balance of estimated costs and revenues, so that the cost to license is kept within bounds. This affects the content and terms of the license.

There are a number of conditions associated with the protection of the technology. The license should include a provision to preserve the validity of the trade secrets by requiring the licensee to take reasonable steps to maintain the confidentiality of the secrets, such as requiring non-disclosure agreements from personnel in contact with the technology, keeping confidential documents in secure storage, and limiting access to trade secrets to those with a need to use them. It is unusual for a license to include sublicensing rights, in part because of the difficulty of maintaining the desired level of control over the IP with licensing at second or third hand. The terms of the warranties and guarantees are also an important part of the agreements, limiting the licensor's potential liability.

Many licenses for new technology also contain provisions for improvements exchanges, or grantbacks, of rights to use improvements to the technology made by the licensee, and vice versa. For experiential technology, such as a manufacturing process, many improvements are developed as part of using the technology in production—of learning by doing. For the licensor the risk is that a licensee, in using the licensed technology, may develop improvements to which the licensor might need to have access if it is to continue to exercise its technology competitively. For the licensee, the risk is that over time it may cease to have access to the most up-to-date technology. In either case, to guard against being blocked from the market in future, a grantback clause may be included allowing one party rights to use such developments by the other. Typically these agreements are optional and reciprocal. Discussing the out-licensing of a major process innovation, BP's licensing director at the time explained, "It is important to note that licensees were not required to exchange improvements. . . . On the other hand, all licensees want some limited exposure to the licensor's improvements. Sohio [later BP] insisted that, to the extent the licensee received Sohio's improvements, it must be willing to reciprocate" (Evans, 1993, p. 76). The details of a grantback in a particular case are a matter for individual negotiation.

Once a contract is agreed upon there is still the major task of contract administration. The licensor must ensure that the terms and conditions of the license contract are met, and that the speed and quality of commercialization maximizes the timeliness and size of the generated royalty revenues. This includes monitoring the adherence to the terms and conditions, assisting and encouraging the commercialization of embryonic technologies, and enforcing the terms of the contract.

Licensing Intermediaries

A distinctive feature of the chemicals industry, as of other process industries such as petroleum refining and petrochemicals, is the use of specialized engineering firms (SEFs) responsible for building and installing complete process plants. These firms consolidate core process technology from a chemicals firm with other technologies and capabilities needed to build a plant, to offer their customers a complete turnkey package. The SEFs work on many projects and become experts in their specialized field (Landau and Rosenberg, 1991).

Specialized engineering firms offer a range of styles of involvement in the licensing agreement. Often the SEF acts as the single contact point for the customer, and the chemical licensor provides technology via the SEF. In a typical agreement, the chemicals firm licenses its technology to the SEF, and the SEF licenses a complete package of technology to the customer, along with construction and installation. This is the structure followed by Firm B, whether the source of the license is a direct contact with the customer or via an SEF. The chemicals firm identifies the customer and performs initial negotiations on the technology to be transferred. It recommends a list of approved contractors to install the technology, from which the customer selects one. The chemicals firm provides a precisely defined package of technology, comprised of patent rights, know-how, and possibly trademarks. This is contained in a specification book, which might be a binder of procedures, engineering drawings, or computer files.

Other firms may use variations on this approach. This depends partly on the source of the agreement. At Firm A, the single contact structure is the norm if an SEF approaches the firm with the licensing opportunity. If the firm develops the licensing opportunity itself it may license directly to the customer, with an engineering and construction contractor involved in a separate agreement made by the customer. There are a number of other forms of licensing partnerships in the industry (Reilly, 1994). As we have seen, other firms have set up their own licensing subsidiaries for major innovations, and these subsidiaries take many of the roles of the SEFs.

The structure of the agreement in this case is for the chemicals firm to license to the SEF and the SEF to have a separate license with the customer. The first license covers the technology—what it is, and where and how it can be used. In the second license the SEF is acting as sublicensor, including the technology and all the other components and services needed to provide a working plant. Warranties and guarantees are a major part of the second license, which are the responsibility of the SEF. This arrangement performs several functions, discussed below.

Determining the share of royalties with the SEFs is an important part of the negotiation process and license structure. It is calculated according to the relative contributions of the partners to the final plant installation, and the degree of risk sharing. A key feature is whether the SEF has exclusive sublicensing rights for its territory. However, it is unusual for the SEF to have rights to sublicense independently of its chemicals partner.

The use of SEFs has a number of efficiency advantages over direct licensing. First, it may provide a single contact point for the customer. The SEFs become expert in project management by accumulating experience in different circumstances across the industry. Also, by using an approved supplier list of several SEFs, there is competition between intermediaries, benefiting both licensor and licensee. This may also allow more efficient negotiation of royalty rates, reflecting the experience of the SEFs in repeated bargaining.

Second, it allows the SEFs to handle licenses that would be too small for the chemicals firm to attempt on its own. The SEFs have developed their own specialist complementary skills in broad areas of technology (in the first place transferred from the petroleum industry) to a far greater extent than an individual chemicals firm, with its firm-specific technology, could manage. This provides the resources for licensing technologies that may be too minor a business prospect for the chemicals firm to support by itself. The SEFs reduce bottlenecks in plant construction, speeding up diffusion.

Third, this helps protect the firm's IP. Although the SEFs sometimes work for a number of chemicals firms, generally they are associated with a single firm in a given market. The chemicals firms each have approved lists of SEFs, which typically do not overlap with competitors' lists. This ensures that confidential information does not leak out to competitors via the SEF. This is expressed by BP as follows: "The core contractor approach safeguards the value of our technology. . . . BP has a deliberate policy to limit the exposure of our core contractors with their agreement and commitment to other similar and competing technologies" (quoted in Royse, 1993, p. 5). This also means that the SEFs provide an efficient means of information transfer by reducing the risks of leakage. The SEF provides a control over the transfer of know-how from the chemicals firm to the customer, who may be a competitor. The chemicals firm may be more open in transferring the required know-how for a project via the SEF, because it acts as a buffer between the chemicals firm and its licensees. It reduces strategic withholding of information, because the SEF is not a direct competitor and can evaluate the validity of an information request.

Fourth, one of the most important roles of the SEFs is in providing warranties and guarantees for the performance of the license. This essentially confines the liability of the chemicals firm to the technology itself, with other guarantees associated with the rest of the technology supply contract being borne by the intermediary. Thus the license structure from chemicals firm to the intermediary may be relatively simple and concentrated on the technology itself, while the license between the intermediary and the customer is a more elaborate agreement, including guarantees for the timely construction and performance of the new plant embodying the technology.

While functionally separate from the generator of technology, the intermediary need not always be a separate company. In some cases it may perform may of the functions of an intermediary as a division of the innovating firm. Thus, Union Carbide's licensing subsidiary, ETS, functions like a specialized engineering firm although it is focused mainly on a particular technology.

Trends in Licensing and IP Management

Most firms intend to increase their licensing activity. In the first instance this is mainly as a means of increasing revenues with which to offset the costs of maintaining the IP portfolio. However, there are also long-term aims to improve the management of the IP assets of the firm and help focus the firm's innovation effort in those areas where it has highest competences. This may involve increased use of in-licensing as well as out-licensing. Global competition means that even the largest chemicals firms can no longer develop all their technology themselves, and licensing will become a necessary way of accessing technology. Also, firms are more likely to need to consider out-licensing, perhaps included in joint ventures and alliances, to commercialize technology.

Part of the rationale behind this is the generally increased stress on IP in corporate strategy in many industries over the past decade or so. With the increased strength of IP protection—both in the United States, following the policy changes during the 1980s (especially the establishment of the Court of Appeals for the Federal Circuit in 1982 to hear all patent appeals in a single court, which increased the likelihood of patents being upheld), and throughout the world, with moves towards harmonization of international IP treatment under the Uruguay round of the GATT in 1994—IP has become more valuable and more important as a competitive tool. It has become more worthwhile to protect IP, to use it for out-licensing or strategic leverage.

Thus there has been a significant increase in the volume of patenting—for example, the number of U.S. patents by the top ten firms increased by 33 percent, from 8,800 to 11,800 between 1990 and 1994. This is set against a background of increasing global competition, in which well-financed and technologically able competitors can challenge worldwide markets, making IP an increasingly important means of protecting the ability to earn value from innovation. The result is that firms have more opportunity to earn rents from their IP portfolios by out-licensing, but this is partly offset by the higher costs of maintaining larger IP portfolios for defensive reasons, and of in-licensing technology.

So far out-licensing is mainly concerned with technology that has been developed for the firm's internal use. The role of licensing in overall firm intellectual capital management—the broad management of the knowledge capital of the firm—is indirect in most firms, as its primary aim is to extend the commercialization of existing technology. There are cases where it is more likely to contribute to a more direct strategic role—for example, negotiating cross-licensing for design freedom for development areas, helping define patenting policy (including what to patent, patent maintenance rules, portfolio monitoring), and ensuring negotiation leverage. There are also strategic differences between the way IP is managed in different firms. Patenting is still often pursued as a matter of course in some R&D departments, with limited consideration of the maintenance cost or strategic value of the patents. In part this may reflect traditional differences between firms in their IP policies.

SPECIAL LICENSING CONCERNS

There are number of concerns facing the potential licensor that reduce its ability to license its technology as widely as it may wish. In many cases licensors are able to alleviate these problems, either by structuring the license agreements or by the evolution of institutional arrangements such as the SEFs.

Control Over Know-How

Perhaps the most critical concern for the licensor is the control over what proprietary know-how is transferred to the licensee, and the risk of losing what, in a process industry, is a primary source of competitive advantage. Part of the problem is that the licensor must be sure that the licensee will not license-on the technology—otherwise the licensor may decide it is unable to grant a license. This depends largely on the patent protection. Most licenses are for a combination of patents and know-how, which helps ensure that the technology is protected and also is valuable enough to earn revenues. A paradox is that patents provide strong protection, but much of the value of technology is contained in the know-how, which is protected as trade secrets. Patents have the advantage that they protect an innovation from imitation even if it is invented independently. Even if the licensee develops improvements in its know-how in using the licensed technology, these may not be usable without the original patents, hence protecting the original know-how.

There remains the problem that know-how transferred with the patents may be useful to the licensee in other areas than those intended in the license. There are also the problems that more may be transferred than intended as the parties work closely together to effect the transfer, or that know-how licensed to a noncompeting customer may leak to a competitor. There are no easy answers to these problems. They may be reduced by careful drafting of license agreements to specify the know-how to be transferred and the field-of-use for which rights are granted, and by close management of transfer procedures. It may be possible to follow policies limiting the know-how available for licensing, offering more patent-only licenses or incorporating only mature know-how. The use of SEFs as licensing intermediaries may limit leakages, as noted above. Yet the use of licensing intermediaries may have its own problems. In the case noted earlier, Firm A decided not to pursue an otherwise attractive licensing proposal for paint-related technology via a licensing intermediary, as it could not ensure that sublicensees would not be its competitors, and it could not be certain that they would not allow know-how to reach its competitors.

Resource Requirements for Transfer

For technology to be useful to a licensee, significant human resources may be needed to transfer the know-how and to be able to work the patents. The licensor must be able to spare these people from its own development and manufacturing needs, and should allow for the opportunity cost in calculating the value of the license. If the requirements are not major then consideration of what is needed to transfer technology may be scheduled in as early as possible. An alternative for supplying these resources is via the SEFs, or the firm may develop specific capabilities in transfer. Similarly, the licensee usually wants a complete package of patents and know-how, so that for developmental technology the licensor may have to devote further development effort to bring the technology to the point where it is licensable. This takes additional resources, which the firm may not wish to spare. The SEFs may help here also. Another solution is the selection of licensee candidates. If these candidates have the complementary capabilities needed to use the embryonic technology then a license is possible. Identifying such candidates is a role for the licensing manager or consultant.

Legal Risks

A further concern is the legal exposure, such as for various forms of patent liability (including patent infringement, indemnification, and warranty) and performance guarantees needed for complete installation of the technology. Partly this is a task for the appropriate drafting of the licensing contract. Risks may be reduced via the use of intermediaries with the necessary specialized capabilities, who can guarantee those elements they provide that are not associated directly with the technology.

SUMMARY AND CONCLUSION

Licensing activity in the chemicals industry is widespread and increasing, in an environment in which the main objective for the firms remains to manufacture and sell products. The different types of licensing behavior observed align with a strategic framework of licensing objectives and structures. Indications of the trend towards greater use of licensing include the increased activity and size of licensing departments and the increasing revenues generated by out-licensing. For the longer term, there is also greater willingness to consider in-licensing. Although royalty fee earnings may still be small compared with the overall scale of operations of the corporations, licensing is seen as a significant contributor to corporate earnings. Perhaps more significantly, licensing is seen as part of a generally increased importance attached to IP strategy, of which licensing is an integral part, and to some degree, a motivator for a more complete approach to intellectual capital management.

BIBLIOGRAPHY

Business Week. (1993). "Union Carbide: Battling Slow Growth by Licensing Technology," *Business Week*, Sept. 19, p. 88.

Contractor, F. (1985). *Licensing and International Strategy*. Westport, CT: Quorum.

Evans, L. (1993). "Case History of Successful Licensing," *Les Nouvelles*, 28:2 (June), pp. 74–78.

Landau, R. and Rosenberg, N. (1991). "Innovation in the Chemical Processing Industries," in National Academy, *Technology and Economics*. pp. 107–120. Washington: National Academy Press.

Reilly, J. (1994). "Choosing a Licensing Partner," *Chemtech*, (June), pp. 42–44.

Royse, S. (1993). "Licensing: A Winning Formula?" *ECN Process Review*, (October), pp. 4–6.

Spalding, B. (1986). "Is It Smart to License Out Technology?" *Chemical Week*, April 9, pp. 29–30.

Telesio, P. (1979). *Technology Licensing and the Multinational Enterprise*. New York: Praeger.

8

Central Control
of Technology Licensing

Russell L. Parr

AUS Consulting and Intellectual Property Research Associates

Should management of intellectual property be controlled by a central corporate-level department or should it be controlled by the business units that have created it? The answer to this question will reflect different corporate cultures. The answer depends on the character of management organization. The answer depends on the nature of the industry. The answer to this question is difficult. However, in this chapter we look at two great companies that are reorganizing the way they manage their intellectual property, and we can gain some insights from their experiences.

ALLIEDSIGNAL, INC.

AlliedSignal ended 1995 with revenues of almost $14.3 billion and net income of $875 million. Balance sheet assets totaled more than $12 billion. The company operates three primary business sectors, including Automotive, Aerospace, and Engineered Materials. Sixteen major business units within these three sectors produce a variety of products for many different markets:

Automotive
> Braking Systems
> Engine Components
> Safety Restraint Systems

Aerospace
> Aircraft Engines
> Environmental Control Systems

Collision Avoidance Radar
Cockpit Data Recorders
Spacecraft Control Systems
Antisubmarine Warfare Systems

Engineered Materials
Nylons
Flourine Products
Oximes
Resins
Specialty Films
Circuit Board Laminates

AlliedSignal employs 87,500 workers and does business in more than 40 countries. It has direct operations and indirect business interests around the world, including the United Kingdom, China, Japan, France, Netherlands, Italy, the United States, and Spain. The company lists among its customers Ford Motor Company, General Motors, Chrysler Corporation, Fiat Group, Boeing, McDonnell Douglas, Airbus, the Department of Defense, the National Aeronautics and Space Administration, and manufacturers in various industries.

In late 1991, AlliedSignal embarked on a reengineering of its organization. It has sold underperforming nonstrategic assets and unused real estate. Administrative functions were combined and personnel reduced. Manufacturing capacity has been fitted to current productivity levels. Non-value-added practices have been addressed by total quality management teams with some practices being eliminated and others combined into value-added activities. Profit margins have been enhanced. Working capital management improvements freed up huge amounts of cash. Fundamental changes have been introduced throughout the company that have powerfully transformed AlliedSignal into a premier company tailored for customer satisfaction and year-over-year double digit financial improvement.

AlliedSignal Technologies, Inc.

AlliedSignal, Inc. has created a new organization responsible for all intellectual property management. It is a wholly owned subsidiary named AlliedSignal Technologies, Inc. (AST). The group owns trademarks, patents, copyrights and technology of each business unit with the goal of central professional and administrative management of intellectual property. AST's primary focus will be on optimizing royalty income, advancing market acceptance of new technologies, converting idle technology into cash, and advocating new strategic planning options.

The initiative for the reorganization of intellectual property has come directly from the top. Lawrence A. Bossidy, Chairman of the Board of AlliedSignal, decided that all assets of the company must contribute to its earnings. This has required operating improvements for businesses that have been retained and disposal of assets that were marginal. Having come from General Electric, Bossidy has a similar philosophy to Jack Welsh, who has long pursued a policy of making each business initiative at General Electric number one or two in its field. Units not making the grade at GE are jettisoned. Like GE's Welsh, Larry Bossidy wants to optimize the value of every asset and his plan includes active deployment of all of the intellectual property of AlliedSignal.

AlliedSignal recognizes an important difference between maximizing royalty income and optimizing it. Maximizing royalty income involves licensing to all comers regardless of the impact such licenses would have on other aspects of the business, and could turn into a free-for-all where the highest amounts of royalty income would be pursued. Optimizing royalty income is different. It requires that consideration be given to the risks that a particular license may have on the operating business of the company. The resources available to service the new license and the long-term strategic impact on the license product and its market must be considered in an optimization mode. In some cases, opportunities for added royalty income are turned down in favor of other options, even at lesser income. Optimization requires a balance of trying to maximize royalty income with avoiding the risk of creating a competitor and the value of addressing a market directly.

A Team Approach

The inputs for doing deals at AlliedSignal come from three parts of the company. The AlliedSignal organization views the technology deal making structure as the three-legged stool shown in Exhibit 8.1. All three legs of the stool must be strong for the resulting license agreement to be sturdy. ASTI con-

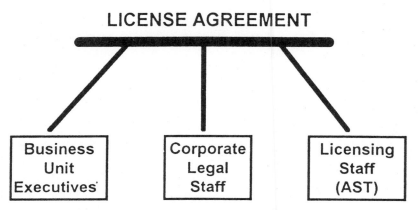

Exhibit 8.1. Licensing Organizational Structure

sults with business unit executives who bring industry insights derived from front-line experience within their industry. They know the customer desires and competitor competencies. They know about the next generation of technology being pursued and they understand industry conditions, derived from front-line experience.

Corporate legal and patent counsel bring their specialties to the structure. Their expertise in international law is vital for turning the desires of decision makers into realities. Licensing professionals bring a unique background into the mix, involving the art and science of technology deal making. Only with input from all three groups can sound licensing agreements be crafted.

Income and Market Acceptance

Besides royalty income from its technology licensing, the company also gains market acceptance for its new designs. In the automotive industry, this is particularly important. Most U.S. automakers want alternate sources around the world for the parts they need. They do not want to be dependent on a single source from a single location. Therefore, AlliedSignal often licenses its technologies so that its customers—automakers—will have a secondary source for the new designs AlliedSignal is selling. The same requirement by Japanese automakers has resulted in numerous license agreements in Japan.

The automotive segment of the business has always managed its intellectual property centrally. The mature nature of the business allows for central management. Conditions change slowly for automakers. The business may be cyclical, but the original equipment manufacturers and their suppliers do not change quickly. The constant factors in this industry allow for development of a centralized and standard method for dispensing new designs. Aerospace is another industry where the players do not often change and demand for product is planned many years in advance.

Management of aerospace intellectual property is also conducted centrally. In its Engineered Materials sector, the company has introduced what it has learned from licensing automotive and aerospace technology.

Out-licensing is the key focus of AlliedSignal. The company looks for license agreements with terms of 10 to 15 years, and almost all of their deals include technological know-how. The deals are mostly driven by designs and manufacturing know-how with the transfer often accomplished by bringing the licensee's technical people to the U.S. operations for education and hands-on training.

Undefined markets and unproven partners in developing nations are definitely candidates for licensing. In certain emerging economies, AlliedSignal would rather license than risk equity capital in newly emerging economies or transitional government structures. In the rapidly developing emerging economies, the People's Republic of China, India, Korea, and so forth, however, equity participation has become the primary focus, and licensing is supporting the equity in joint venture thrusts.

AlliedSignal does not pursue cross-licensing of its patent portfolio. Cross-licensing is only conducted regarding particular technologies involving a limited number of patents where AlliedSignal is seeking specific inventions.

Converting idle technology into cash is another goal for AlliedSignal Technologies, Inc. The same philosophy that drives selling off underutilized businesses or real estate applies to technology. AlliedSignal has significant research and development capabilities. Not all of its inventions have been incorporated into company operations.

These inventions are underutilized assets that ASTI will be looking at for the generation of new AlliedSignal income.

Strategic Planning

Management at AlliedSignal Technologies is also exploring the potential for becoming an integral part of the strategic planning processes followed by the business units. One of the core planning processes used by ASTI is strategic planning. The process is used to identify opportunities and assess the company's market positions in relation to its competitors. As business units consider their strategy options, the licensing executives at ASTI prepare strategies to take maximum advantage of the corporation's technology. This is a broadened scope of activity for the licensing function that should be followed by more companies. Key assets of companies have always been the focal point of strategic planning. The growing awareness of intellectual property as key to future success will bring these assets directly into the planning process.

There is an old joke that worries many licensing executives. *If you take a starving dog and make it healthy and strong, it will not bite you. That is the principle difference between a licensee and a dog.* Many licensing executives worry about creating new competitors. ASTI is not worried about this old joke. It believes that to license is to exercise prudence. First, third party licensees are not given rights by agreement to use the licensed technology in areas of primary importance to ASTI. Secondly, licensees become dependent on the licensor for the next generation of improvements. When priced properly, the royalty rate can induce a licensee to decide to continue to license next generation technologies from the original licensor. A licensee can save enormous amounts that would otherwise be needed to conduct its own research and development. R&D expenses saved by a licensee are very useful for gauging royalty rates. When structured properly and equitably, licensing deals provide long-term relationships and benefits to both the licensor and the licensee; in fact, at AlliedSignal, there are agreements with companies that have started almost 40 years ago and some even started before the Second World War. Creating new competitors is not a major worry of the AlliedSignal licensing organization, as licensees are seen as long term partners for AlliedSignal.

EASTMAN KODAK COMPANY

Kodak ended 1994 with $13.6 billion in revenues and $554 million in net income from continuing operations. The company is divided into seven primary business sectors—Consumer Imaging, Business Imaging Systems, Digital and Applied Imaging, Health Sciences, Motion Picture and Television Imaging, Office Imaging, and Professional and Printing Imaging.

As with AlliedSignal, a significant reorganization is underway at Kodak. In 1994, Kodak sold its clinical diagnostics business, Sterling Winthrop pharmaceutical and over-the-counter drug business, and the household products and do-it-yourself businesses of L&F Products. The company has refocused itself on imaging.

Eastman Kodak is the world leader in imaging technology. It spends enormous amounts on research and development. Between 1992 through 1994 Kodak spent over $2.7 billion on research and development. The company is the world leader in imaging technology—especially traditional photography.

Kodak's patent portfolio exists primarily to protect the company's market position. Central management of Kodak's intellectual property in photography has served it well. The market for its products is well established and the competitive environment does not change rapidly. Therefore, Kodak has adopted a licensing philosophy in its photography business where technology licensing to outsiders is conducted for the benefit of the entire industry. Kodak's leadership position in traditional photography means that it experiences direct benefits from almost any actions that help expand the traditional photography industry. Generally, the company will consider granting licenses to all comers but requests for technology licenses from competitors get careful analysis. When a direct competitor requests a license, opportunity costs and other competitive issues, such as market share, are scrutinized, and royalty negotiations are driven by a fair market value standard. In other instances, where license requests come from noncompetitors, royalty rates are determined by considering industry standard rates. Royalty rates based on industry standards do not reflect the impact of competitors on Kodak's business. Royalty rate negotiations with competitors must be analyzed to reflect the unique conditions existing between Kodak and the competitors who request licenses.

The management of Kodak's technology requires that a dynamic balance among the different business units be maintained. Kodak's many different business units share the same technology. Instances can arise where a license agreement many benefit one business unit while harming another. The result is that technology management at Kodak requires input from both front line and corporate levels. Kodak's technology management is conducted as a team effort with participation from corporate groups and business units. The symbiotic relationship of the different business units and the company technology is of paramount concern when licensing decisions are made.

Accelerated Market Acceptance

Forces driving Kodak's licensing practices in its traditional lines of business are those that will encourage widespread adoption of new technologies in the marketplace. Licensing at Kodak focuses on system inventions that in the photography business include camera, film, printing paper, and chemical formulas for making the film and developing it. In 1963 Kodak introduced the *Instamatic*, in 1972 the *Pocket Instamatic* and in 1982 the *Disk Camera*. In each case Kodak licensed many companies to participate in these new product offerings. Outsiders were licensed to manufacture camera for both Kodak and for themselves. Kodak generally follows a strategy that believes the more cameras in the market the greater its potential for gaining sales of other related products from film to developing services.

Kodak believes that a larger overall market, with a variety of licensed participants, will maximize its sales and profits much more than monopolizing the technology. Admittedly there are risks associated with inviting others to exploit your technology, but Kodak believes that its competitive products and lead position in the market will serve it well in an expanded market. In Kodak's traditional business of chemical based imaging the oligopoly nature of the industry allowed for relatively straightforward implementation of established licensing practices. As imaging moves quickly toward a digital foundation new challenges and complexities are being met head-on by Kodak.

Photo CD Technology. Recently Kodak faced the complexities associated with new digital technology when it developed a licensing strategy for its Photo CD product. The product was a new concept and its market was undefined. The identity of potential competitors was unclear. None of the factors affecting Kodak's traditional business applied. Instead of operating in a mature market, Kodak was entering a new arena.

Launched in 1992, the Photo CD stores photographic images on a compact disk. The images can be displayed in different ways. In essence, the product is a digital photo negative. The images can be printed from digital color printers, viewed on personal computer monitors, broadcast for television reception, transferred electronically, and displayed on standard television sets. Kodak's patent portfolio for this invention covers the creation, capture, manipulation, storage, and display of the images. The invention involves

creating images from data processing instead of through chemical processing. It also involves the conversion of photographs captured using traditional
means—film—into digital images.

The company initially expected to concentrate its efforts on home market
where consumers would view their still photographs on their televisions or
home computers. This was the focus of Kodak's commercialization efforts.
It considered most other applications as secondary. The philosophy behind
granting licenses in the secondary market negotiations was a desire to directly profit, in the form of royalty income, from use of the technology by
others.

The First Strategy

As just described, the initial commercialization plan had two components: 1)
Kodak would development the home-use for itself and 2) Gather royalty income from all other users of the technology outside the home-use market.
Commercialization categories for Photo CD technology included different
patent portfolio licenses for each group:

1. Software developers, including Microsoft, Apple, and Adobe would
   be licensed with the expectation that the technology would be incorporated into their utility and application software products.
2. Manufactures of Photo CD players would be licensed to make
   equipment for the home market.
3. Software publishers, whose focus was on entertainment and education would be licensed to create new products that used Photo CD
   technology.
4. System integrators, who provide systems that facilitate the authoring of software games, applications and other types of software
   products would be license.

Participants in each category were offered a portfolio of patents they
needed to participate in their product area at terms that would allow Kodak
to benefit directly from royalty income. A reasonable plan was devised and
implementation began.

Reality Can Be Rude

The primary market for the Photo CD was slow to embrace the product.
Consumers did not seem to take to the idea of viewing still pictures on their
televisions screens. But good news was not far away. The markets Kodak
had considered of secondary importance to its strategy were very interested.
Kodak had underestimated the demand from desktop computer applications

outside the home market. Other uses of the technology became the dominant commercial force.

The new opportunities brought new challenges. Software companies were reluctant to pay royalties for patents. Traditionally they were used to dealing with copyrighted intellectual property. They were also reluctant to spend development money to incorporate Photo CD technology into their products when demand for it was yet to materialize. Considering the required development costs and uncertainty regarding demand, royalty payments were vigorously resisted. Other companies in businesses outside the home-use market also balked at paying continuing royalties because acceptance in their markets was yet to be established.

Kodak realized that its expectations for royalty income were premature. It first had to face market acceptance and had to establish industry standards. For Kodak this was new territory. In its chemical based businesses market acceptance and industry standards were a given. In the digital arena these fundamentals had to be created. The response to changing conditions was accomplished quickly by establishing a team comprised of business unit and corporate staff personnel.

Revised Strategy

Faced with both new opportunities but reluctant licensees, Kodak decided to open licensing. The new strategy provided interested parties with complete access to the technology. Kodak decided to adopt a strategy that would advance the technology's acceptance and then allow them to indirectly benefit from offering complementary products and services. Kodak now expects to benefit from demand in the expanded market for the following products and services:

Digital cameras
Film scanners
Digital color printers
Paper used in digital color printers
Compact disk recorders (CD writers)
Recordable compact disks
Integrated systems for creating software programs
Retailer systems for converting Photo CDs into printed pictures
Photofinishing services to convert film into a Photo CD

As business conditions changed, the licensing policies evolved quickly. Changing licensing policies to reflect changing market conditions is not a surprise. The speed at which these changes took place however, illustrates a fundamental change in intellectual property management for Kodak.

Expanding their licensing policies for the Photo CD technology has opened a floodgate of opportunities for Kodak. Recent stories in *Licensing Economics Review*, a technology journal based in Moorestown New Jersey, demonstrate the willingness of other parties to adapt new technologies when the proper licensing policy is in place.

From the March 1995 issue of *Licensing Economics Review*:

> All-electronic cameras are a new product that will be introduced by The Eastman Kodak Company. The cameras will cost between $200 and $300. Photofinishing will not be required to turn the pictures captured in the camera into printed documents. The pictures will be generated by printing images on printers that are expected to cost about $300. Widespread use of this technology is expected within five years by Kodak. The company already makes digital cameras aimed at professional photographers but is planning to primarily serve the general consumer. Already the company is selling digital print stations that allow customers to scan photographs, adjust the image, and print out the changed photo. Kodak plans to participate fully in the next generation of desktop publishing where color photographs will be scanned into documents composed on personal computers and printed on low-volume printers. The maintenance of color during such a process is challenging so the company has joined forces with Microsoft, Motorola, and Apple to meet the challenges. Kodak will bring its color management systems to the party, and the others will provide expertise in software, electronics, and computers.

From the April 1995 issue of *Licensing Economics Review:*

> Eastman Kodak Co., seeking to push ahead in digital technology, opened up access to its proprietary Photo CD system and forged alliances with other top technology players. The company hasn't been able to leverage its expertise in pictures to gain marketing advantage in the digital arena. It recently adopted a new strategy to move forward. Among the recent announcements is a plan to create retail kiosks with Microsoft Corp. that will let customers manipulate and print photographs and put them on Photo CD disks. Kodak has also said IBM will market Photo CD products.
>
> Kodak had jealously guarded Photo CD, a means for storing and editing images on compact disk. The company announced that it will allow Photo CD technology to be licensed by software developers, eliminating royalty fees. Adobe Systems, Inc. will include the technology in future versions of its best-selling PhotoShop software, allowing customers to put their own images on Photo CD instead of relying on film developers or printers to do it for them.
>
> Kodak's move to form alliances is considered likely to come under heavy pressure from the computer industry, which resented Kodak's hoarding its imaging technology. The new strategy reflects the realization by many that complex technologies cannot be fully exploited by one company. Kodak's Chief Executive Officer, George Fisher told reporters "We used to try to do it

by ourselves. We've learned very quickly that in this digital world, the opportunities are just too massive for any one company to do it on its own."

As Kodak forms its partnership it plans to trumpet its technology by putting a new "Kodak Digital Science" logo in yellow, red and blue onto its products. As part of the new strategic alliances, Kodak said that it is teaming up with Sprint Corp. to create a system for storing and distributing images over telephone lines. Currently, moving a digitized image over phone lines often takes a long time and results in a poor image.

Kodak, with its color management technology and image search and retrieval platforms, hopes it can solve those problems and become the standard while earning fees for transmitting images. Simultaneously, using IBM's networking and data management capabilities, Kodak will help develop a means for distributing and selling pictures and documents over the Internet. The company is also working with IBM to develop a system to store photographs on the magnetic strips of credit cards. A store clerk will be able to put the card in an IBM reader and see whether the photograph matches the customer carrying the card. Citicorp already agreed to use the system in tests. Kodak also said that it would work with Hewlett-Packard Co. to develop inkjet printers capable of printing high-quality images.

In yet another agreement, Kinko's copy centers will begin putting photographs on Photo CD disks for customers, in competition with photofinishers who may feel slighted by Kodak.

Credibility for New Technology

Kodak's licensing policy for the Photo CD technology was adapted for three reasons. The first was to gain market acceptance for its technology in new fields as quickly as possible. The second was to gain credibility for the technology. The third was to help establish industry standards for digitally-based imaging.

Kodak believes that its Photo CD product will be most successful if many others make compatible products. The quickest way to create a large market is to have many uses for a product and the quickest way to accomplish that is to have a large number of companies selling products that are based on the underlying technology. When home use of the technology was contemplated, additional participants in the market were not critical to success. When the secondary markets became primary, Kodak needed help in expanding demand and addressing the different forms of demand and the different means of serving that demand.

Another benefit of licensing the technology widely had to do with credibility. As other prestigious companies in consumer electronics, telecommunications, software, and computers adopted the technology, the reputation of Kodak's Photo CD technology grew. Kodak needs no such assistance in traditional photography but its management wisely saw that the trademarks and reputations of others, in diverse fields, would do for its new technology what Kodak could not do alone.

CENTRAL CONTROL BUT SHARED AUTHORITY

Typically, corporate staff and executive management at many large companies have decided intellectual property management issues for their business units. This can work well for mature industries where changes come slowly. As business unit conditions change, however, it becomes vitally important to allow for the rapid implementation of new ideas and policies. Such rapid actions often do not always come from the corporate staff level. The traditional business model has changing conditions first recognized at business unit levels. Staff and executive management are informed and new topics are added to huge corporate agendas. Eventually corporate staff determines a new policy and the business units implement it. However, a fundamental change in how intellectual property is managed is now going on. Intellectual property is key to business unit success and the responsibility for its management is being shared at the business unit level. Corporate level input however is still vitally important.

In large corporations like Kodak the wide use of technology among different business units requires that a top-down viewpoint be maintained. The new structure of technology management is a team approach where input from the front lines must be balanced with forward looking corporate strategies.

The fantastic expenses associated with developing new technologies and the fast pace at which it becomes obsolete does not allow for delay in response to changing market conditions. Because business units are the first to experience and understand changing market conditions, they are now being relied on more than ever for technology management decisions.

Control of key decisions and policies continues to filter down to business unit managers. Lately we are seeing more instances where business units are charged with deciding about intellectual property management. Part of this trend is due to employee empowerment. Part is due to employee downsizing and the fact that fewer corporate staff are available to play such roles. The trend seems a good one. The managers responsible for product inventions are often best suited for management of the underlying intellectual property.

Corporate Culture

Successful licensing can become super successful depending on the openness of the corporate culture. In the case of AlliedSignal we asked where the ideas for licensing deals come from? The answer was—Anywhere and everywhere. Included in this answer are:

Salespeople in the field
Corporate Legal Staff
Corporate Licensing Staff

Research and engineering managers from business units
Special teams charged with devising new strategies
Directors of Business Development for business units
Chairman of the Board
Requests from outsiders

For ideas that are generated from such a diverse group to become a reality there must be an open culture where employees at all levels can expect their ideas to be considered seriously. The growing practice of employee empowerment, where decisions at lower organization levels are encouraged, is ideal for supporting the generation of new licensing opportunities. As corporations work to inspire their employees to act on their own, the conferences that are designed to foster such new thinking should alert employees about recognizing licensing opportunities. No one is saying that employee empowerment should allow local plant managers to conduct licensing negotiations but encouraging all levels of management to be alert for licensing opportunities is an important part of successful licensing programs. When all members of an organization feel that their ideas are welcome, the floodgates open.

Most large companies work hard to educate their researchers about the proper way to assure protection of their inventions. They publish internal books and pamphlets that discuss all aspects of patenting inventions. Sometimes companies use seminar programs to educate newly hired researchers. Similar strategies can serve companies well if they are pursued from the point of view of licensing. Corporate cultures that include employee empowerment are a growing trend. The benefits derived from such cultures are well documented. Companies would do well to make sure that technology licensing awareness is part of the process used to empower employees.

Industry Conditions

Management hierarchies and industry conditions will also have an effect on the way intellectual property management is conducted. In large companies that operate in mature industries corporate management and staff control of intellectual property works well. The benefits of such an arrangement include the capacity to support a department of licensing professionals—people who are expert at the art and science of licensing.

Licensing strategies that are initiated from business units are best for industries in which new technologies are emerging quickly. Market acceptance is important for young industries and the managers at the business unit level usually 'are first to experience the impact of quickly changing conditions. They are also the most knowledgeable about specific markets and competitive threats. In dynamic industries the rules governing participation change fast. For these industries, business units must be focused on licensing strategies and central control is less advisable. In mature industries, conditions change more slowly and licensing strategies can be firmly established because there is less need for rapid responses to changing conditions. Such industries require less conscious attention by business unit managers and a more central focus from corporate control can work well.

Technology management in the future will involve more input from business unit management because the proliferation and use of divergent technology in all industries means that fewer industries can consider themselves to be mature.

Passive management of intellectual property at the corporate level for the single goal of protecting markets is dead. The new paradigm of intellectual property is active management with a myriad of goals and benefits that can only be realized by integrated efforts that include business unit managers.

9

Gaps Analysis

Russell L. Parr

AUS Consulting and Intellectual Property Research Associates

In the last decade, DuPont Corporation has implemented a major restructuring of its diverse business holdings. As part of the restructuring of the
corporation, an extraordinary number of corporate levels, departments, and
functions were eliminated. The company has reduced its work force size
from 180,000 employees to 107,000. As part of the restructuring the methods by which the company manages its business holdings has changed. Now,
managers of its strategic business units perform as they would if they were
overseeing an investment portfolio. Most operating and strategic activities
for each unit are handled at the unit, and centralized corporate departments
and overhead functions are minimized. DuPont does not maintain what
would be considered an extensive corporate staff, and so most of the technology management function is handled at the business unit level.

This new shift of intellectual property management responsibility can be
attributed to several factors. One of these factors has to do with the number
of employees remaining at corporations after the common practice of down-
sizing has been implemented. Reduced numbers of corporate staff means that
fewer people are available outside the business unit for such activities. Employee downsizing also has yielded a trend toward pushing responsibilities
once retained by corporate headquarters downward into the organization, and
intellectual property management is one of the jobs that business unit managers are reclaiming. Another reason we are finding intellectual property
management at business units has to do with time. The pace at which industry conditions change is not slowing. Reaction to market forces must be
immediate and must reflect the front-line insights possessed by business unit
management. Too many months can pass before business unit management
and corporate management agree on the best course of action to take in response to changed conditions. Time lost is never regained, and neither is lost
market share, sales, product launches, or any of the many other losses to a

135

business that result from delay of action. Another reason that business management is now responsible for intellectual property management has to do with competency. No matter how diligent corporate staff is at studying the conditions of different business units they will never appreciate the subtle nuances of each separate industry as well as the front-line managers do. Appreciation for this factor is growing and the people responsible for creating intellectual property are now responsible for almost all aspects of its commercialization and management.

DuPont is a large and diverse business. Revenues for 1994 reached nearly $40 billion. Earnings for the same year exceeded $2.7 billion. Broad segments of the business include chemicals, fibers, polymers, and petroleum. Within these broad categories different business segments include the manufacture of:

- Engineered polymers, such as elastomers, fluoropolymers and ethylene polymers
- Specialty chemicals, such as titanium dioxide
- Fluorochemicals
- Polymer intermediates
- Coatings for paper, plastics, and textiles
- Specialty fibers
- Agricultural chemicals

Within the listed business segments are numerous strategic business units, each of which focuses on different products that DuPont manufactures for different industries. In addition, its Conoco division conducts oil exploration and refining along with natural gas production and transportation.

Such diversity presents very different challenges that must be addressed on case-by-case bases. Each business unit is responsible for itself. Corporate headquarters staff at DuPont is still available to provide guidance but usually only at the request of the business units. Key executives from DuPont headquarters provide management consulting and guidance that focuses on the core competencies possessed by each of the strategic business units while identifying weaknesses that must be addressed by each unit. While the guidance provided can address many different areas of business activity the implications for technology management and licensing are significant. One of the analytical methods used by DuPont to guide its business units is called Gaps Analysis.

DuPont–Merck

Application of the Gaps Analysis by DuPont a few years ago indicated to the company that to be a winner in the pharmaceutical business in the future the core gaps—fundamental weaknesses—that existed in its drug related business had to be addressed. While the company had a nearly full pipeline of research efforts, it realized that it lacked the important knowledge necessary to gain approval from the Food and Drug Administration for the drugs it hoped to bring to market. The company also realized that its marketing know-how and network in the pharmaceutical industry was severely limited, and it was almost nonexistent overseas. As DuPont considered the future its pharmaceutical division would face, it realized that the identified weaknesses could be filled by a strategic alliance with Merck.

Merck & Company, at about the same time, had a research pipeline that was less than robust. Still Merck possessed extraordinarily important expertise in guiding new drug applications through the Food and Drug Administration approval process. Merck also possessed another strength that would solve another of DuPont's weaknesses—Merck had a well-established and respected marketing network in the United States and overseas. The resulting negotiations gave birth to the joint venture known as DuPont–Merck. DuPont brought the potential for development of new drug products to the alliance and Merck brought the regulatory and marketing expertise needed for commercialization.

GAPS ANALYSIS

The Gaps Analysis is a forward-looking analysis that seeks to identify weaknesses that a company may have to deal with in the future. Gaps Analysis is also called the Future-History Approach. This will be explained later; for now, think of the approach as studying the future as if it were the past. Gap's Analysis can be especially useful in focusing on technological gaps that will exist, and it is a powerful way to help guide the licensing department as to the types of individual patent licenses and technology portfolio licenses that it should begin to develop. While the description of this analysis may sound simple, implementation is challenging. More importantly, the benefits of thoughtful application can be powerful.

Implementation of Gaps Analysis requires four primary steps:

1. Describe the future industry and economic conditions that will exist 10 to 15 years from now—*Future Game*.
2. Describe the business characteristics of a hypothetical company that will dominate in the scenario described in the first step—*Future Winner*.
3. Assess the current competencies and business characteristics of your company—*Current Assessment*.
4. Compare your company to the Future Winner to find areas where important future competencies are lacking—*Gap Identification*.

Exhibit 9.1 highlights the primary components of Gaps Analysis.

Future Game

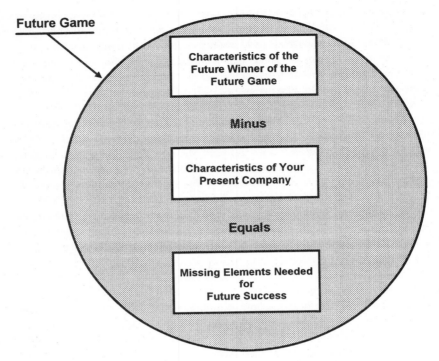

Exhibit 9.1.   Gaps Analysis

Future Game

The first step in the process is to define the future game, where the game is defined as the economic and industry environment in which the company will compete. This involves describing future products, customers, competitors, technologies, and manufacturing techniques, as well as the future production factors that will be necessary to play in the game. The business environment must be described as it will be from ten to fifteen years from now, but from the vantage point of someone who has just experienced the future being described. It involves describing the future in detail as if it were already history—which is why Gaps Analysis is often called the Future-History Approach.

It is important to admit that you are guessing at the future but not to let that admission deter you from confidently describing it. Admitting that the future game being described is based on informed speculation frees you from the constraints that typically work at a subconscious level to stifle imagination. Business forecasts and projections are usually scrutinized and critiqued by others, often at higher levels of management. Such experiences can leave psychological scars that restrict full expression of the imagination. Latitude in describing the future game should be unrestricted. The only caveat is to remember that the goal is neither to create a science fiction novel nor to estimate sales volume for the next three years given prevailing circumstances. Somewhere in between, and more toward science fiction side of the continuum, lies the future that must be described.

The resulting Future Game should include descriptions of the market that is expected to develop, the products that are expected to serve the market, the technologies that will be in your products, the competitive environment, the economic conditions, the people who will be needed to produce the product or service for the anticipated market, the facilities that will be required, and the funding that will be needed, as well as the intellectual property in the forms of trademarks and technology that will serve the anticipated future. Detailed descriptions are needed for each key area:

- Customers
- Markets
- Competitors
- Products
- Services
- Production Facilities
- Marketing Networks
- Distribution Channels
- Trademarks
- Technology

Accomplishing such a task can seem daunting, but is instructive to compare the present situation to that which existed ten years ago.[1] For each of the areas listed describe the characteristics, in detail, for the different factors as they were ten years ago. Compare things as they were to the same things as they are now. The trends and shocking differences between ten years ago and today should be expected to continue. Comparison of the past with the present provides not only a practice session for defining the Future Game but insights into the subtle and not-so-subtle changes that occurred in the past ten years as well. The areas that have changed the most in the past are likely those that will continue to change and should represent the focal point in your Future Game. The only constant is change, so one thing you can count on is that the business characteristics existing today and those that

---

[1] For some industries a period of ten years or less is sufficient, but other industries can only discover fundamental industry shifts by looking further back. The target historical period should be just long enough to illustrate how much both basic factors and assumptions about an industry and a specific business have changed.

will exist in the future will be different. To start the ball rolling with visions of the future consider the implications to your company of computer systems that can talk to their users. Joseph F. Coastes, a self described futurist and president of Coastes & Jarratt, a Washington, D.C. consulting firm, says that he expects "the future to bring a proliferation of artificial intelligence that sees, understands words and talks back. These technologies are almost upon us."[2]

The River of Time

Albert Einstein described time as a river. Inherent in this description is the idea of traveling back in time—going upriver. Performing Gaps Analysis does not require time travel but immersing yourself in the details of the past obviously can improve your comparison of the past and the present, which in turn enhances details you imagine in the Future Game. Two novels can help you develop the proper frame of mind.

In two novels by Jack Finney—*From Time to Time* and *Time and Again*—the protagonist agrees to participate in a government experiment that sets him in the New York City of 1890. Surprisingly, there is no time machine at the government facility. The hero travels through time not by riding inside a whirling machine but simply by willing himself into the period.

Finney posits that different time periods exist simultaneously. Existing at a past time in a given place depends on the expectations of the time traveler. In order to expect to reach 1890, the protagonist surrounds himself with thoughts and tangible goods from 1890. He reads only newspapers from 1890, he listens to the music, dresses in the clothing, lives in an apartment that is decorated with furniture of 1890. When he leaves his building he expects that city travel will be possible only on foot or in horse-drawn carriages. He expects to see street lamps fueled by gas and knows that the arm of the Statue of Liberty is on display in Madison Square—its builder is trying to raise enough money to erect the statue on a permanent base somewhere in New York harbor. When the hero of the tale finally leaves his building he steps onto the streets of New York, but the time in the *river* at which he enters is the year 1890.

In order to compare your current company with its past you must immerse yourself in that past. Starting from a macro viewpoint is more efficient than considering the implications of a specific change. List the competitors the company had ten and twenty years ago. How many dropped from the radar screen? What new companies became competitors? Was it a surprise? Why did they enter the field? How were they different from the competitors that dropped out? How do products compare? What technologies were being

---

[2]"Pondering What World Lies Ahead—The Good and the Bad of Life in the 21st Century." *The Philadelphia Inquirer*, page G1, July 25, 1995.

patented by you and your competitors? Which patent portfolio ultimately served its owner the best? Here are key areas on which to focus.

- The products were different. To appreciate the differences collect and read product catalogs of the past. Better yet, decorate your office with old products and use them.
- Customers' needs have changed. Learn about the ways in which your products were used by its customers and what utility they gained from your products.
- The machinery used to build the products was different. In fact, the entire process may have changed.
- Raw materials and subassemblies are different. To understand the scale of that difference, get a production parts lists, purchase order information, and assembly drawings. Some raw materials of the past may have been eliminated completely from current products—that could happen again.
- Read old customer lists. You may see names that no longer sell anything you currently produce. Who took their place and why?
- Describe distribution channels. Ten years ago specialty stores may have sold your products. Today the easiest route to consumers may be through mail order catalogs.
- Find Wall Street research analyst reports and study the key factors they cited when they recommended your stock and the stock of your competitors.
- Pull all newspaper and trade journal stories about your company, industry, and products from the library archives. Learn about the issues of the past and decide if they actually turned out to be issues at all.
- Talk to employees who retired ten years ago about every aspect of the company and how the business was run. At a gathering of retirees a careful listener can learn a lot about past details. The interviews should be with retirees because their memories are a snapshot of the past, unmuddied by the changes that followed. Current employees who have been with the company for ten years or more will not be as clear about the past because the changes they lived through, which lead to the present, have contaminated the purity of their past memories.
- Compare the patent list of today with the patent list of the past and note the significant differences in the types of technology protected and which types prevailed.

As you research the past, additional avenues for investigation will undoubtedly present themselves. The process of looking into the past and comparing it to the present is a method for training the mind to make connections between two times. This training will pay off as you ultimately attempt to visualize the future in relationship to the present.

Change Happens Slowly

In essence, markets for products do not change fundamentally. Customers desire safety, security, freedom from hunger, shelter, attractiveness, wealth, and specific product utilities. This has and always will be true. The products that continue to serve them throughout the years are still made of some form of materials and components. The physical embodiment of products is fundamental but shapes, sizes and the types of materials used have changed and will again. Employees have been and will continue to be needed to run the different business enterprise assets, but their skills and number will be different. Many elements of the future game are a given and can be assumed to remain static. By carefully selecting areas that are expected to remain static energies can be focused on key factors with the greatest potential for change. As you approach this analysis the most important realization will be that technology is the fundamental reason for change, and that will continue to be true. This may seem obvious but the subtle ways in which technological change has altered your company will only become apparent when a diligent investigation is conducted. Subtle change is like the details of a major project. Left unattended, details can kill you.

Future Winner

Step two of the Gaps Analysis requires a description of the likely winner of the future game. For each of the characteristics that were previously defined, the competencies that are possessed by the winner of the future game should be described in detail. With the future game defined and broken into manageable pieces of markets, products, and production facilities, the theoretical winner can be described in relation to these characteristics. Note that there are many ways to meet the challenges, so the future can take many different shapes, and there are many ways to win.

One way to start defining the theoretical winner is to study a respected competitor or group of competitors, as is commonly done in benchmarking. An interesting approach to benchmarking is to look at the competitive strategic alliance actions and licensing policies of competitors. If you look at what a competitor is doing with regard to the technology that it is licensing or the strategic alliances upon which it is embarking, you will see a very clear symbol of its plans, goals, and objectives, and how it is positioning itself for the future game. Such an analysis can be instrumental in helping to focus your definition on the shape of the future game and also to get a glimpse of what the competitors of the future game will possess in the way of the technology know-how, alliance strengths, and core competencies. The reason to focus on licenses (especially exclusives) is that the technology transfer represents a type of strategic alliance because the exclusive licensor has allied itself with the exclusive licensee. However, benchmarking should not dominate Gaps Analysis. You must be careful not to imitate the companies perceived to be setting the standards. In defining the Future Game and the Future Winner no standards yet exist. Your implementation of steps 1 and 2 of the analysis are to set the standards. Benchmarking allows others to set the standards and that is not the goal of Gaps Analysis. Use benchmarking as a tool in helping to define the future winner but not as the compass by which to guide your company.

Current Assessment

The third step in the process is to analyze your current situation critically, looking carefully at all the characteristics that will be important for winning the future game. The comparison between the core competencies that are possessed by the theoretical winner and those you currently possess clearly identifies the gaps and points up everything that must be done or obtained to fill the gaps and become the theoretical winner of the future game.

Filling Gaps

While there may be many ways to fill the gaps, licensing the technology that will be needed is certainly a key option. Licensing strategies dominate this book, but other gap-filling methods are available. Additional options can include mergers and acquisitions, joint ventures, minority interests in third party companies, strategic alliances, cross licensing, making changes in the human side of the question. These usually include hiring the technical people—consultants and contractors—needed to develop the missing technology or increasing current employee capabilities through education or training.

Beyond Licensing—Filling the Gaps

Some of the alternatives to filling the gaps include:

- Direct licensing of the technology you need for a royalty payment.
- Cross-licensing of patent portfolios to obtain the technology you need.
- Acquiring companies that now have or are likely to obtain the technology you will need in the future.[3]
- Forming strategic alliances

---

[3]A major problem here is that buying a company often includes acquiring divisions and properties in which you have no interest. The process of selling off undesirable divisions can become time consuming, deflecting management energies from the primary goals that triggered the acquisition.

- Obtaining research grants and alliances with research institutions and universities.
- Contracting for technology development with private companies.
- Contracting for technology development with individuals as consultants.
- Adding technical staff with the expertise needed to fill gaps.
- Acquiring minority ownership interests in companies possessing the needed expertise.

Special Problems with Strategic Alliances

Licenses can help fill gaps but the mere possession of the rights to use patents may not be enough to allow for development of the enabling technology that will be needed to win the future gain. Alliances have become popular among many companies. Some of the reasons include more shared risk where partners each contribute capital funding, access to the different core competencies of the alliance partners, and shortening of the time needed for development because of the shared expertise.

Alliances are considered to exist when two companies come together to work on a single project. An alliance is less formal than a joint venture, where two companies come together to form a third company that lasts into perpetuity. Strategic alliances are not to be entered into easily. They are possibly the most complex business combination that can be created. Results to date show that few have achieved their intended goals. Moreover, as with a marriage, the breakup can leave the former partners with strong animosity toward each other. Dr. Bob Gussin of Johnson & Johnson described the key characteristics associated with establishing successful strategic alliances at the June 27, 1995, Rutgers University Strategic Alliance Conference, *Managing Strategic Alliances*. He explained that both partners need to conduct or have:

1. A clear understanding of the goals to be attained.
2. A clear strategy for reaching the defined goals.
3. Milestones by which to judge the progress of the alliance.
4. Extensive up-front planning.
5. Defined roles of responsibility.
6. Frequent communication between the partners at the operating management level.
7. Enthusiastic and continuing support from upper management.

Dr. Gussin indicated that the list just recited may seem obvious but the lack of attention to these important details is where disasters originate. An initial discussion between J&J and a joint venture partner seemed to indicate that the future partner had 200 products ready for market. J&J agreed to form an alliance principally because of the potential to introduce new products in a short time. J&J had plenty of long-term research of its own but wanted access to technology that was ready to go. The truth of the alliance was that 200 research efforts were ready for publication in science journals; it was almost 20 years before a product actually hit the market from the alliance. The stumbling block was poor communication. *Ready to go* meant different things to the negotiators. There was no clear understanding between the partners—seemingly fundamental and obvious in hindsight but nonetheless an Achilles Heel.

In another alliance, J&J realized that the scientists had no common ground. One side of the partnership thought that the scientists from the other side were stupid. The other side's scientists thought that their new partners were crazy. For an alliance to work there must be some continuity and basis for understanding. This conflicts with the fact that you are only entering into an alliance because of your need for new technical competency, yet there must be room for that technical competency to be understood. The driving force of technology transfer is the need to gain access to broad technologies in diverse areas, but each side must have the ability to understand the other. Dr. Gussin indicates that partners must be picked carefully and that it is important that both companies have respect for each other. Personalities and culture become more important in alliances than in any other type of business combination or operating structure.

At the same conference, Dr. Gene Slowinski of Rutgers University reported on a recently completed study that focused on the reflections of alliance managers. He studied strategic alliances that involved 50 companies. He found that only 50 percent of the alliances survived after three years. He also found that only half of those surviving were meeting the expectations that had been established.

Dr. Slowinski indicated that alliances work when partners take small steps together. He refers to this as Phased Relationships, defined as the serial motions of a successful alliance involving management predicated upon completion of milestones. Continued movement forward depends on an evaluation of a partner's ability to go to the next step. Phased relationships involve limited early investment, which is not followed by additional investment until successful phases have been accomplished. A phased relationship leads to a successful strategic alliance when logical decision criteria for assessing progress are established and maintained.

Successful strategic alliances are those where both partners develop internal networks through their parent organizations so that resources from both companies are cultivated for the support of the activities of the strategic alliance. Strategic alliances must compete for the partners' ever more severely restricted resources. In-house projects are likely to get more management focus. Parent company management, which is not directly related to the strategic alliance, is not likely to support the strategic alliance unless political networks are nurtured and cultivated and the parent company is reminded about the mutual benefits that will be gained from supporting the strategic alliance. Unless both partners in a strategic alliance cultivate their internal networks to provide the needed resources, the alliance is doomed. A support network is needed from both partners.

The research conducted by Dr. Slowinski supports the professional experiences and observations of Dr. Gussin and indicates that the most important reason for alliance failures is that there is a mismatch between the strategic versus tactical intentions of alliance partners. Unless the alliance involves the core businesses of both companies, it is likely to fail. When a company is in a strategic alliance that represents its core interests with another company for which the alliance represents only a peripheral interest, the likelihood that commitment will not be maintained by the peripherally involved company almost guarantees the alliance to failure from the start. A successful alliance addresses the core business interests of both partners.

Strategic Alliances Will Be Needed

Strategic alliances are difficult to organize, control, and make successful, but they will become more important. In the future, access to patent rights in the form of licenses and cross-licenses will not provide the broad expertise that companies will need for the future game. Alliances will need to be formed in order to help a licensee practice the patent rights licensed. In the future, when broad and diverse technical competencies are required, a license to practice the new technology will only be the beginning. The licensees will need education to allow the technology to be applied successfully. Companies that need new technical capabilities also will need enabling technology and the means by which to commercialize the new technology into its product offerings. Therefore, the future may bring less naked licensing and more licenses that are preceded by alliances.

The most important aspects of a successful strategic alliance is that both parties have mutual needs and common objectives. These two characteristics are dynamic and ever-changing. If the partners are lucky the needs and objectives of both sides will change together and the alliance will survive.

Regardless of how deficiencies are filled, Gaps Analysis is a method for finding the intellectual property that will be needed in the future. The entire process does not have to be completed before benefits are realized. Just defining the Future Game can yield important information about a company's future. IBM was slow to see that the future had little use for mainframe computers. Western Union was slow to see that the future would include email. Don't be slow. Define the future so you will be part of it.

10

Strategy for the Times: Intellectual Property Can Drive Corporate Profitability

James P. O'Shaughnessy

Rockwell International Corporation

Many American companies have long been content with "invention" strategies for building their patent portfolios. These strategies are remarkably similar in concept from company to company: certain people in the organization—inventors—make inventions and others in the organization—patent attorneys—obtain patents on them. These activities are repeated until the company develops a lot of inventions and acquires a lot of patents covering them. Management has felt comfortable with this approach, if for no reason other than it has been the standard operating procedure throughout most industries for as long as most can remember.

Invention strategies have led to unsurprising qualitative uniformity among most corporate patent portfolios. This proves true whether the company is large or small, whether its products are described as high tech or no tech, whether it operates in industrial or consumer markets and without particular regard to its geographic location. Retrospectively, however, this turns out to be quite predictable.

THE COMPOSITION OF INVENTION-INSPIRED PORTFOLIOS IS PROSAIC

The commonality in the makeup of most portfolios is seen when auditing the patent holdings of major US industrialists. These audits invariably reveal patents falling into two broad categories, each of which can then be divided into two subgroups.

The first broad category of patents consists of those which are not very helpful to the company, essentially valueless patents. The two subgroups in this case are best described as relating to "junk" and "productivity-enhancing" technologies.

The term "junk," though potentially offensive as overly judgmental, is applied advisedly so there can be no doubt about the ability of patents in this category to return any conceivable value to the company. Value in this sense refers to asset value from a strategic viewpoint.

Patents should be regarded as corporate assets protecting technological or other corporate prowess having the capacity to support or gain new sources of competitive advantage for the company or to sustain an existing source of competitive advantage for it. It is axiomatic today that some source of competitive advantage is essential to corporate vitality if not viability.[1] Without a competitive advantage of some sort, no company is likely to endure in the cauldron of modern, vigorous competition endemic in every sector of every major market. Yet even those companies currently enjoying strong competitive advantage in their markets cannot be smug about it. All companies, wherever located and irrespective of market mechanics, face inevitable "value migration."[2] These are the realities impacting all corporate strategies and affecting their capacity to develop and deliver value for the company.

Though value migrates in many cases initially to benefit the organization, that phase of corporate existence is generally relatively short lived. For virtually every company for virtually its entire existence, the real battle is ebbing the flow of value away from it. Outbound value migration—econoporesis, if you will—can be the result of changing, evolving or maturing customer wants or needs. This form of corporate atrophication is the consequence of a shift away from the products[3] of a given company and toward those of a competitor in the same industry or a shift away from all product offerings of the entire industry toward revolutionary replacements. The consequence is the

---

[1]One of the best and most comprehensive analysis of these concepts is found in M. E. Porter, *Competitive Advantage—Creating and Sustaining Superior Performance*, Free Press (1985) (hereafter, "Competitive Advantage"). *See also, Strategy: Seeking and Securing Competitive Advantage*, C. Montgomery & M. Porter (ed.), HBS Press (1991), a compilation of insightful articles on the general topic.

[2]A. Slywotzky, *Value Migration*, HBS Press (1995). Slywotzky chronicles the woes of many companies and several industries as he proves his thesis of sure and often too swift a process of migration of value from those companies having the enviable status of contemporary market or corporate leaders. An exceptionally telling example is the metamorphosis in the computer industry. In one decade, over $100 billion in market value was lost by some and claimed by others as the face of that market changed forever.

[3]I will not make a sharp distinction between products and services. The fundamental premises and recommendations in this chapter do not materially differ between product versus service strategies, though there will be obvious tactical differences in their application.

same: the loss is not just of business but the source of competitive advantage that underlies the ongoing economic strength of the company.

Junk simply lacks the ability to alter either the calculus or dynamics of the marketplace. If a line of products (or services) loses its relevance in the market, the technology and patents protecting it can have little if any intrinsic value.

Thus, "junk" becomes synonymous with patents that afford no protection for the business design of the enterprise, no shelter for the investments made to promote its business plan. But, it is not so much that junk emerges from barren soil in all events; patent portfolios are dynamic corporate assets. Just like the treasures we all have tucked away in the basement or garage, these patents may once have had substantial value to the company—at a time when they bore relevance to the sources of competitive advantage at the heart of the enterprise. The problem now is that they have lost that value. They have become irrelevant to the company's business.

Most of us can usually see the junk for what it is and many of us can do something about it. As evolving assets, patent portfolios require periodic review and pruning to remove underperforming assets. If no other benefit is gained from the exercise, their removal saves the cost of the fees to maintain them in force, an expense multiplied many times if there is a large foreign dimension to the portfolio. Accordingly, the objectives in dealing with this category are at least two-fold: minimize if not eliminate altogether the initial acquisition of junk, but then spot it fast and rid the portfolio of it as efficiently as possible.[4]

The second subgroup mentioned above may also provoke some controversy, but perhaps only over the semantics. Here, productivity-enhancing technology refers to those inventions which arise out of the solutions to problems confronting the industrialist. These solutions more often than not tend to be relatively unique, insofar as the problems to be solved exist in a relatively unique environment. For example, one challenged to solve a prob-

---

[4]The "junk in the garage" metaphor is equally apropos for those who hold on to technology, wholeheartedly believing it must have some value, if not to them then most assuredly to their competitors. Though it may be argued that everything has relative value, this proposition is much like the view that a garage sale is a decent way to dispose of old junk and "profit" from it. However valid the belief that this represents latent value, it cannot seriously be contended that it rises to the level of market or corporate altering value.

The related "strategy" of seeking patents on technology simply to prevent a competitor from patenting or exploiting it also needs too be questioned. How often will a company devise a way to do something that is so inferior to its preferred approach that it rejects adopting the technology while at the same time the very same technology is so significant to a competitor that it cannot do without it? For sure, as we will see, there are beneficial strategies to be formulated and executed to secure value by preempting the opportunity space of competitors. But as we'll also see, that strategy is marketplace driven not product or process feature driven. The failure to make this distinction is likely to lead to a substantial "junk" component in the portfolio.

lem concerning the company's throughput of raw material in a manufacturing process to create a specific product necessarily must take into account the plant, equipment and labor force (perhaps other variables as well) that define the source of the problem and constrain its acceptable solutions.[5] The eventual answer to the problem of how to increase productivity may be very creative and have a notable impact on the company's profitability. Nonetheless, a patent on it is no better than worthless in most cases; in many cases, it may be positively harmful to the company.

A competitor having a different set of plant, equipment and labor force variables is unlikely to be able to use a solution to a problem existing in a different environment. Of course, there may be room for adaptation of the solution, but its wholesale adoption is normally foreclosed. On the one hand, the grant of a patent—the legal right to exclude others—is of little value when those most likely to use the technology are already practically excluded. In other words, the right to prevent someone from doing something he is unlikely to do anyway confers little inherent benefit. On the other hand, patenting this category of technology exposes the knowledge of how the industrialist-patentee so capably competes in the market, many times in circumstances where the technology is unpoliceable. Once again, little value is likely to be derived from these tactics. Thus, normally, this category of patents can usually make only minor contributions to the company and, from an asset management vantage, these patents are almost as worthless as junk.

This position runs counter to the once conventional wisdom, but experience bears out its validity. This category of productivity-enhancing technology most often is not broadly patentable. For those productivity-enhancing innovations that are—those which support strong market-preemptive positions—they are more likely to fall into the second category of technology discussed below. Moreover, just how many intractable productivity problems does any one industrialist actually face? To the extent a company is constantly confronted by one productivity dilemma after another, its problem doesn't lie so much with an inadequate patent or technology strategy; it faces a more or less severe competitiveness problem to be overcome simply if it is to remain in business.

No company can build a formidable portfolio, having the ability to alter the marketplace factors it faces every day, on a foundation of productivity-enhancing technology. The sooner that reality is faced, the sooner the company can begin to craft a patent portfolio having market-influenceable value.

This leads to our consideration of the other broad category of patented technology, again comprised of two subgroups. In this instance, we deal with strategic technology and more specifically corporate strategic technology and

---

[5]See R. L. Ackoff, *The Art of Problem Solving*, John Wiley & Sons (1978), for a timeless study of problem solving concepts in general.

market strategic technology. Though the two share some common traits, their acquisition and deployment are profoundly different.

The factor common to these groups is found in the concept of *strategic* technology. Technology is strategic in this sense when it supports an existing or emerging source of competitive advantage (dubbed by some a strategic advantage). The subject of competitive advantage is beyond the scope of this article.[6] Suffice it to say for our purposes that there are a number of ways an enterprise may garner a competitive advantage in its market, but three tend to predominate. They are differentiation, cost leadership and niche or focus marketing.

Corporate strategic technology underlies a specific source of competitive advantage enjoyed by the company. It may be the technology defining the source of differentiation of a product or service, the technology providing the source of demonstrable cost leadership in an industry or sector, or the technology barring the niche to entry by competitors. Regardless, it is recognized as the technical "corporate jewels," technology that distinguishes the company from all who envy it and its marketplace position. The absolute degree of competitors' jealousy over the company's possession and effective use of corporate strategic technology thus becomes one of the more significant benchmarks of its value while at the same time signifying the strength of the intellectual property protecting it.

Market strategic technology is the kissing cousin of corporate strategic technology. It too has the capacity to influence market dynamics. It is technology any participant in the involved market would love to have because that company could adopt or adapt that technology to its own advantage in the production or delivery of its own goods or services. Patents covering this type of technology have the correlative ability to shelter broadly the investments made by those who offer for sale the related goods or services, insofar as any entrant to the market could promote its own, perhaps different, product or service to meet market desires while enjoying the advantages of the related legal protection.

Market strategic technology differs from corporate strategic technology in one important way—its holder can share with another the rights to this category of technology without simultaneously yielding its unique source of competitive advantage, except of course for the very presence of the other company in the competitive market sphere. In other words, rights to corporate strategic technology, if shared, would immediately and significantly erode the source of competitive advantage enjoyed by the holder; those respecting market strategic technology can be shared without inevitably suffering those consequences.

---

[6]See those references cited at footnote 1 for valuable background on this topic.

The "invention strategy" summarized above yields relatively predictable results, confirmed when one examines the patent portfolios of almost any major company (and some that aren't so well endowed). The four categories are almost universally represented in about the same relative proportions. The patents that are not so helpful, those covering junk and simple productivity-enhancing technology, predominate. They account for about 80% or more of most portfolios. Corporate strategic technology adds at most another 15–20%. This relationship reflects the reality that most companies derive most of their effective patent protection from relatively few patents. Simple math tells us that market strategic technology is essentially nonexistent.[7] Yet this is the category best suited to contribute highly leveraged value to its proprietor in the modern era—market strategic technology has the ability today to alter corporate fortunes as much or more than any other asset of the company, technological or otherwise.

The pitiful contribution of market strategic technology to the overall composition of most portfolios is the consequence of reactive strategies. Invention strategies foster the development of market strategic technology only by serendipity. It takes an "innovation strategy" if the industrialist is to benefit from the enormous potential to be unleased by a strong position in market strategic technology. But simply expecting proactivity to replace reactivity is not enough to shift from invention-inspired to innovation-driven strategies; the mere hope itself is too reactive. It takes an entirely different focus, a focus on what's important to customers and what's valuable to those who are asked to part with their hard-earned money if the company is to prosper.[8] That is the subject of the next section.

THE TEXTURE OF INNOVATION-DRIVEN PORTFOLIOS IS RICH

Invention strategies were adequate for the industrial era. Make an invention, then patent it; accumulate lots of inventions and patents and everything will turn out alright. Despite its logical simplicity, this approach worked for most for many years. But, in the new technological era, that strategy is outmoded.

---

[7]There are some very large companies everyone would agree exemplify the high tech image, whose patent portfolios of literally thousands of patents contain a small handful covering market strategic technology. Incredibly, the proportion representing corporate strategic technology is only about 10%. Perhaps it is the large absolute number of patents that dilutes the significance on a percentage basis, but even the raw numbers are surprisingly small.

[8]Imparato and Harari, *Jumping the Curve: Innovation and Strategic Choice in An Age of Transition*, Jossey-Bass (1996) (hereafter "Jumping the Curve"). The authors express their advice with the suggestion to "build the organization around the software and build the software around the customer." In their jargon, "software" is equated broadly with knowledge—knowledge about business and the business organization. Their point is the importance of the customer as the central focus of these efforts.

The assets of the industrial era that counted most were real and personal property, and the capital they represented or that underlay them. The individuals and companies initially conquering those industrial frontiers reaped the greatest wealth and power. Those left behind, no matter how industrious, were often unable ever to catch up and rarely acquired the same market stature. In today's world, we have seen already the emerging force of intellectual property as a factor that shifts wealth and power or more dramatically as the acquisition or loss of other types of property in the bygone era. This is the new landscape for innovation strategies and those who master its vagaries the fastest and most comprehensively stand to garner the greatest benefits. If history can provide a valuable lesson on this account, the idle have much to fear as the swift seize these new opportunities.

Innovation strategies differ fundamentally at almost every level from invention strategies. Invention strategies have concentrated on the features of products or processes as the objects of attention ultimately defining the efforts to obtain patents or other forms of intellectual property protection. On the contrary, innovation strategies use the product, process or other manifestation of the technological urge as the focal point that suggests the opportunity space enveloping it.[9] Viewed from a somewhat different point of view, invention strategies centered on the product whereas innovation strategies concentrate on the market opportunity surrounding the product. These opportunities need to be explored to see how innovation strategies outperform invention strategies every time.[10]

A competent business design for a company or marketing plan for one of its products takes into account a host of variables. The "If-you-build-it-they-will-come" design doesn't work in today's markets. Likewise, a competent innovation strategy must look beyond the attributes of the product and the

---

[9]R. Simmons, *Levers of Control*, HBS Press (1995), describes the concept of opportunity space and the way corporate strategies may expand or constrict it.

Most "successful" executives achieve that very status because they are able to solve problems or seize opportunities constrained by suboptimal conditions. Options they wish were available are for some reason often foreclosed. Thus, tradeoffs become necessary simply to get business done and workable as opposed to ideal plans are put into motion. One of the theses of this chapter is that the development of a position respecting market strategic technology expands the opportunity space for devising business plans under improved, even if still suboptimal, conditions.

[10]This is not at all a call to eschew the benefits that can be obtained from "patenting inventions" as they arise in the ordinary course of research and development. That dogmatically myopic view would be as inane as awaiting the final development of those inventions before doing anything to secure protection for them. The "invention strategy" has a place in modern corporations, but one needs to be critical in defining that place. More to the point of this chapter, that approach—the invention strategy—assuredly needs to be dominated by "innovation strategy" thinking not merely supplemented by it.

obvious ways others may attempt to copy or emulate it.[11] The primary focus for either strategy—business design strategy or innovation strategy—must begin with, end and reside in the market for the goods which are the proxy for corporate revenue. It is the market and the market only which is the arena for success or failure of the product and its underlying technology, whether enabling, sustaining or core. That market may be object oriented but its business potential is controlled by the individual decisions of a cast of influential participants.

Every market is populated by a number of actors with distinct and well defined roles. In addition to the company, there are its suppliers and its customers. Intersecting those relationships, the company also encounters substitutors and complementors. These interlaced relationships need to be fully analyzed and folded into every innovation strategy to maximize its value to the company.[12]

The disparate roles of a company's suppliers and its customers are often recognized but then promptly forgotten in most invention strategies; little more than lip service is paid to their importance and influence when constructing the intellectual property portfolio. Suppliers are thought to serve the primary purpose of providing the raw materials the company requires to do what is more important—convert them into something having *real value* to the company's customers. Customers also are perceived to have a distinctly important role—recognize that value and *pay for it*.[13] When it comes to devising a business design, these relationships are thought by invention strategists to be the province of someone else. Substantial value goes unclaimed when thinking this way.

---

[11]One of the common invention-strategy strategies when seeking patent protection for a new product is to evaluate feature substitution: build protection around alternative features or attributes of the product to prevent ease of substitution of an equivalent product by a competitor. An innovation-strategy strategy examines the more comprehensive question of wholesale product substitution: how to construct protection around the combined problem/solution set which, in the limit, contemplates revolutionary replacement for the protected product, not merely its evolution. This is the core of the topic we'll explore later in connection with the phenomenon of disruptive technology.

[12]A. Brandenburg & B. Nalebuff, "The Right Game: Use Game Theory to Shape Strategy," *Harvard Business Review*, July–Aug. 1995. The authors present a provocative description of market interactions in explaining the value of viewing them allocentrically rather than egocentrically. In applying game theory, they sum up their advice with the pity aphorism, "Successful business strategy is about actively shaping the game you play, not just playing the game you find." Market strategic technology has the power to alter immensely the game every company plays in its markets, especially when the opportunities in those markets are evaluated in the context of all the players in them.

[13]A better view is stated in Schonberger, *World Class Manufacturing: The Next Decade*, Free Press (1996); Grant, "Realize Your Customers' Full Profit Potential," *Harvard Business Review* Sept–Oct 1995.

Every company has a value chain.[14] It is made up of the inputs to production that eventually are converted into the goods or services the company offers into its market. As between the company and its suppliers on the one hand and the company and its customers on the other, there are specific, distinct linkages among their value chains. The supplier's goods link into the company's value chain as raw materials for its production of value-added goods while the goods it produces then link into it customer's value chain in the same way by adding discernable value to its operation. Equally true, each of the company's suppliers and customers has its own respective set of suppliers and customers, each-too with its own value chain defining what is important to it. It is almost always advantageous to examine closely these downstream customer relationships. Positioning the company to take advantage of the way its products are used by its customers' customers can set the company apart in its competition with others for that business. The same is true, perhaps to a somewhat lesser extent, when considering the value of the company's upstream supplier relationships.[15]

An innovation strategy identifies these linkages and builds around them a market strategic technology position for the company. This type of strategy is crafted to return value from relationships the company has with its suppliers and customers at the points of interaction or intersection of the value chains at their linkages. In doing so, the company can alter the way it receives its critical manufacturing inputs from its suppliers and improve its importance or leverage with its customers. In both instances, the company's market strategic technology position allows it to claim this marketplace value, value it has created for itself through a properly devised innovation strategy. This form of business differentiation serves to distinguish the company from its "competitors" who lack a portfolio as richly textured.

The industrialist also must fully examine the relationship with its "substitutors." Substitutors include, but should not be limited in concept to, the ever-present competitors of the company. A substitutor is one whose goods or services can be substituted by the customer for those of the company—the classic competitor. But, in the constellation of actors in the market, substitutors may also exist on the supplier or upstream side of the market, competing for resources customarily obtained by the company from its supply network. In this situation, the two rivals for scarce resources may not be competitors at all in the markets for their finished goods but the competition for critical supplies may be as limiting a factor constraining the company's ultimate success as if the two were head-to-head competitors for common

---

[14]See *Competitive Advantage*, note 1.

[15]Overall, this can be as simple as thinking about the product on a continuum, from the earliest identification of the raw materials that comprise its makeup to its eventual integration into the business environment of the ultimate user, and assessing at every step the value-added contributions involved in its conversion from components to an eventual tool of production.

customers.[16] The loser in the competition for limited inputs to production faces the same prospects for economic failure as the company having all the supplies it needs but which is unable to sell its converted goods to customers.[17] A sophisticated innovation strategy takes into account this broader perspective of substitutors; it is not limited to the conventional, narrow view of "competitors."

While the full range of substitutors has not been completely appreciated in the historical development of intellectual property portfolios, complementors and their fundamental marketplace role have generally been overlooked altogether in the eyes of invention strategists. The popular intellectual property model of yesteryear normally analyzed the features of the product that distinguished it from "competitive products" and then sought to obtain protection in some zone around those important features. In this way, it was thought or hoped that competitors would be foreclosed from using the same advantages to win business from the common customers. Complementors have not typically entered the equation at all.

Complementors in the market are those companies who, in selling their own products, either push or pull the product of another company through the complementor's market at the point of sale. A good example is a company selling a computer mouse. It has a complementary relationship with the computer manufacturer who designs his product for use with a mouse and another complementary relationship with the software company that sells programs to enable use of the mouse. In this environment, there is a sense of symbiosis. The mouse manufacturer should sell a lot more "mouses" if the computer manufacturer sells a lot more computers using them, whereas the software company should also do well by taking advantage of improvements offered by both of its complementors. Potential benefits accrue in favor of the mouse company through mutuality of these marketplace interests.

The combination of all four categories of players, plus the company at the heart of it all, defines a robust and constantly changing arena where all participants are vying to exploit the value to be found in the market common to them. It is like a chorus of as many voices whose harmony is drawn out melodically and clearly by the customer who orchestrates market action with

---

[16]An apt example of upstream substitutors—competitors for raw material inputs—is Coca-Cola and Tyson Foods, each of which consumes large quantities of carbon dioxide without which neither could get its product to market.

[17]Loss in this context is not limited to the absolute inability to acquire necessary raw materials, immediately driving the company out of business because it is unable to make product at all. The inability to obtain manufacturing inputs on adequate commercial terms, including price or priority, quality or conformity to specifications, can hamper successful conversion of those raw materials into saleable product customers will buy in the cycle necessary for prosperity. Ancient cultures show us that "death by a thousand cuts" has the same eventual result as swifter means. The metaphor is fully applicable in this business setting.

its funds. An innovation strategy can profoundly affect the sounds in this marketplace. An intellectual property position built on this foundation can deliver substantial value to the company that invests its time and energy in securing a dominant position. That strategy needs to be as dynamic as the market itself, for as noted above, value migration is almost always migration out of the company while the potential for disruptive technology to sweep away even hard-won advantages is ever present. This is the environment in which market strategic technology must be developed, deployed and vigorously exploited for maximum value.

INNOVATION STRATEGY WILL ADD INESTIMABLE VALUE TO CORPORATE FORTUNE

There are a number of situations in which innovation strategies have the potential to return substantial value. We will look briefly at a few to bring home the points generalized above.

The Effect of Disruptive Technology Can Never Be Underestimated

Every industrial market, whether high tech or low tech, is eventually swept by disruptive technology.[18] Disruptive technology is the revolutionary technology that obsoletes the dominant design laying hold of the current market, rendering the products that yesterday satisfied customers irrelevant to their needs today. Scholars have undertaken long-term studies tracking this phenomenon through product sectors like typewriters[19]—from the manual Rem-

---

[18]J. L. Bower & C. M. Christensen, "Disruptive Technologies: Catching the Wave," *Harvard Business Review*, Jan.–Feb. 1995 (hereafter, "Disruptive Technologies"). Bower and Christensen explore the concept of disruptive technology, in particular its relationship to the U.S. disk drive market and the effect it had in allowing Connor Peripherals to capture from Seagate Technology the exploding market for shrinking drives during the 1980's. After Bower and Christensen published their article in January 1995, Seagate made an offer in September 1995 to purchase Connor for approximately $1 billion. It is fanciful to speculate now on how the presence of market strategic technology in Seagate's portfolio might have affected first the course of market competition between the two and later their negotiations over purchase price. *See also, Profiting from Innovation*, Howard and Guile eds., Free Press (1992); Hamel and Prahalad, *Competing for the Future*, Harvard Business School Press (1994); Leonard-Barton, "Wellsprings of Knowledge," Harvard Business School Press (1995); "Jumping the Curve," note 8.

[19]J. M. Utterback, *Mastering the Dynamics of Innovation*, HBS Press (1994). Utterback traces the plight of participants in many industries, as they evolved from market infancy through a lively middle phase to a transition in which dominant firms and designs are swept aside by newcomers with different visions and better products. Some of the industries on which he reports include float glass, rayon, and computer components, in addition to typewriters. His is an interesting viewpoint, especially when compared and contrasted with Slywotzky's view in *Value Migration*, in which the latter explicates comparable concepts during what he terms the three distinct phases of market evolution: migration in, stability, and migration out.

ingtons of the turn of this century to pc-based word processors that may still be dominant at the turn of the next century—and shorter-term analyses of sectors such as the disk drive market.[20]

There are common historic lessons taught by these studies of disruptive technology from which wise people will profit. Two are unmistakably clear: disruptive technology will overtake *every* market, the question is not "if" but "when;" the disruption will doubtless be borne on the energy of an outsider, almost certainly one who does not currently enjoy the position of the dominant design, whether business or technology design.[21]

Another trend has been signalled by these analyses. The company having the dominant position has suffered, sometimes irretrievably, by its lack of vision; not so much from the inability to see or sense the approach of the disruptive technology but the lack of vision to have prepared properly for its arrival. One cannot plan effectively or expect to be positioned for success by waiting until the change has been wrought.

When it is clear that a disruptive technology is afoot in the market, it is too late to counter it effectively. Once the trend has been spotted, the opportunity to have done something to offset its marketplace effects has dissipated. And, those who have been displaced have had little of technological value to offer once the disruptive technology has taken hold. What is there of value if all the disrupted (i.e., displaced or more popularly termed, "dislocated") company can offer is junk, productivity-enhancing technology or last week's corporate strategic technology in a market where the strategy has now failed? Is the disrupted technologist to offer money to the new rival for the privilege of sharing the budding riches of the evolved marketplace? And why would the disrupting technologist want to take a competitor's money, at least directly, if the business design allows him to capture the market share that eventually will collapse the competition? In sum, the old guard has had nothing of real value or interest, *unless* it has had the foresight to have developed market strategic technology to be used as the ante to the new market and its expanding opportunities.[22]

---

[20]*Disruptive Technologies, supra.*

[21]It is sobering to note the statistics supporting the proposition that market pioneers "succeed" at a rate only slightly greater than 10% of the time, when measured by the ability of the first entrant to hold market leadership through full maturation of that market. Nearly 50% fail outright while the remainder are overtaken by later entrants to the market. G. J. Tellis and P. N. Golder, "First to Market, First to Fail? Real Causes of Enduring Market Leadership," *Sloan Management Review*, Winter 1996. From a marketing point of view, the "wait-and-see" approach may be commendable. However, from an intellectual property point of view, such an approach surely will be deadly in the future.

[22]Some contend that IBM has bucked this trend and serves as the most visible if not only example of a company that has retaken a leadership position after having suffered the fate of a disrupted company. I cannot agree. IBM's reemergence in the pc-based word processing mar-

Thus, in this new realm, market strategic technology and the intellectual property rights safeguarding it pave the way to the company's continuing participation in its old market, whether undergoing reformation or radical change by the disrupting technologist. But it goes without saying that any company desiring an innovation strategy as the hedge against the market disruption it foresees must take steps before the situation crystallizes. This impels the view that innovation planning must be an ongoing function in the company, informed by the same type of market intelligence other sectors of the business use to predict trends. Indeed, trend prediction itself may leave the company in second place or worse if it waits for the trend to be easily detected by its competitors too. Thus "fad analysis" becomes an important complementary tool.

But, whether fad or trend is sought to be predicted, the most valuable point to see clearly is the shift from normalcy that seeds market change. Here is one of the most powerful adaptations of an innovation strategy designed to prevent value migration from the company as it is challenged to anticipate the incalculable: shift prediction. Of course, the prediction requires programs designed to enable the company to engage in over-the-horizon thinking and derive for itself the kind of "luck" characterized by the confluence of preparation and opportunity. But the real prize is to have secured an intellectual property position as close to the shift as possible to reap the rewards inherent in the eventually maturing trend or fad and its commercial exploitation.

Market Strategic Technology Can Blunt a Technology Attack

Every going concern must anticipate the inevitable value migration away from its business design brought on by disruptive technology. There are other reasons to find value in an innovation strategy designed to develop market strategic technology.

It has become commonplace in some industries for companies to shop their patent portfolios around, accompanied by threats (veiled or not so veiled) that licenses need to be taken by less dominant (i.e., technologically weaker) players in the market to avoid costly and potentially disruptive litigation. This strategy has proven successful for a small handful of companies.

---

ket is primarily the result of its size and diversity. When the market for electric typewriters cratered, IBM's position in it fell as precipitously as everyone else's. The Selectric typewriter that had dominated the design for both product and market was as dead as every other entrant's offering. That IBM was already in the computer field, unlike Xerox for example, and that pc-based word processing became the evolved form, is a tribute to the benefits of size and diversity as opposed to construct or plan laid previously for the acquisition of targeted market strategic assets designed as a hedge against inevitable value migration when disruptive technology fundamentally alters a market.

Their success has spawned similar efforts further down the industrial food chain.[23]

Giving the devil his due, these strategies make perfect sense from an asset analyst's vantage. The portfolio is an asset created (whether by an invention or innovation strategy) through corporate investments and it needs to be treated as any other asset of the company from ROI and ROA viewpoints. If it has the ability to achieve a return on its asset value, whether intrinsic or extrinsic, it is not only in the best interests of the shareholders to maximize asset return but that action is required of management acting on behalf of all stakeholders in the company. Those on the receiving end may not find the motives quite so lofty, but it is not as though they have no recourse if they have been sufficiently prescient.

A company visited by the negotiating team of the large portfolioist usually finds itself in much the same position as the disrupted technologist previously described. What does it have to offer but money? Junk and productivity enhancing technology are usually of no or little value while it is heart-wrenching to have to part with corporate strategic technology, especially when the erosion in the value of the company's sources of competitive advantage now benefits a major competitor. This company desperately needs market strategic technology to serve as the basis for a cross license preserving the company's vital technology while at once having the kind of value any participant in the market would see—and pay for.

As with the case of disruptive technology, an innovation strategy designed to create value in market strategic technology cannot operate *ad hoc*. A plan needs to be adopted to develop these assets in advance of the anticipated business and legal problems. Equally true, the results of having technology assets strategic to an adversary's market or position in it can profoundly affect the nature of negotiation. Best of all, a comprehensive approach to the development of market strategic technology and correlated intellectual property rights is a leveraging strategy.

Market Strategic Technology Can Divert a Litigation Threat

There is another interesting variation on the foregoing theme. A company does not need to be in one of the small handful of industries in which these forms of cross licensing are practiced. The rise in patent litigation is unlikely

---

[23]This is not to be confused with the customary practice of policing one's patents or the assertion of one's rights in the face of infringement. The text refers more particularly to the "strategy" of asserting a vast number of patents based on the proposition that the company against whom they are asserted must deal with the larger landscape issues posed by the portfolio or a major segment of it. Sometimes this is accompanied by the related assertion that the company simply couldn't compete in the market if it were not using some form of the protected technology; thus its presence as an effective competitor is ample proof of infringement. Irrespective of the approach or its motivation, the prescribed antidote is the same—counter the charge with one's own brand of market strategic technology rights.

to subside. Technology continues to underlie competitive survival, if not out-right advantage, while courts grant injunctions to protect market share and substantial damage awards to cover economic injuries. With the advent of meaningful relief has come the quest for it. Any company selling a product containing or based on new technology is at risk of becoming a defendant in a patent infringement lawsuit.

Many defendants may harbor different views, but most patent infringe-ment litigation is prompted out of genuine beliefs that a wrong is being suf-fered and that it can be proven. Beyond motivation, it remains as true today as ever that it is usually only the close case on the merits that gets close to trial or is actually tried. Where the situation clearly favors one side or the other, that case typically will be resolved quickly for practical reasons, leav-ing one side or the other disappointed over its lack of bargaining leverage.[24] Most cases, however, still proceed too far in the expensive process of patent litigation. This entails not only the obvious expense of legal fees; the ex-pense represented in lost opportunity costs or the inability to make and ex-ecute a business plan oftentimes dwarfs the actual litigation cost.

The ability to avert or to resolve quickly a brooding or actual dispute can have enormous value, far greater than the actual cost of resolution.[25] The ability to negotiate a speedy resolution is almost always facilitated when the party accused of infringement holds rights in market strategic technology of interest to its adversary. Like the disrupted technologist studied above, hav-ing nothing but money to throw at the problem may be inadequate in some situations, such as those where share rather than income is the litigation dri-ver. This can also be true if the patent holder, like the disrupting technolo-gist, calculates that it is going to get that money anyway just by pursuing its established strategy, because share eventually spawns income.

Going to the central point of this chapter, the motivation to settle the dis-pute based on a transfer of rights is clearly advanced by the presence of mar-ket strategic technology that can be added to the negotiating mix. Otherwise,

---

[24]This discussion presumes customary business judgment is being exercised. Ordinarily, the prime business objectives to be attained through litigation are preservation of market share or creation of a stream of income in respect of the patented technology. Litigation is normally only a strategy or perhaps only a tactic to achieve such a goal. Sometimes, perhaps frequently, other business objectives may arise which rival in importance the vindication of the company's legal rights. In the conventional exercise of business judgment, the suggestions of this chapter con-cerning the development of market strategic technology are apropos. They also have a place in attempting to control the actions of an adversary with a different focus.

[25]These costs should be evaluated in the context of retained value to complete the perspective. Even a "winning" defendant (a seeming contradiction in terms) has little to show for success. The cost of proving oneself right can be high and the result bittersweet. Almost universally, fully burdened litigation costs are Pyrrhic. But, when the situation is altered by the acquisition and deployment of market strategic technology, the company still has an asset of value, even after the conclusion of the litigation is resolved by licensing—it continues to hold rights that retain the ability to return additional value.

except for money, the company accused of infringement has little to offer except its own corporate strategic technology, the transfer of which can lead to devastating results if the consequences is also to lose the distinct competitive advantage it represents.

MARKET STRATEGIC TECHNOLOGY TO FILL OUT THE HAND OF THE EMERGING COMPANY

Having looked thus far at the advantages of possessing, and the problems of not possessing, rights in market strategic technology from the viewpoints of large companies in the disruptive technology setting, of a smaller company in the typically unbalanced setting of cross-licensing negotiations and of any company confronted by claims that it is an infringer, let's now shrink our view and look at companies in the initial stages of formation or development or too resource poor to seize all the opportunities they see laying before them. Here too developing and deploying market strategic technology and rights respecting it create important benefits.

Market Strategic Technology as the Catalyst of Strategic Partnering

There is no longer any doubt that our society has passed into the technological era—the industrial era is as dead as the agricultural and hunter/gather eras preceding it.[26] As capitalists of the industrial era sought to capture financial strength based on real or personal property, technologists play out the same theme based on the intellectual property value found in innovation. Just as in earlier times, when physical frontiers seemed boundless, so too do the frontiers of knowledge capable of effective application seem limitless. There are times when one feels euphoric because there are simply too many good opportunities to pursue, or distraught because those opportunities that languish are likely to be seized by others.

Against the backdrop, there are enterprises that have fundamentally sound but embryonic technology that must be developed and a demonstrable market for that technology once it reaches that stage. In this sense, they are the disruptive technologists-in-waiting. Many lack the resources, sometimes financial but as often others as well, to bring to fruition the potentially disruptive technology quickly enough for it to have market impact. It is equally true that good ideas themselves remain a dime a dozen. Something additional needs to be done to move from the realm of ideas to their realization.

---

[26]Note especially, "Jumping the Curve," note 8.

A program centered on developing control over these disruptive technologies is likely to be fruitful to the extent it focuses on developing market strategic technology assets. No one would dispute the value of that type of control to the extent it translates into a consequent control or dominance in the market itself. But it is not necessary to be dominant—as often as not simply the ability to be influential in the market is all that is required to realize a high degree of return no matter how it is measured.

In the case study section that follows, we will explore an example of the successful use of these principles. For purposes of this overview, the central point is found in the understanding that fledgling companies or projects can soar if borne on the wings of market strategic intellectual property. This undeniably facilitates the ability to attract capital. As importantly, your author's experience demonstrates that the ability to attract a strategic partner often is more advantageous than merely bringing adequate capitalization if you can also attract other essential resources, including the ability to codevelop the technology and, in bringing it to market realization, provide an effective platform for distribution and sale of products that use it.

Having a position in the essential market strategic technology paves the way for these results. Evaluations of the opportunities may be undertaken more readily, with at least the same degree of predictability that most people require for risk analysis. The sense that investments will be made under the shelter of an existing position in the technology assists in providing the degree of comfort that most need to avoid wild speculation on the likelihood that the development project will provide the predicted rate of return. This position in the market strategic technology necessary for success thus supports the rationale for a strategic partnering relationship.

The benefits to the technologist in this scenario stem from the ability to evaluate the contribution to be provided by the technology as it is transferred from the lab to the market. Just as the parties in the cross-licensing situation described above regularly rely on a qualitative rather than strictly quantitative evaluation, so too can the parties in the strategic partnering relationship come to an appropriate sense of qualitative value. Though this approach may be somewhat imprecise, the concept of value nonetheless can be pinned down with at least the same degree of precision as customarily can be seen in financial projections on which business decisions of at least the same magnitude are made every day. In this context, the party offering to the joint enterprise the value found in its market strategic technology position can expect its partner to make contributions of human and financial capital having equivalent value. These are usually the inputs sought by the technologist, but now it has leveraged its market strategic technology by receiving from its partner contributions it otherwise could not have afforded to purchase. We will see in the case study section how this technology strategy played out favorably for a company in the industrial field.

Start-Up Companies Seeking Equity Financing

As we continue to look at ventures that are even smaller and in earlier stages of development, the emerging company or start-up offers another glimpse of where and how market strategic technology assets can have value vastly in excess of their cost of creation. The classic example of a start-up is thought to be the result of the vision of an individual or small group of tightly knit entrepreneurs who strike on an intriguing idea. The firm has taken the idea beyond mere conception and usually has a working prototype or at least can adequately demonstrate proof of principle. The firm invariably has or is in the process of acquiring protection—often patent protection—for its technology, customarily in the category of corporate strategic. The firm is tantalized by the likely financial success of the product or line if only it could be commercialized and distributed properly. For these purposes, the firm turns to sources of capital.

First-tier investors, such as venture capitalists or sophisticated individual investors, still can be found to fund emerging businesses, given the right combination of factors. While technology or technologically based products continue to capture the attention of these investment sources, typically it is only those with at least a working prototype who need apply. At this level of investment, founders of the business ordinarily must yield from 40 to 70 percent of the business to those who fund it. Mezzanine investments may result in lesser equity positions once the company has grown, but many are unlikely ever to get to that stage without the initial infusion of capital.

Irrespective of the absolute loss of equity, most start-ups suffer the prospects of yielding control and majority equity interest when bringing venture capital into the firm. Savvy investors will ensure that all the company's assets are covered by the investment agreement, and this will include technology rights and similar intangibles. In this environment, the development of an initial position in market strategic technology can be the difference between a successful or unsuccessful venture, from all points of view.

The average funding negotiation is couched in terms of risk and reward, with different sides of the table focusing on different aspects of this linked concept. All other factors being equal, investors demand high rewards for assuming high risk. Two undeniable facts support the investors' logic that high levels of equity are justifiable—the future is uncertain and many of these ventures fail without returning a single dollar.[27] Experience suggests that arguments against that position will prove unproductive. No matter how convincing an argument can be mustered, it cannot effectively neutralize the shibboleths of uncertainty and the history of failure chanted as the mantra of investors. The better approach is found in classic game theory—changing the game itself.[28]

---

[27]See note 21.

[28]Brandenburger et al., "The Right Game: Use Game Theory to Shape Strategy," *Harvard Business Review*, July 1995.

Expanding innovation horizons can benefit the emerging company materially in at least one of several possible ways. The customary portfolio initially developed by the typical emerging company is adequate, if not strong, in its corporate strategic component. Complementing it with the development of a market strategic component paves the way for an entirely different negotiating dynamic. If they are able to achieve a better technological position by developing a market strategic component for the portfolio, the company founders bring additional value to the negotiating table. The addition of value can deflect the conventional arguments of risk and reward, success and failure, for in this setting the potential investors must also take into account the presence of technology assets that transcend the focus of the company's emerging business.

Negotiations can proceed along somewhat related lines depending on how investors attribute value to the market strategic component of the portfolio. If significant value can be allocated for these assets of the business, the calculus of risk and reward can be altered toward a lesser equity stake insofar as a ratable portion of the investment is represented in these corporate assets. On the other hand, if the investors are unwilling to accord enough value to the market strategic assets represented by this technology, the business plan can be revisited with a view to separating these technology assets from the core of the business and maintaining them in a holding company that serves as the licensor to the business. Having allocated minimal value to them, potential investors will be hard pressed to argue their essential value to the enterprise.

Of course, in practice it never develops quite as simply as this and there are always competing and compelling arguments about the need to keep the company as strong as possible by retaining all relevant assets within its direct control. However, the ability to create the proper relationship between the emerging operating company and a holding company licensor is often easier and more effective than arguments over the value of these intangibles in the environment of a company with a mission but few or no customers. Also, it has proven workable to give investors the opportunity, directly or by options, to invest in the holding company. Some of these issues are explored in greater detail in the cases studies below.

MARKET STRATEGIC TECHNOLOGY AS THE BASIS FOR DEBT FINANCING

The capital markets that are now accessible to most new ventures are almost exclusively equity-based, in the sense that investors who may be interested in contributing capital are interested in doing so for a portion of the equity of the enterprise and the future success it potentially represents. Currently, there is virtually no market for debt financing, because the permissible return on debt investments is not seen as adequate to cover the risk. However, for new companies that have progressed further along the path of their business plans to more stable market footing, debt capital may be a realistic objective.

Lenders have been persuaded to consider off-balance sheet assets in their evaluation of asset-to-debt ratios sufficient to justify—that is, to meet regulator approval of—loan placement. Intellectual property can qualify a borrower's efforts to secure debt financing by increasing the asset value of the enterprise. Banks and other lenders have become more astute, requiring at least a threshold valuation of these assets just as they routinely require appraisals of other assets. This gives the company the opportunity to increase the value to be accorded its technology, and the rights it holds to it, by developing a position in market strategic technology to complement its current corporate strategic component of the portfolio. These technology assets warrant a considerably higher valuation, or at the least can support it, adding to the likelihood a lender can be convinced these assets could add to its security.

CASE STUDIES

We've examined the concept of market strategic technology from a number of vantage points and shown how its acquisition stands to improve the position of its holder.[29] The remainder of this chapter looks more specifically at licensing strategies for the transfer of technology and examines licensing vehicles useful or adaptable to the acquisition or disposition of market strategic technology for those inclined to trade in it. The following case studies exemplify generally the implementation of some of these principles.[30]

Case 1—The Multifaceted Approach

Acme was a substantial company with significant market presence in an industrial market dominated by its chief rival, Giant. Together they had the

---

[29]There are many ways a company can develop market strategic technology, but that discussion is beyond the scope of this chapter.

[30]These case studies are based on the experiences and observations of your author while in the private practice of intellectual property law and as a principal of Innovatech Co. In every case, the actual plans and programs devised and implemented are highly confidential. Thus, these case studies are reported in a way that masks the identities of the companies from which they are drawn as well as the markets and industries in which they operate and the precise details of their strategies.

It should also be appreciated that these examples of the principles described above are presented in a vastly simplified version, designed to convey concepts rather than tactics. The programs from which these examples are taken typically required several weeks, sometimes more than a month, to assemble the pertinent background information and craft the appropriate strategy, the full development of which can easily take one year or more.

lion's share of the business for their competitive widgets, with the balance divided among several other companies. In this industry it was common to spend in excess of 15% of gross revenue on research and development but Giant was so much larger than Acme that, in actual dollars spent, Giant's R&D budget dwarfed Acme's and amounted to a large percentage of Acme's entire income.

The involved market was customer driven to the extent that customers set the overall expectation of product features for successful widgets, but Giant was able to influence the market through its ability to steer customer desires toward or away from certain product features. It did this through its dominance of the market and its ability to bring new features, usually minor improvements, to market quickly. Giant exercised this influence to drive product demand toward the features it built into its widgets. Though it could not actually control customer spending, in this way Giant had been successful in capturing a larger share of the expansion of the market than Acme could command despite having a very competitive widget of its own.

Acme was concerned that it would never be able to pace Giant but was more concerned that it would fall behind in share to the point that its R&D effort could not continue turning out widgets that met customer expectations of product features while maintaining cost parity with Giant. Giant had an immense and growing patent portfolio and Acme feared that at any time a breakthrough in the enhancement of Giant's widgets would cost Acme its place in the market. Acme was relatively confident that it would be able to keep up with Giant as widgets go through the current evolutionary phase of improvements. However, because Giant had the capacity to fulfill virtually all of the market demand, Acme saw that it was likely to be squeezed from the market at the next stage of product revolution. Already many smaller competitors with small share fled the market as it proved to be unprofitable for them to continue competing.

Acme commissioned a planning team to design a program allowing the company to work smarter though not necessarily harder in its competitive struggle in the widget market. Several strategic initiatives were devised to meet the challenge.

Customers were primarily system integrators who must respond to their own market imperatives if they expected to obtain premiums for their goods in the hands of consumers. Thus, one of the first places the planning team focused was the latter interface.

The planning team set the objective of developing a technology position, both addressing the use of widgets as components in the final systems made by its customers and studying the range of system applications in which the components are used. These applications vary with product features incorporated into different models of widgets and this aspect of the market was examined as well. Product functionality was assessed from the vantage of the downstream user and the range of demands on functionality likely to emerge over the short to intermediate term. Acme thus began to position it-self to deal on a different footing with its customers by influencing their linkages with their own customers. This advantage was sought through Acme's acquisition of a market strategic technology position capable of af-fecting the transaction between Acme's customers for widgets and their use of widgets in systems they sold into their market.

Successful technology strategies are multifaceted. However helpful it may have been to create a position at the customer–consumer interface, Acme had to be prepared to take Giant on head to head. This promised to be more dif-ficult.

The initial step in this facet of the technology strategy began with a trend analysis of Giant's technology. This phase of the strategy was supplemented with publicly available information from patent office filings around the world, and Acme's own quite competent technical staff interpreted it in light of their understanding of Giant's products. Using established trending tech-niques, the planning team was able to see certain areas where priorities ap-peared to have been established by Giant. Other information, such as recent hiring trends, taught the team much about where Giant seemed to be apply-ing resources, and this was used to correlate with other information, such as new product announcements and information distributed to shareholders. Armed with its own understanding of current technological boundary condi-tions and the rate at which they were changing, Acme was able to predict several likely technological approaches Giant seemed to be committed to as it deployed its own resources. Surmising where Giant was likely to be going, the planning team set Acme on the path of developing a market strategic po-sition as close to a collision course as could be predicted.

Recognizing the impact of disruptive technology and the likelihood that it would be brought to market by a company other than those with the cur-rently dominating design, the planning team crafted a program intending to capitalize on the work of others in the field. This began with a review of what was possible, coupled with some over-the-horizon thinking on what was probable from among those possibilities. The one thing about disruptive technology in this kind of long-term look at the market is the high proba-bility that one simply will guess wrong. However likely that prospect was, the planning team believed that Acme's staff couldn't be entirely wrong on every guess of what the future was likely to hold for this industry.

Thinking about many possibilities of future developments, Acme also de-termined what probably had to happen if those competing in the market were to be successful in getting there. Using regression techniques, we plotted the paths technology would need to follow if Acme's technologists were reason-ably close in their predictions of how the markets would unfold. Working with probabilities in light of several plausible scenarios, the paths did not nec-essarily become clearer but we were able to see much better where they con-verged and overlapped. Acme concentrated on developing market strategic positions in those regions of convergence. In this fashion, though the company may have been mistaken in its ultimate predictions of what the future would hold, it would be positioned as a gatekeeper to the future by being at the most probable paths of travel from the current market to the next tier.

Case Study 2—A Cross Licensing Preemption Strategy

Acme's widget business unfolded as its management hoped and its competition with Giant appeared under control. Acme realized that it had to diversify and so purchased the assets of Marvel, an old-line manufacturer in the gizmo business.

Soon afterwards, Acme suddenly received a notice from Rambo, a competitor in the gizmo market. Now Acme faced claims of patent infringement concerning both certain product features and methods for making its new gizmos. Rambo threatened to shut down Acme's business unless Acme entered into a broad cross-license and paid a significant balancing payment to Rambo. Rambo had been around the gizmo market for decades and had considerable experience in asserting its portfolio against many others in the industry. Anecdotal information indicated that Rambo had a history of success in getting its way in these negotiations and that it had received handsome payments from most of the industry.

Acme saw no realistic choice but to negotiate with Rambo. Management was advised that Rambo had a plausible case, primarily due to the breadth of its portfolio. Even if Acme found a way around the patents Rambo had asserted, there was a decent chance that the company would step into another problem. In examining the portfolio it acquired when it purchased Marvel the planning team had determined that it was heavily skewed toward old products and processes for making them. Marvel had allowed its intellectual property to lag its marketplace position and little negotiating value would be found in its technology.

Rather than litigate under these circumstances, Acme capitulated and negotiated the best deal it could get. The result was a five year cross-license with customary guillotine provisions upon expiration, along with a large transfer fee due in installments over the first two years.

Immediately upon closure of the negotiations, Acme's management examined what they had to do to avoid being in the same position during renegotiation. Acme had already embarked on a program to bring new technology to Marvel's line. Management directed the planning team to develop a strategy that would safeguard this technology in the next round while also minimizing the need to pay Rambo.

The planning team began with a review of Rambo's entire portfolio to see what technology held by Rambo was likely to have value to Acme. This included a projection of any crossover with the evolving trajectory of Acme's process and product feature technology. Several of Rambo's patents were identified as having significant interest for at least the term of the existing cross-license and having a probable longer-term value beyond that. Though Acme thought that it might be able to avoid these patents by designing around them over the five-year term, the initial view was it might be a better use of resources to use the few of Rambo's patents that had greater value than to embark on a radical redesign now.

The planning team concluded that it would be imperative for Acme to develop a position in market strategic technology. Two approaches were eventually adopted.

Acme's first step was the development of market strategic technology directed broadly to the gizmo market. Acme strove to improve its technology stature in this way to have an equal if not superior bargaining position when the companies were to meet at the next negotiation. Given its previous experiences in blunting the market rush posed by Giant, Acme pursued a similar program for creating a market strategic position in gizmos.

But a hedge was also important. For this purpose, Acme evaluated Rambo's diversified business in products other than gizmos. This investigation revealed additional opportunities to develop a market strategic technology position targeting a different segment of Rambo's value chain. Investigations revealed that Rambo's manufacturing facilities were relatively old in comparison with others in the field. Though Rambo was able to keep its costs of production under control because it had low manufacturing burden, it was apparent to the planning team that Rambo would be forced to modernize its plant and equipment soon.

The planning team decided to examine opportunities to develop positions in process technology. Though it was considered overly ambitious to predict exactly what technology Rambo might choose to adopt, there were certain paths Acme believed would be explored by anyone in the field. Acme worked assiduously to acquire a position in those avenues of manufacturing technology that would be the easiest or most efficient for implementation, in the expectation that Acme would force Rambo into more complex or costly production techniques or require a license from Acme to implement what were believed to be the most efficient processes. In doing so, Acme believed that it would gain a superior bargaining position in its next negotiations with Rambo and perhaps drive Rambo to negotiate even before the expiration of the current five year agreement.

Case Study 3—The Idea Rich But Undercapitalized Enterprise

Xenith was a moderately sized but highly successful manufacturer of light industrial equipment. It had current sales of about $100 million and could sustain ongoing research and development of its current line of products. The company had a particularly creative staff of engineers who thought ahead to the ways the market was likely to change. Xenith predicted that new product features would be demanded, as would additional functionalities. Xenith projected the probable demand for these future products and created pro forma financial predictions. The company was encouraged that it would be able to more than triple its size in the next five years if it could bring in even half of the development projects necessary to take these ideas to fruition.

Xenith was at once encouraged by the opportunities it saw and discouraged because it could not divert funds from current projects to finance the next round of product development. Xenith was worried that others would eventually see the same opportunities and they would be snatched by a better funded company or one willing to risk its current position by shifting resources from existing production.

Xenith looked for investors to fund its development work but had not been able to attract capital on terms acceptable to the board. Xenith decided that the best way to pursue the development program was with a strategic partner with which it shared a common market interest. However, the company was concerned that it was not in the best negotiating position and faced the prospect that it would have to give up too much of the upside of a successful development program to secure the necessary financial backing from a partner.

The planning team saw an opportunity to do some preliminary development of threshold market strategic technology and to secure a position before approaching a potential strategic alliance partner. In doing so, Xenith improved its position in two important ways. First, it would more likely attract a serious partner on terms of parity because it would be more apparent that Xenith had assets of value to contribute to the coadventure. The value of these market strategic assets would be used in the negotiations to balance the capital and other resource contributions sought from the partner. In this way, Zenith considerably leveraged its technology assets by receiving value from its partner exceeding the cost of creation of the intangible. Second, Xenith retained control over the development process. Having secured its technology position before joining in partnership with another, the technology yet to be developed will arise under the umbrella of Xenith's pre-existing technology rights. Accordingly, Xenith established, retained, and reinforced its controlling technology position.

Case Study 4—A New Venture Strategy

Newco was formed to capitalize on the revolutionary ideas of one of its founders, a retired athlete, for a new athletic product he would promote. There was no doubt that the product would have widespread consumer appeal and could be manufactured at a low prime cost. Pro forma financials were extraordinarily favorable. Newco had a prototype and had proven the validity of its manufacturing procedure. However, Newco had run out of capital and needed funding if it were to survive.

Newco made the rounds of commercial lenders. Even when it pledged the assets of the small group involved in the start-up, no bank was interested in lending the necessary capital. Newco next turned to the equity market and Veeco expressed an interest. Veeco examined the business plan and agreed that there was good potential based on paper but expressed a concern that marketing and distribution limitations might leave the company unable to execute its plan.

Veeco said that it was willing to make the necessary investment but insisted that it acquire 2/3 interest in Newco to justify the risk. Veeco said that it was imperative it have controlling interest because, though impressed with the technical ability of the Newco founders, it was convinced that the company had inadequate experience in business to make Newco a market success.

Newco heard from other new ventures about the possibility that an investor would attempt to negotiate for a controlling interest because of the risk of business success. While Newco members could do nothing about the obvious problem due to their collective lack of business experience, they had put in place a plan to neutralize efforts by investors to secure a controlling equity interest.

Newco saw the importance of expanding its technology position. Though still interested in the athletic market because of the company's ability to capitalize on its founder's popularity, they saw other applications in the medical field in general and particularly in physical therapeutics. Newco prepared itself for the situation it faced in negotiations with Veeco by developing a broader base in market strategic technology, thus establishing a commercial breadth exceeding its immediate business plan.

Newco resumed discussions with Veeco, recognizing that it could benefit from more experienced management but resisting Veeco's insistence that the founders relinquish equity control of the company to acquire that talent. Newco offered several counterpositions based on the strength of its market strategic position. Eventually, the parties settled on multitiered investment coupled with the formation of another entity, Holdco, created to hold the intellectual property Newco had previously developed. Newco was restructured as a manufacturing and marketing company in which Veeco acquired a slight controlling interest. The founding group was granted warrants that could be exercised in several years, allowing it to regain control by shifting the slight balance initially in favor of Veeco. Holdco was entitled to licensing royalties of varying percentages depending on the phase of the business plan in which Newco operated as it moved into the market. Holdco was also in a position to attempt to penetrate other markets in which its products might find a niche with the opportunity to fold these opportunities into Newco. Veeco held a small but not insignificant position in Holdco.

Though this created a complicated tax planning problem for the founders of Newco, they found the ability to keep control of their company reasonably within their grasp outweighed the accounting headaches. If Newco were successful, after a transition phase Veeco would move toward a passive investment position once its management skills in bringing new ventures to market were no longer essential, returning equity control to the founding group. That success would simultaneously translate into greater royalty income for Holdco, in which Veeco also participated. Were Newco to founder and fail to reach marketplace success with its athletic product, Holdco would still be in a position to generate income based on its broader based strategic technology holdings. It would remain to be seen whether that would prove to be a successful financial hedge, but that possibility gave Veeco the comfort it needed to consummate the transaction.

CONCLUSION

Market strategic technology has the capacity to generate highly leveraged value for its proprietor. That value can manifest itself in many ways. We have examined briefly a few situations such as the value to be derived when market strategic technology underlies a source of competitive advantage, particularly an emerging one when disruptive technology is afoot, and the value it can deliver in negotiations with adversaries. Case studies provided other examples.

One can imagine other scenarios in which intellectual property covering market strategic technology will enormously affect the futures of the company. But its acquisition and its ultimate value don't come easy. It takes a well-though innovation strategy, conscientiously devised and spiritedly implemented, along with the right focus over time.[31] But, for those with foresight and fortitude, the returns promise to be the difference between sinking fortunes and thriving prosperity in the new era lying before us all.

---

[31]Like other corporate strategies, the innovation strategic approach suggested here will increasingly come under the scrutiny of boards of directors. Strategic audits are now recommended, in which periodic oversight by the board is exercised in much the same way as financial audits are undertaken. *See*, G. Donaldson, "The New Tool for Boards: The Strategic Audit," *Harvard Business Review*, July–Aug. 1995.

Donaldson does not address the issue of periodic audits of innovation strategies, as the author is interested in the corporate strategies with which business consultants are more familiar. For those companies with proactive innovation strategies, they will predictably fall within this ambit of review because of the linkage between innovation and general business strategies. For those companies without such a strategy, predictably the audit of the business plan or design will highlight that omission with the view of commissioning the work necessary to achieve a world class innovation strategy. In either event, businesses should ready themselves for this new level of corporate oversight.

Part II

Royalty Rates

11

The Importance of Context in the Derivation of Royalty Rates

Suzanne P. Sullivan

The ICM Group

INTRODUCTION

Technological change has continued at a fast pace in the 1990s. The news media constantly herald new technologies that will enable us to do things better, faster, and cheaper. Knowledge-based companies are being pushed harder and harder to keep up with the frenetic pace of their competitors. Companies that formerly prided themselves on their reliance on internal development are now finding a "not-invented-here" mentality difficult to maintain in such a fast-paced and increasingly competitive environment. Escalating development and commercialization costs, combined with crowded technology fields, are forcing companies to scour the marketplace and license technologies from others that will enable them to leapfrog the competition and maintain a dominant market position. This increase in licensing activity has led many companies to view out-licensing as an alternative and lucrative source of revenue generation, rather than merely a means to recover sunk R&D costs.

A license is a permit or authorization granted by one firm to another. In a licensing agreement the owner of the property retains title to the property, assigns certain rights to another for a specified period of time, and receives some sort of compensation. In granting a license, the licensor allows the licensee to do something the licensee could not do but for the permission granted. As a consequence, the licensor is entitled to receive a fair share of the incremental profit the licensee is likely to obtain—that is, the incremental profit the licensee will make over and above what it would have made without the benefit of the license.

> The licensing process is an art practiced in negotiation between two or more parties. The process is frequently difficult since its success requires that the parties agree on the exploitation of often highly valuable intellectual property rights in which both have, claim or want an interest. The range of interests, intellectual property rights, and exploitation arrangements is limitless, making the process of negotiating a mutually desirable agreement, from the myriad possibilities, indeed an art.[1]

Although the negotiation of a license may well be an art form, the result of that negotiation is an agreement that will have an economic impact on both parties.

In the past, technology commercialization, of which licensing is a major component, was usually handled by a few people in the firm—often the CEO or a patent attorney. There were few guidelines or norms, and success depended on the background and experience of the individual directing the commercialization activity. Often licensing agreements were negotiated on an ad hoc basis. As long as licensing held only limited importance to the firm, such a hit-or-miss approach was acceptable. As licensing has become more common, particularly in knowledge-based companies, commercialization activity has spread over the entire company, and managers with no valuation expertise are being required to calculate the value of intellectual property under a variety of different licensing scenarios.

Before embarking on royalty rate calculations, there are three fundamental questions, which, when answered, will enable the decision maker to bring the appropriate level of resources and precision to bear on the calculation: (1) Why is this valuation being undertaken?; (2) What are the resource constraints?; and (3) Who is the intended audience? This chapter is intended to highlight the importance of context in valuations and how it can affect the determination of the appropriate methods of calculating royalty rates in licensing arrangements. This chapter will not attempt to explain in detail the exhaustive list of valuation methodologies, as previous literature has provided more than ample information. Rather it will establish several typical valuation scenarios to help the reader to understand the trade-offs between precision and resource constraints.

The decision whether and how to conduct a valuation can be made at three different times: (1) when a technology is first identified as having commercial potential; (2) when a potential licensee has been identified; and (3) when a competitor has infringed on a company's intellectual property and that com-

[1]Arnold, Tom, "Basic Considerations in Licensing," *les Nouvelles*, September 1980.

pany wishes to seek damages in litigation. We might call the first of those decisions the preliminary, or precommercialization, assessment; the second the prenegotiation evaluation; and the third the litigation determination.

The synthesis developed here relies on licensing research found in the economics and technology literature, on observations of industry practices, and on interviews with licensing executives. It is meant to help managers choose among the available royalty rate valuation methods based on the context of the decision.

UNDERSTANDING CONTEXT

The valuation of intangible assets is an inexact science that often relies heavily on assumptions about future events. Conducting an accurate valuation requires using an appropriate methodology in conjunction with reasonable assumptions, because different valuation techniques will give different magnitudes of value. Choosing the appropriate valuation methodology is important in order to calculate value as accurately as possible. The first step in valuing an intellectual property is to determine the objective of the valuation. If the objective is a sale, the assumptions might be very different from the assumptions related to a licensing agreement. In turn, these differences could lead to dramatically different values.

For licensing, the three circumstances in which royalty rate determinations are often made are precommercialization, prenegotiation, and litigation. Understanding the context of each of these situations, and the associated constraints, will lead to a more accurate determination of the appropriate royalty rate valuation method.

Precommercialization

The commercialization process in many knowledge-based companies consists of a series of technology checkpoints or hurdles that must be passed in order for technology development, and ultimately commercialization, to take place. The first step is to determine whether a technology is developmentally feasible and commercially viable. Technologies by themselves have little commercial value. It is the application of the technology in a product or service that is commercially attractive. Once possible applications have been identified, the next step is to estimate the size of the market and the potential revenues. In this assessment stage, information is usually inadequate and scarce, resources are limited, and the overall riskiness of a new venture is high. Not surprisingly, complete accuracy is not a requirement for success, but a good initial estimate of value is. The goal is to determine ballpark estimates of market size, development costs, and resulting revenue streams. At this early stage, it is generally not known what the best commercialization path for this technology is; therefore it is important to remember that licensing is only one commercialization alternative available.

Technology managers cite limited resources, particularly time, as the biggest constraint in conducting valuation assessments at this stage. Often a company is approached by a potential licensee looking to license the intellectual property of the patent holder. In response, the patent holding company executives ask the technology manager to determine the value of a potential licensing revenue stream. Such a request is usually couched in the form of preliminary estimates, with a short turnaround time. In addition, the person asked to value the technology may or may not have previous valuation experience. Research and development and marketing managers often are asked to calculate potential royalty rates and revenues. These individuals are not always the same ones who will later negotiate a licensing agreement. Because time is short, the need for precision is low, and previous valuation experience also may be low, at this stage it is desirable to use several different valuation methods that are quick and easy to estimate the potential income streams.

Prenegotiation

Once the precommercialization alternatives have been evaluated and licensing chosen as the desirable commercialization path, then the search for licensees begins. Once a potential licensee has been located, a firm enters the prenegotiation stage. From the preliminary assessment, the firm has a preliminary estimate of licensing revenue and needs to buttress those numbers with additional information before beginning negotiations with the potential licensee. Although each licensing agreement is unique, some standard factors should be taken into account by both parties when determining a royalty rate:

- *License terms.* Is the licensing agreement to be exclusive or nonexclusive? In an exclusive arrangement, the licensor assumes more risk while granting the licensee more opportunity, largely by limiting potential competition; therefore the royalty rate for an exclusive agreement is usually higher.
- *Competitive advantage.* The usefulness or amount of competitive advantage the technology offers to the licensee is of utmost importance. Technologies that offer a significant head start on the competition are more valuable than those that offer only opportunities for playing catch-up. Technological capabilities that will enrich the licensee firm and allow it to enhance its strategic position are the most valuable.
- *Cost savings.* If a licensee would otherwise have to create its own market position by developing around the licensor's patent, or by developing its own technology at a significant cost, then licensing-in

the technology saves the licensee money and therefore would justify its paying a higher royalty to the licensor.

- *Legal protection.* The nature and amount of protection that a licensor offers to the licensee as part of the license agreement is a major consideration. The royalty rate will be higher for a patent that is proven to be enforceable and whose infringement is easy to detect. The licensee must be assured not only that adequate legal protection is in force, but also that the licensor is prepared to enforce and is capable of enforcing this protection against infringers.
- *Technology maturity.* Is the technology fully developed and able to be used immediately in the design or manufacture of products, or does it require further refinement or development before it can be commercially applied? Fully developed technologies command a premium over technologies that require additional development.
- *Commercial success.* Technologies proven to have marketplace appeal and to significantly increase sales are more valuable than technologies still untested in the marketplace or those whose commercial success is not an issue.

Whenever possible it is useful for both parties in a licensing negotiation to quantify all of these factors and include them in the royalty rate calculation. The person responsible for the negotiations tends to be heavily involved in the royalty rate calculations and generally has previous licensing experience. This expertise, which is difficult to obtain, is helpful in evaluating market comparables, industry norms, and potential competition. Because the company is about to enter into a financial obligation, the need for precision is higher, and the company is willing to spend more time to get a more precise estimate of value, there usually are only moderate resource constraints.

Litigation

There may come a time when one firm markets a product or service utilizing another firm's intellectual property without its consent. Intellectual property disputes are increasing as courts recognize the rights of the inventing firm and award significant damages. Before 1982, legal suits involving disputes over the rights of intellectual property were heard in the federal district where the dispute occurred. Intellectual property cases are often technical and complex, and for many years courts interpreted such cases as a way to eliminate competition. Not surprisingly, many courts ruled against the intellectual property owners. On October 1, 1982, a federal court of appeals was established for the sole purpose of determining intellectual property cases. Since the creation of this IP court, judicial interpretation no longer equates intellectual property with anticompetitive behavior. Most judicial decisions have upheld the rights of the intellectual property holder.

These changes constitute a reversal with enormous implications. The number of significant domestic and international intellectual property cases decided since 1982, along with the dollar amounts of the settlement, make it clear that intellectual capital has become an asset with significant value to the firm.

One of the most important aspects of an intellectual property dispute is the determination of damages; that is, how much was the firm damaged by the unauthorized use of its intellectual property? Calculating economic damages requires a high level of accuracy. The view of any expert as to the size of the damage caused by an infringement naturally will be refuted by the opposing side, so precision is vital. Companies that engage in intellectual property disputes are represented by highly experienced patent attorneys, economists, or licensing experts (or all three), with the goal of providing a very precise damage calculation. Because the cost of losing is so high, a firm's expenditures of time and money may be almost unlimited in this situation.

CALCULATING ROYALTY RATES

There is no one right way to calculate a royalty rate. However, it is important to define the parameters around the circumstances of the valuation, which in turn will help define the level of precision required for the calculation. Alternative valuation methods will provide different determinations of value, based on differing levels of precision. Fundamentally, there is a trade-off between precision and resource costs (people, time, and dollars). Some of the more commonly used royalty rate development methods are briefly described below. Exhibit 11.1 provides a summary of royalty rate valuation methods, their strengths and weaknesses, and when each method is appropriate.

The 25 Percent Rule

This rule says that a licensor should receive a royalty of at least 25 percent of a licensee's pretax gross profit. This is analogous to a royalty rate of about 5 percent of the licensee's selling price. Although this calculation is easy and inexpensive, it leaves some fairly important questions unanswered. What does "gross profit" really mean? Should selling, administrative, and overhead expenses be included in the analysis? Intellectual property that is used to create a product that requires little marketing effort is far more valuable than intellectual property used to create a product that requires a highly specialized sales force. Two patented products might cost the same amount to produce, and yield the same gross profit, but one might require much more after-sales support than the other. The additional sales support required for a product makes that product less profitable to the licensee, and therefore it is unlikely that the two products would command the same royalty. The 25 percent rule does not take such factors into account and thus a firm may unintentionally omit them from consideration.

Exhibit 11.1 Alternate Royalty Rate Valuation Methods

Method	Strengths	Weaknesses	Context
25 Percent Rule	- Easy - Inexpensive - Ballpark estimate	Does not consider: - true profitability - risk/return of investment - low level of precision	- Precommercialization - Provides initial ballpark estimate of value
Market Approach	- If data are available, provides credible way to determine industry range or average royalty rate	- Assumes current industry norms are correct - High cost of obtaining accurate data - Requires active market of similar transactions	- If data is easily obtainable then this is ideal for precommercialization - If data not readily available but possible to find, then prenegotiation
Return on Sales	- Quick - Easy - Inexpensive	- Low level of precision - Difficult to determine proper allocation of profits between two parties Does not consider: - value of complementary assets - risk/return of investment	- Precommercialization - Provides initial ballpark estimate of value
Return on R&D Costs	- Easy - Inexpensive - R&D costs easy to determine	- R&D costs rarely equal IP value Does not consider: - low level of precision - value of complementary assets - risk/return of investment	- Use only as last resort during precommercialization stage
Income Approach	- Highly credible methodology Does consider: - value of complementary assets - risk/return of investment - market size - competitive assessment - requires cross functional input	- Accuracy of valuation highly dependent on precision of assumptions - Getting consensus on appropriate assumptions may take some time - Time consuming to get accurate data - Need detailed knowledge of marketplace and environment	- Because is more resource-intensive, good for prenegotiation and ideal for litigation
Lost Profits	- Highly credible methodology - Very precise valuation Does consider: - value of complementary assets - risk/return of investment - market size - competitive assessment	- Requires very precise assumptions - Time consuming and costly to get accurate data - Need detailed knowledge of marketplace and environment - Requires independent expert - Takes a long time - Often must rely on infringer's costs of production	- Litigation

183

Market or Industry Norm Approach

The market approach consists of obtaining a marketplace consensus of the value of similar transactions—for example, an industry royalty rate or the royalty rate of a similar intellectual property. Market size, growth potential, net profits, investment risks, and complementary asset requirements are all absent from consideration. For industries that negotiate license agreements frequently, industry rates might be easy to find. In such cases, this methodology provides a quick and easy way to estimate average royalty rates. For most industries, however, these rates are difficult to find. It may require interviewing a variety of technology managers or patent attorneys to just get a range of royalty rates, for example from 2 to 8 percent of net profit. Such estimates will require further refining to determine the appropriate royalty rate for a particular situation. One of the main drawbacks of this methodology is that the licensor assumes that the negotiators of these earlier royalty rates had correctly considered and interpreted the many different factors affecting royalties.

Return on Sales

The return-on-sales method calculates a royalty rate based on net profits as a percentage of revenues. Again, this method is quick, easy, and inexpensive, but it also has several inherent weaknesses. Perhaps the biggest weakness is the lack of precision in dividing net profit between the licensee and licensor. This method also fails to take into consideration the value of any complementary assets or intellectual property that is invested in the enterprise. Finally, this method does not consider investment risk at all.

Return on R&D Costs

Another possible method of calculating appropriate royalties is to determine how much money was spent on the development of the intellectual property and add to that a fair return on cost. Again, this methodology is easy and inexpensive, but it is perhaps the most misleading of the methods. The amount spent on development is rarely equal to the value of the property. If the goal of a licensing agreement is to provide a fair rate of return on the value of the intellectual property, then a proper royalty should provide a fair return on the value of the asset regardless of the costs incurred in development.

Income Approach

The income approach focuses on the income-producing capability of the property. The underlying theory is that the value of the intellectual property can be measured by the present value of the income stream to be received over the life of the property. The level of sophistication of the assumptions about the future income stream, and the capitalization or discount rate used, can provide estimates with different degrees of precision. One of the advantages of the income approach is that it does take into consideration the value of complementary assets, market information, and the risk of the endeavor. Obtaining this information, however, usually requires cross-functional input into the decision making process, and reaching consensus on the assumptions may take some time.

Lost Profits or Reasonable Royalty

Calculations of damage to intellectual property through forgone profits and royalties usually include lost profits resulting from infringement, and/or a reasonable royalty for the use of the patented invention.

To claim lost profits, a patent holder must prove that infringement has caused it to lose sales. Useful guidance is provided by a well-known U.S. patent case, *Panduit v. Stahlin Bros.* (1978).[2] This case spawned the so-called Panduit tests, which require a patent holder to demonstrate all of the following in order to claim lost profits:

1. that demand existed for the patented product;
2. that there was no noninfringing substitutes;
3. that the patent holder has the manufacturing and marketing capacity to exploit the demand; and
4. that the amount of lost profits can be quantified.

The Panduit tests take a commonsense view of patent infringement—that there was a demand for the patented items and that the patent holder could and would have satisfied this demand but for the infringement. If a patent holder cannot demonstrate the circumstances listed above (for example, there are noninfringing substitutes in the marketplace), but infringement has been clearly established, the patent holder is entitled to a reasonable royalty on the infringer's sales. The choice of reasonable royalty compensation reflects, at least in part, the difficulty of demonstrating lost profits. A reasonable royalty is established using any or a combination of the previously mentioned methodologies.

The main goal of a damages expert is to determine what information was knowable at the time of the infringement. The high cost of calculating economic damages in litigation cases is largely due to the high level of precision required in the calculation.

SUMMARY

This chapter highlighted the importance of context in valuations and how it can affect the determination of the appropriate methods of calculating royalty rates. The valuation of intangible assets is an inexact science that relies heav-

---

[2]*Panduit Corp. v. Stahlin Bros. Fibre Works Inc.,* 575 F.2d 1152 (1978).

ily on assumptions of future events. An accurate valuation requires a combination of appropriate methodology and reasonable assumptions, both of which are determined by the circumstances around which the valuation will occur. The creation of three typical valuation scenarios, precommercialization, prenegotiation, and litigation, has attempted to highlight the trade-offs between precision and resource constraints (people, time, and dollars) that often face technology managers. In the precommercialization assessment stage, information is scarce, resources are limited, and commercialization is a highly risky endeavor. At this early stage, a valuation is performed merely to determine ballpark estimates of market size, revenue streams, and development costs. Once a potential licensee has been located, the firm enters the prenegotiation stage. Here, a firm is looking to expand upon its preliminary estimates of revenue from the precommercialization stage, and fortify these numbers prior to entering into a licensing agreement. Finally, in the litigation stage, a firm is attempting to claim or rebut damages relating to intellectual property infringement. Because the cost of losing is so high, in this scenario the need for precision and accuracy demand a high resource commitment.

As licensing becomes more prevalent in the business world, performing intellectual property valuations will become common place among technology managers. Deriving a royalty rate is not difficult once the following three questions have been answered: (a) Why is this valuation being undertaken? (2) What are the resource constraints? and (3) Who is the intended audience?

The fundamental message of this chapter is that there is no right royalty rate calculation methodology. Instead there are a variety of methodology choices, and all of them can be appropriate based on the many varied circumstances under which intellectual property valuations occur.

BIBLIOGRAPHY

Boulton, Richard, and Mark Bezant. (1995). "The Calculation of Damages for Patent Infringement." *Managing Intellectual Property*, p. 32–38. Sussex: Euromoney Publications.

Kempner, Richard, and Ian Sampson. (1994). "Many a Slip." *Managing Intellectual Property*, p. 15–26.

Khoury, I. A. (1994). "Valuing Intellectual Properties." Midland, Michigan: The Dow Chemical Company.

Schwab, Jeffrey A. (1995). "Licensing Overview and Guidelines For Royalty Rates." *Managing Intellectual Property*, p. 20–21.

Smith, Gordon, and Russell Parr. (1994). *Valuation of Intellectual Property and Intangible Assets*. New York: John Wiley & Sons.

Sullivan, Patrick H. (1993). "A Preliminary Survey of Royalty Rate Setting Practices in the US Computer Hardware Industry." Haas School of Business, UC Berkeley.

Sullivan, Suzanne P. (1993). "Insights Into Commercializing Technology." *les Nouvelles*, 28.1, p. 30–35, March 1993.

12

Techniques for Obtaining and Analyzing External License Agreements

Michael J. Merwin and Colleen M. Warner

Ernst & Young LLP

When licensing executives or business development managers in any industry negotiate a deal, the goal is the same—obtaining the most favorable terms. Having access to information regarding earlier license agreements involving the other contracting party, the same product, or similar intellectual property provides a better negotiating position. For a company just entering the licensing area, this background information can help it progress more quickly along the learning curve, thus avoiding first-time mistakes. A better understanding of previous contracts will assist a company in learning how deals are structured, as the case study later in this chapter will illustrate. For the experienced negotiator, this information provides an extra edge in completing an important deal. The key to being successful in negotiating a license agreement is doing the background work and being prepared.

Having said this, the question then becomes how to get this information. In the past, three means to this end have included:

1. *Internal Agreements.* Typically, companies rely on past transactions when structuring a new agreement. Past agreements are modified to meet new circumstances. This methodology has proven successful, but it does not eliminate the need for additional research. Of course, for the first time licensor or licensee internal agreements cannot be applied.
2. *Financial Analysis.* Performing a financial analysis has become a more widely used tool for determining the payment terms of an

agreement. Although there are many important clauses in a license agreement, the payment terms often become the focal point. A financial analysis can highlight what a licensee might be willing to pay or what a licensor would require in order to recover the investment.

3. *External Agreements.* Existing agreements, including those involving the other contracting party, can be very useful in assessing the licensing trends in an industry. Historically, this information has been difficult for companies to obtain.

The methodology companies can employ to acquire external agreements is described in greater detail in the next section. The remainder of this chapter then discusses how the information available in these agreements can be utilized to develop a framework for negotiating a new agreement.

RESEARCHING AGREEMENTS

Obtaining copies of competitors' license agreements is often viewed as a desirable yet legally unobtainable goal. However, the truth is that thousands of license agreements are made publicly available through individual company filings with the Securities and Exchange Commission (SEC). A company is required to publicly disclose a license agreement that is a material part of its business. SEC regulations stipulate that "any franchise or license or other agreement to use a patent, formula, trade secret, process or trade name upon which [the] registrant's business depends to a material extent" must be incorporated in the firm's public filings.[1]

Although the actual license agreements are only made publicly available through one source, the SEC, the information can be accessed through a variety of channels. Evaluating which sources to use in conducting a search for license agreements goes beyond a simple price comparison. Exhibit 12.1 summarizes the primary sources available, including some of the advantages and disadvantages of its utilization.

As illustrated in Exhibit 12.1, a search for publicly available license agreements can be a difficult but manageable process. The first source listed, Disclosure Information Services (Disclosure), requires the least amount of work on the part of the company doing the research. In fact, the process can be as simple as dialing a 1-800 phone number and requesting research on a particular company. For an hourly fee, Disclosure will then search the microfiche copy of that company's filings for the information requested; a separate fee is then charged for any documents ordered. This can be a very

---

[1] *1991 SEC GUIDELINES; Rules and Regulations*, Warren, Gorham & Lamont, Boston, MA (1995), Section 229.601(b)(10)(ii)(B), p. Reg S-K.69.

Exhibit 12.1 Licensing Agreement Sources: Advantages and Disadvantages

Source	Advantages	Disadvantages
Disclosure Information Services	• Requires fewer company resources • Available everywhere	• Can be expensive • Requires an understanding of what is available
On-line & CD-Rom Data Bases • Dialog • Nexis • Lotus One Source	• Requires fewer company resources • Available everywhere	• References only the most current 10-K • "Full Text" does not include exhibits
Securities and Exchange Commission Reference Room	• Most thorough and comprehensive source • Full text copies of actual agreements	• Only available in a limited number of areas • More time intensive

useful service when a company is attempting to obtain a specific license agreement or if the company being researched is not very active in licensing. However, if the company being researched has a large number of publicly available license agreements spanning several years, an undefined Disclosure search can be expensive and inefficient.

In order to have a more directed research process, many companies turn to one of the many on-line and CD-Rom data bases now widely available. These data bases allow a company to research a specific company or an entire industry to determine licensing activity. However, it is important to note that all data bases are not the same. It is very important that a company have a thorough understanding of the system they choose, because many only provide access to the most recent 10-K. As a result, a search in one of these systems would miss many important agreements that may be in effect currently but were signed a year or two earlier. In addition, though many of these data bases claim to offer full-text documents, this usually means full text of the annual report or 10-K. The exhibits, including license agreements, are usually not included, which means that copies of the actual agreements are not available from these sources.

The most thorough and comprehensive research involves an examination of the public filings at the SEC. This research process should include a search of a company's 10-K as well as its other filings, such as the registration statement. Unfortunately, this is also a very time-intensive process that can be performed only in selected cities.[2]

Based on these advantages and disadvantages, these three sources should not be viewed as alternatives, but rather as instruments to be used collectively in an attempt to both *identify* and *obtain* copies of publicly available

---

[2]SEC reference rooms are located in Chicago, New York, and Washington, D.C.

license agreements. Ernst & Young LLP (E&Y) uses all three resources in conducting licensing research by first beginning with the on-line and CD-Rom data bases and then conducting the actual company-specific research at the SEC, supplementing this research with Disclosure if a specific file is not currently available at the SEC reference room.

The on-line and CD-Rom data bases are used to further research a specific company or industry to determine the extent of licensing activity. This first screening is very helpful in narrowing the list of companies to be researched at the SEC reference room. For instance, in an attempt to search for any publicly available license agreements in an industry, the first step might be to select those companies that are categorized according to the relevant Standard Industrial Classification (SIC) code. However, this simple step may result in the identification of hundreds of companies. Because conducting the research at the SEC reference room can be very time consuming, it is more efficient to first perform an on-line or CD-Rom data base search to narrow the list of companies to those active in licensing.

Exhibit 12.2 illustrates the E&Y licensing research process. This process has resulted in the acquisition of over 4,000 license agreements from ap-

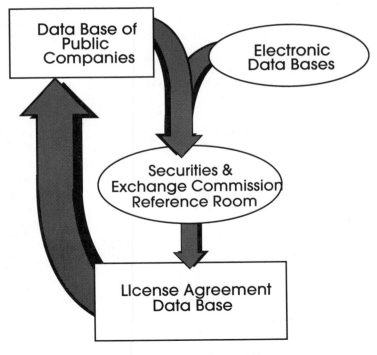

Exhibit 12.2   Licensing Research Process

proximately 2,500 companies in over 50 different industries. The types of agreements, as well as information regarding the payment terms, are provided in Exhibits 12.3 through 12.6.

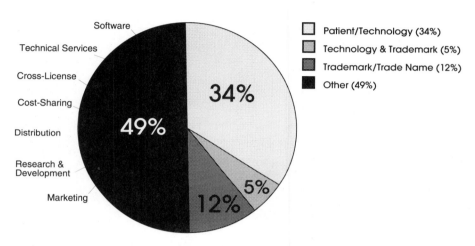

Exhibit 12.3 Type of Agreement

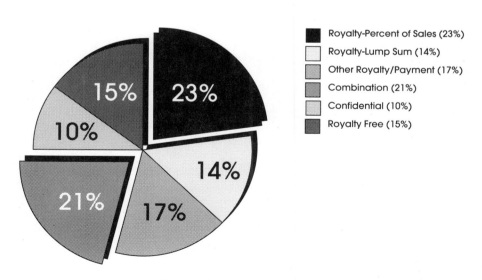

Exhibit 12.4 Forms of Compensation

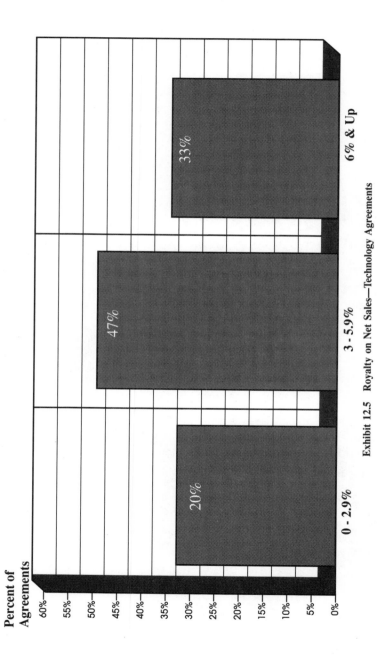

Percent of Agreements

60%
55%
50%
45%
40%
35%
30%
25%
20%
15%
10%
5%
0%

20%

47%

33%

0 - 2.9%

3 - 5.9%

6% & Up

Exhibit 12.5   Royalty on Net Sales—Technology Agreements

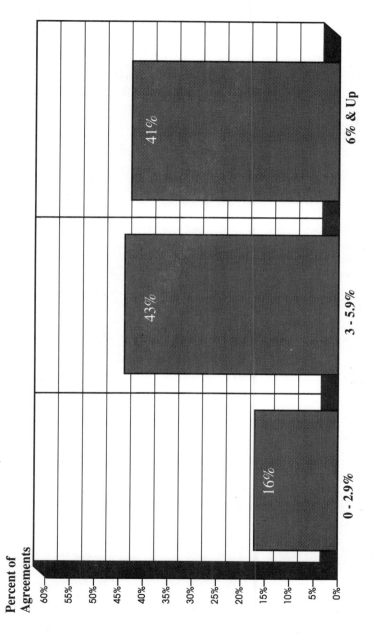

Exhibit 12.6 Royalty on Net Sales—Trademark Agreements

ANALYZING AGREEMENTS

Of course, the research to identify other license agreements is just the first step of the process; an equally complex task is developing a framework for comparing these agreements. If successfully completed, the research will result in the acquisition of pages and pages of legal documents. The next step of the process involves a thorough analysis of each of the license agreements in order to assess the comparability of the agreements. To facilitate this analysis, a framework must be developed, identifying key factors that must be examined in order to ensure that an accurate comparison is being made.

In order to assess the level of comparability, license agreements should be evaluated according to internal as well as external standards. Internal standards typically refer to the contractual clauses, while external standards refer to the economic conditions governing the transactions.

The remainder of this chapter will introduce a framework that can be utilized in evaluating the comparability of technology license agreements, focusing on the internal standards. In addition to a general discussion of these standards, examples are provided from two agreements involving a major Japanese consumer electronics manufacturer. Finally, a case study will be presented, illustrating how this framework can be used in evaluating trademark licenses.

Framework for Analyzing License Agreements

This section provides a summary of some of the more significant factors affecting the comparison of license agreements, including technology, term, territory, exclusivity, sublicense, termination clauses, trademarks or trade names, technical assistance, payment terms, and relationships. Exhibit 12.7 summarizes each of these factors for the two examples involving the Japanese consumer electronics manufacturer.

Technology. Although the technologies licensed need not be identical, they must have similar applications—one agreement cannot be for the manufacture of components while the other agreement licenses the technology for an entire system. Both the extent of research and development that was necessary to develop the technology and the ease in which a competitor can duplicate the technology are relevant. For example, if the technology or process is patented, how hard is it to design around the patent? The age of the technology is another factor influencing its value. Technological change is so swift in some industries that a difference of one or two years may have a dramatic impact on the technology's worth. Therefore, the technology being licensed should be viewed from the perspective of an internal as well as an external standard.

The agreements summarized in Exhibit 12.7 highlight the importance of evaluating the comparability of the technology being licensed. Even though

Exhibit 12.7 Comparability of Two Agreements

Standards	Agreement #1	Agreement #2
Technology	Right to use worldwide patented technology to make, use, and sell FM stereo receivers and tuners and FM radios.	Right to use worldwide patented technology to make and sell compact disc players and certain other products.
Term	Effective January 1, 1988 Expires January 1, 1993	Effective January 1, 1988 Expires after 5 years—renews automatically for 5-year terms
Territory	Licensor is a U.S. corporation and Licensee is a Japanese company—no specific market area is given	Licensor is a French company and Licensee is a Japanese company—worldwide market
Exclusivity	Nonexclusive	Nonexclusive
Sublicense	Nontransferable and nonassignable	Nontransferable, licensor can assign; licensee cannot assign or sublicense without consent
Termination Clauses	Licensor can terminate for default, bankruptcy, reorganization, takeover of licensee, or force majure	Licensee can terminate at the end of each 5-year term; either party can terminate for default, bankruptcy or force majure
Trademarks of Trade Names	No	No
Technical Assistance	None	None
Payment Terms		
• Lump Sum	None	Equivalent of 1.1 billion yen in French Francs
• Royalty	0.2% of net sales in U.S. $— credits given for apparatus sold in certain combination	1.3% of Net Selling Price in Francs or other currency acceptable to Licensor
• Minimum	None	None
Relationships	No other relevant agreements	Licensor waives all claims it may have against Licensee for prior use of the products

both agreements have the same licensee and are for the same industry, the technologies being licensed vary considerably. Agreement #1 is for older technology and is more component oriented, while Agreement #2 is for newer technology to manufacture entire compact disc players.

Term.   As mentioned above, the age of the technology at the time of licensing can influence the value. Furthermore, the length of the agreement can have an impact on the other clauses. The negotiation process may be different for a ten-year agreement than for a two-year agreement.

The length of the agreement is only a minor issue in determining the comparability of Agreement #1 and Agreement #2. Both agreements are for five years; however, the licensee in Agreement #2 has the option to renew the agreement for successive five-year terms.

Territory. Technically, an evaluation of the markets involved qualifies as an external standard. However, attention should be paid to the territory being licensed when evaluating the internal standards. For instance, a license agreement with a potential competitor might have different terms that an agreement licensing the use of the technology in a confined geographic market. The agreements in Exhibit 12.7 are with licensors in different countries, but are both geographically unrestricted.

Exclusivity. A license can be granted on an exclusive basis in a variety of ways. Exclusivity can refer to a licensee's right to use the technology in a geographic area (sales in a specific country or region), a market area (sales to Original Equipment Manufacturers), an industry area (sales to the automobile industry), or a combination. In most cases, an agreement that provides a licensee with the exclusive use of a technology is more valuable than a nonexclusive license. Neither agreement in Exhibit 12.7 provides the licensee with the exclusive rights to the technology.

Sublicense. License agreements that permit the licensee to generate income not only from the manufacture and sale of the licensed technology, but through the sublicense of the technology as well, can differ substantially from agreements that prohibit sublicensing. Agreement #1 and Agreement #2 both restrict the licensee's right to sublicense.

Termination Clauses. The majority of agreements contain clauses that allow either party to withdraw from an agreement if there is a breach in performance. Far less common are clauses that allow one or both parties to terminate an agreement unilaterally without cause. For only one party to have this right would place the other at a significant disadvantage and presumably would reflect a strong bargaining position by one of the parties. All other things being equal, a licensee would typically not pay as high a royalty if the licensor had this right.

The agreements in Exhibit 12.7 are essentially comparable in their provisions for the termination clauses. Although Agreement #1 allows only the licensor to terminate for breach, bankruptcy, and so on, the substance is the same, because the licensor has no other obligations other than allowing use of the patented technology, thus eliminating the possibility of the licensor defaulting. The licensee's option to terminate after each five year term in Agreement #2 is really a decision not to renew as opposed to an unconditional termination.

Trademarks or Trade Names. Agreements that license both technology and the corresponding trademarks or trade names may command higher royalty rates. This of course assumes that the trademarks or trade names have value in the licensee's market; if the trademarks or trade names have no value; the royalty may not be affected. Because Agreement #1 and Agreement #2 both license technology for consumer products, an area where brand recognition is very important, the inclusion of a trademark or trade name would most likely have skewed the royalty rate.

Technical Assistance. Frequently, license agreements have provisions whereby the licensee receives technical assistance from the licensor. When comparing two agreements, it is necessary to examine the type of assistance, frequency of assistance, and supplemental charges, if any, related to the assistance provided. Neither agreement in Exhibit 12.7 has a technical assistance provision.

Payment Terms. Licensing fees can be computed in a variety of ways; therefore, the payment structure must be considered carefully. The most common forms of payment include a flat royalty rate, a sliding royalty rate based on sales volume, lump sum payments, or a combination of the three. Besides the structure, the basis on which the royalty is computed may also differ. Royalties can be paid on a dollar per unit basis, as a percentage of sales or even as a percentage of profits (this is not very common).

As previously mentioned, a combination of the different payment structures is often used in establishing licensing fees. A lump sum might be used as an initial payment or a royalty prepayment. Other factors also affect total compensation, such as minimum payments and, in the case of international licensing, the existence of foreign exchange risk.

The fact that the structure or basis in two agreements is different should not lead to the conclusion that the agreements are not comparable. However, the analysis may be more difficult and require more data to determine if the agreements produce similar income when placed on a common basis. For example, when comparing a royalty based on sales to a royalty that pays on an amount per unit basis, additional data must be gathered so that the income generated can be calculated on the same basis.

Agreement #1 and Agreement #2 both use a straight royalty as a percent of sales. However, Agreement #2 combines this with an initial lump sum payment, thus complicating the comparison of the royalty rates.

Relationships. Although it is not a contractual clause, it is imperative that the relationship between the licensor and licensee be considered when evaluating agreements to obtain an arm's length comparable. It is not uncommon for a company to enter into a license agreement that offers less than favorable terms, in order to achieve a greater goal, such as becoming an exclusive supplier for the other party.

Agreement #2 illustrates this point. It cannot be assumed that the agreement truly represents an arm's length transaction because part of the agreement includes the licensor waiving all claims it may have against the licensee for prior use of the products.

The summaries in Exhibit 12.7 provide a quick opportunity to evaluate the comparability of the two agreements. However, as discussed above, the differences in the technology and payment terms, as well as the relationship between the licensor and licensee in Agreement #2, diminish the comparability. It is important to remember that because each situation is based on the particular facts and circumstances involved, an in-depth analysis should be performed on a case-by-case basis.

CASE STUDY

This case study involves a company in Mexico that manufactures casual sportswear for women and children. During a recent trip to the United States, the president of the company noticed the popularity of clothing bearing the trademarks of athletic footwear companies. He realized that this could be an exciting new growth area for his business. The sales of U.S. athletic footwear such as Nike, LA Gear and Reebok, have just begun to increase in Mexico due to the lowering of duties under North American Free Trade Agreement (NAFTA). The president hoped to capitalize on this growing popularity as well as the additional exposure that will be generated by the 1996 Olympics. He assigned his business development manager to determine the costs and conditions of negotiating a trademark license agreement with a U.S. athletic footwear company.

The manager began by retaining a marketing company that was experienced in licensing. The marketing consultant provided information on all aspects of the business, including marketing plans, basics of licensing arrangements, legal considerations, and a financial model to help determine the feasibility of the project.

The model required that estimates be made of the projected sales volume and the manufacturing and licensing costs. The manager was able to supply estimates of sales and his costs but could only guess what the licensing costs might be. The marketing consultant suggested conducting a comprehensive search of public sources to identify the terms of similar license agreements. Through an analysis of these agreements, they hoped to determine the royalty payments and other associated costs of the license.

Expanding on the list of potential licensors developed by the marketing firm, an on-line data base search was conducted to identify companies to be further researched. The data base search indicated that six potentially comparable agreements were publicly available. Close examination of the companies' filings at the SEC revealed an extensive amount of licensing activity—one company had filed over a dozen license agreements. A further analysis was performed utilizing the full-text copies of the identified agreements.

Exhibit 12.8 summarizes the 14 agreements analyzed; specifically, it lists the products included under the scope of the license and the corresponding royalty as a percent of net sales. Because the agreements resulted in such a broad range, 3.5 to 10 percent, a more detailed analysis of the agreements must be completed to determine the reason(s) for the differential.

The manager notices that the products can be separated broadly into textile and nontextile products. Therefore, the agreements are sorted into two groups based on the type of product that bears the logo. The first category consists of agreements pertaining to sportswear and other clothing and the second encompasses accessories and nonclothing items such as sunglasses, skateboards, and exercise equipment. As illustrated in Exhibit 12.9, this segmentation helps to identify some differences in the rates charged for the trademarks.

Although the sportswear royalty rates still vary from 3.5 to 10 percent, the nontextile products have a much narrower range of 7 to 10 percent, with 5 of the 6 agreements at 10 percent. This provides a useful analysis for the company in determining what might be a *typical* royalty rate in the industry for accessory products. Because of the wide range for the sportswear royalty rates, a more detailed analysis of the contractual terms will be necessary to determine the reason for the disparity. In order to determine which characteristics are having the greatest impact on the royalty rate, the manager prepares a chart of what he believes to be the most significant factors. These clauses include lump sum payments, guaranteed minimum payments, date of the agreement, term or length of the agreement, and geographic markets.

In order to identify the differences between low-rate and high-rate agreements, the manager prepared a table summarizing the five key factors iden-

Exhibit 12.8 Fourteen Agreements and their Royalties as Percentage of Sales

#	Product	Royalty Rate
1	Socks, leg and ankle warmers, head and wrist bands	10% 7% on multipack socks
2	Sunglasses and optical frames	7%
3	Sandals and beach thongs	10%
4	Men's shirts, shorts, and sweatclothing	10%
5	Skateboards	10%
6	Plastic headwear, excluding children's toy market	10%
7	Adult exercise equipment	10%
8	Footwear, apparel, and fashion accessories	3.5%
9	Women's and children's shoes, socks, hosiery, purses, and bags	6%
10	Fashion dolls, doll clothing, and accessories	10%
11	Girl's woven and knit sportswear and activewear	5%
12	Junior sportswear, including fashion activewear	6%
13	Socks and women's legwarmers	10%
14	T-shirts, sweat shirts and pants, and active type shorts	10%

Exhibit 12.9   Royalty Rate Comparison of Textile and Nontextile Agreements

#	Product	Royalty Rate
Nontextile Agreements		
2	Sunglasses and optical frames	7%
3	Sandals and beach thongs	10%
5	Skateboards	10%
6	Plastic headwear, excluding children's toy market	10%
7	Adult exercise equipment	10%
10	Fashion dolls, doll clothing, and accessories	10%
Textile Agreements		
1	Socks, leg and ankle warmers, head and wristbands	10% 7% on multipack socks
4	Men's shirts, shorts, and sweatclothing	10%
8	Footwear, apparel, and fashion accessories	3.5%
9	Women's and children's shoes, socks, hosiery, purses, and bags	6%
11	Girl's woven and knit sportswear and activewear	5%
12	Junior sportswear, including fashion activewear	6%
13	Socks and women's legwarmers	10%
14	T-shirts, sweat shirts and pants, and active type shorts	10%

tified above and sorting the agreements in ascending order according to the royalty on net sales. The manager's first guess was that lump sum payments might be causing the difference in royalties. However, an examination of the data in Exhibit 12.10 does not confirm his expectations. The lump sum payments vary slightly but not enough to explain a nearly 200 percent difference in royalty rates.

However, the exhibit does indicate that all of the low royalty rate agreements are licenses to use the trademarks outside of the United States. It appears that in most cases the trade names have significantly less value in markets outside the United States. In the Far East the rate is at 3.5 percent, while in Canada three of the four agreements have royalty rates of 5 to 6 percent with the remaining one at 10 percent. All of the license agreements for the U.S. market have a 10 percent royalty rate.

Although the manager felt confident that the data showed that differences in geographic market had a significant impact on the ultimate royalty rate, he has not yet satisfied that the full differential had been explained because of the one agreement for the Canadian market that had a 10 percent royalty rate. Examining the five agreements for the foreign markets more carefully, he decided that the agreement from the Far East should be disregarded because it is in a vastly different geographic market. He felt it was a logical conclusion that the trademarks have more value in Canada because of its proximity to the U.S. market. However, this does not explain why three of the agreements are in the 5 to 6 percent range while one is at 10 percent.

Exhibit 12.10 Five Key Factors of Various Agreements

#	Royalty Rate	Lump Sum	Guaranteed Minimum	Date	Term Length	Term Renewal	Market
8	3.5%		$0 1st year $17,500 2nd year $26,250 3rd year $35,000 4th year $43,750 5th year	9/1/83	10/1/88 5 Years	Automatic 5 Years	Indonesia, Hong Kong, Singapore, Malaysia, Philippines
11	5%	$5,000	$12,500 Initial term $25,000 1st renewal $37,500 2nd renewal	1/1/86	12/31/86 1 Year	Automatic 1 Year	Canada
9	6%		Can$ 60,000 1st year Can$ 90,000 2nd year Can$ 120,000 3rd year Can$ 150,000 4th year Can$ 180,000 5th year Can$ 210,000 6th year	4/1/84	1/1/88 3 Years 9 Months	Automatic 3 Years	Canada
12	6%		$36,000 1st year $45,000 2nd year $60,000 3rd year $75,000 4th year	12/1/85	7/1/88 2 Years 7 Months	Automatic 2 Years	Canada
1	10% 7%	$15,000	$60,000 Initial term $120,000 1st renewal $160,000 Next renewal	7/1/87	9/30/88 1 Year 3 Months	Two options 1 Year if over Net Sales minimums	U.S.
4	10%	$12,500	$50,000 per year	11/15/86	9/30/88 1 Year 10 Months	Three options 2 or 3 Years if over Net Sales minimums	Canada
13	10%			4/1/86	6/30/87 1 Year 3 Months	Automatic 2 or 5 Years if over Net Sales minimums	U.S.
14	10%	$10,000		6/1/86	9/30/87 1 Year 4 Months	Mutual Agreement	U.S.

Determining the cause for this royalty rate differential is important to the manager because his internal financial analysis indicates that the company would be able to successfully market a product line bearing the athletic trademark at a 5 or 6 percent royalty, but would most likely not be able to achieve an acceptable profit margin at the 10 percent rate. As a result, he once again reexamined the four Canadian agreements according to the contractual clauses summarized in Exhibit 12.10.

After completing this analysis, the manager concluded that the contractual clauses in the agreements do not explain the differing royalty rates. For instance, the lump sum payment and the guaranteed minimum payment for all of the agreements is among the highest for the Canadian agreement that has a royalty rate of 10 percent of net sales. Typically, the royalty rate as a percent of net sales for this agreement would be expected to be among the lowest, not the highest.

Finally, the manager was left with the conclusion that the royalties are tied to the term of the agreements. Although the length of the agreements did not appear to have a significant effect on the corresponding royalty rate, the time frame does appear to play a role. The eight agreements summarized in Exhibit 12.10 were all enacted in a span of less than four years, between September 1983 and July 1987. However, this four-year period can be further segmented into two time frames, September 1983 to January 1986 and April 1986 to July 1987. The manager felt that it was more than a coincidence that the earlier time period coincided with the lower royalty rates, while the later period coincided with the higher royalty rates. Exhibit 12.11 below summarizes his observations.

Based on this analysis, the manager conducted further research into what the licensor's market position had been during these two time periods. This research highlighted the fact that the athletic footwear company had pursued a very aggressive advertising campaign in the mid-1980s, dramatically increasing its market share and financial returns in 1986 and 1987. As a result, the manager concluded that during the two time periods, significant differences existed in the profit potential for the licensed trademarks, strengthening the licensor's negotiating position and thus explaining the differences in the royalties charged.

Although the most recent trademark license agreements call for a royalty on net sales of 10 percent, the manager concluded that because of the geographic differences, the current value of the trademarks in his undeveloped market was comparable to the value of the marks during the 1985–86 period. Based on the fact that the trademarks were not as widely recognized in his geographic market, the manager felt that he could negotiate a license agreement with the athletic footwear company that would incorporate a royalty on net sales not exceeding the 5 to 6 percent range.

Feeling confident was that he was in a secure position for negotiating the payment terms for the license agreement, the manager was curious as to

Exhibit 12.11   Agreements per Royalties, Dates, and Markets

#	Royalty Rate	Date	Market
First Time Period			
8	3.5%	9/1/83	Indonesia, Hong Kong, Singapore, Malaysia and the Philippines
9	6%	4/1/84	Canada
12	6%	12/1/85	Canada
11	5%	1/1/86	Canada
Second Time Period			
13	10%	4/1/86	U.S.
14	10%	6/1/86	U.S.
4	10%	11/15/86	Canada
1	10%, 7%	7/1/87	U.S.

what type of assistance his company could expect from the licensor. In order to prepare for this aspect of the negotiations, the manager decided to further review the four agreements from the earlier time period to determine if there were any ancillary services that the licensor provided to those licensees. Exhibit 12.12 summarizes the services that the athletic footwear company provided and the corresponding requirements for the licensees.

The four agreements summarized in Exhibit 12.12 provide some important information for the manager about the various services the footwear company had been willing to provide to licensees. The services ranged from advertising copy, merchandising assistance, and samples to no assistance at all. However, the manager now also knew that in those cases where assistance was provided, the licensee had to commit to spending a certain amount to advertise the product. This analysis gave the manager insight into the types of services for which he might be able to negotiate, and also what the licensor's expectations for his company's performance would be.

After completing the many months of research and analysis, the manager was now in a position to prepare his report for the company president. Based on the analysis, the manager believed that his company should pursue the license agreement with the athletic footwear company. In order to facilitate this process, the manager prepared a report summarizing his recommendations for how this agreement should be structured:

- Because Mexico has only a limited amount of U.S. media exposure, the manager felt that the company should only be willing to pay between 5 and 6 percent of sales for the use of the athletic footwear logo.
- Although the licensor may pursue lump-sum payments, the manager recommended that the company negotiate any lump-sum payments

Exhibit 12.12   Agreements per Licensor Services and Advertising Requirements

#	Licensor Services	Advertising Requirement
8	**Know-How** • Marketing and merchandising assistance upon request • Marketing and merchandising advice, when techniques or products available • Permit attendance at sales meetings involving products **Tangibles** • Samples of each product • Copy of Technical Guidelines and Trademark Guidelines • Copy of advertising and promotional materials used by Licensor • Copy of commercials and preparatory work used by Licensor	• 4% of net sales during first annual period • 2% of net sales during additional annual periods
9	**Know-How** • Marketing and merchandising advice, when techniques or products available • Permit attendance at sales meetings involving products **Tangibles** • Samples at factory cost, Copy of advertising and promotional materials used by Licensor • Copy of commercials and preparatory work used by Licensor **Operations** • Act as buying agent with vendors	• $25,000 per contract year
11	**Know-How/Tangibles** • Copies of sketches and ideas for collections of products	• 3% of annual net sales • Minimum advertising expenditures: $7,500 during 1986 $15,000 during 1987 $22,500 during 1988
12	**Know-How/Tangibles** • Copies of sample lines for collections of products **Operations** • Approval of articles	• 3% of annual net sales • Minimum advertising expenditures: $15,000 during 1st year $20,000 during 2nd year $25,000 during 3rd year $30,000 during 4th year

to serve as prepayments of the royalties based on net sales. In addition, the licensor will require guaranteed minimum payments; however, the manager recommended that the company negotiate either a grace period or a low minimum for the first year.

• The company should anticipate an agreement that will have a one to three year duration with renewal options that might extend the agreement another two to six years.

- It would be possible for the company to pursue a certain level of marketing assistance and know-how from the licensor; however, it would have to be prepared to accept requirements pertaining to advertising expenditures. Therefore, a cost/benefit analysis should be performed before the contract is negotiated based on the expected advertising payments and the expected return for the licensor's assistance.

CONCLUSION

This chapter provides a guide to using unrelated license agreements to develop a framework for negotiating a new agreement. It began with a discussion of the three primary sources available for information on license agreements: Disclosure; on-line and CD-Rom data bases; and the SEC reference room. A list of advantages and disadvantages was provided for each resource, with the ultimate conclusions that the most thorough search strategy would utilize a combination of the three.

The remainder of the chapter focuses on how the information available in these external license agreements should be analyzed in order to assess the comparability of the agreements. A framework for this analysis was presented, highlighting some of the significant factors that affect the comparability of the agreements. The framework emphasized the internal factors, contractual terms, but also included external factors, such as the relationship between the licensor and licensee. The chapter concludes with a case study illustrating the use of external license agreements in preparing for the negotiation of a new license agreement, beginning with the search for external agreements and culminating with the analysis of these agreements.

13

Advanced Royalty Rate Determination Methods

Russell L. Parr

AUS Consulting and Intellectual Property Research Associates

This chapter will discuss different methods that can provide insight into royalty rates. Both qualitative and rigorous financial models are described. Two of the methods are taken from court decisions. Underlying this discussion is the idea that intellectual property is an investment asset. Licensing strategies often seek to gain the highest rate of return on intellectual properties. Royalty rates should reflect the same factors that drive the rate of return requirements associated with all other business assets.

INVESTMENT RISK AND ROYALTY RATES

Royalty rates and business risk are related—there is a fundamental relationship between the two. The amount of business risk associated with commercializing a technology will have a direct bearing on the amount of royalty that a licensee will pay. Unfortunately, this belief cannot be proved. So many different factors come into play when determining royalty rates that proof of a simple correlation is not easily accomplished. The hypothesis that royalty rates and business risk are related is still valid, but many other factors that also affect royalty rates disguise the relationship with risk.

It is important that the determination of a royalty rate for licensing technology addresses the important factor of risk. Therefore, this chapter will present models for use in gauging royalty rates relative both to risk and to many other factors.

This chapter first explores an analysis of technology licenses negotiated in business climates of different risk, beginning with an attempt to correlate royalty rates and business risk.[1] The results of the analysis lead to the conclusion that royalty rates cannot be categorized by general measures of industry risk, and so the financial terms of technology licensing must be determined on an individual basis, with consideration given to the specific business risks associated with a specific technology transfer.

INTELLECTUAL PROPERTY IS AN INVESTMENT ASSET

The value and rate of return associated with all types of investment is driven by three fundamental factors:

1. Economic benefits derived from the property,
2. Duration of the benefits, and
3. Risk of receiving the benefits

Higher-risk investments typically provide higher rates of return as compensation for the risk levels accepted by investors. When investments are sure to provide a rate of return, both risk and the amount of investment return are low. The debt obligations of the U.S. Government are an example of this sort of investing. When risk is high, the rate of return must be high as well. Exhibit 13.1 shows investments of varying risk and the corresponding rate of return they provide.

Intellectual property is very valuable. In fact, it is the most important asset that any company owns. Without intellectual property, a company cannot differentiate itself and must fight in a commodity-oriented environment where competition is fierce and profit margins are slim. Intellectual property can make the difference between being stuck in a commodity market and enjoying fast growth and high profit margins. Part of the power of intellectual property is due to its unique proprietary aspects. Many companies implement different programs for strategic advantage but only intellectual property can truly represent a barrier to competition.

The first companies practicing Just-In-Time inventory management enjoyed profit advantages, but only until their competitors adopted the same program. It happened again with Total Quality Management campaigns, Customer Is Number One programs, Frequent Flyer Bonus plans, Management by Wandering Around techniques, and scores of other programs. Lasting improvements resulted for the companies adopting these programs but the programs and benefits could be and were easily copied. Only intellectual property can provide both enhanced corporate value and a barrier to compe-

---

[1]This analysis is derived from a workshop developed by Russell L. Parr and Patrick H. Sullivan, Ph.D., and presented on October 16, 1994, at the annual conference of the Licensing Executives Society (USA & Canada) at the Hilton Waikoloa Village, Hawaii.

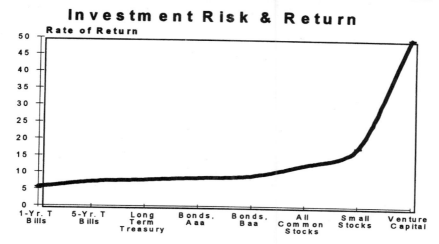

Exhibit 13.1   Investment Risk & Return

tition. Such an asset is extremely valuable. Because intellectual property has such enormous value it seems logical that the fundamental factors driving value as listed above should also apply to intellectual property.

Intellectual property should be looked at as an investment asset with royalties representing a form of return on investment. As such we would expect royalties to relate to risk. To test this hypothesis we have attempted to correlate the royalty rates associated with 41 technology licenses with different measures of investment risk. On the next page is a summary of the licenses that were used in the analysis. The summary is titled *Summary List of Technology Licenses—Royalty Rates & Industry Risk*. The information has been gathered from past issues of Licensing Economics Review, published by AUS Consultants, Moorestown, NJ. For each license the table shows the licenser, the licensee, the technology licensed, the industry into which the technology was licensed, the negotiated royalty rate, and a qualitative measure of the business risk associated with the deal.

Qualitative Risk Measures

Each transaction was categorized by investment risk into one of three risk categories—low, moderate, and high. Transactions were considered low risk when the technology transferred was commercially proven and expected to be easily exploited by the licensee. The high-risk label was assigned to transactions involving technology requiring additional development and testing before commercial exploitation was possible. An example of high risk is the transfer of embryonic biotechnology from a university laboratory to a company that must satisfy FDA regulations and develop large volume production capabilities. A low risk example is one where the technology transferred is commercially proven and successful exploitation by the licensee is not in serious doubt. Moderate risk transactions were those that fell somewhere in between these two extremes.

The licenses perceived to involve *low* business risk included 10 deals with royalty rates ranging between 1 and 10 percent. The average royalty rate in the group was 5.6 percent, and the most frequently reported rate was 3 percent.

The licenses perceived to involve *moderate* business risk included 15 deals with royalty rates ranging between 2.5 and 10 percent. The average royalty rate in the group was 4.9 percent, and the most frequently reported rate was 5 percent. In comparison to the low risk deals, the bottom of the royalty rate range for the moderate risk deals starts two and a half times higher than the bottom of the low risk range. The average for the moderate deals is lower but the most frequently reported royalty rate for moderate deals is 1.67 times that reported for low risk transactions.

The licenses perceived to involve *high* business risk included 13 deals with royalty rates ranging between 3 and 15 percent. The average royalty rate in the group was 6.5%, and the most frequently reported rate was 4 percent but it should be noted that a 10 percent royalty was reported for this category more often than for the other two categories. The high risk deals show a royalty rate range with significantly higher bottom and top boundaries. The average royalty rate reported for this group is also highest among the categories. The most frequently reported royalty rate does not support the general hypothesis but the high frequency of 10 percent royalty rates does.

This qualitative analysis (where business risk is ranked by informed perception) shows that high risk business environments are generally associated with higher royalty rates. Each category shows characteristics that loosely relate royalty rates to investment risk. The next step in the analysis is to try to find more precise correlation using statistical techniques.

Beta as a Measure of Risk

The volatility of publicly traded company stock is often represented by a statistical factor known as *beta*. It is a measure of company stock price volatility relative to the entire market for company stock investments. The volatility of a broad portfolio of stocks is defined as having a beta equal to 1.0. Individual stocks with betas greater than 1.0 rise and fall faster than the broad market. These stocks are riskier than investments in a broad portfolio of stocks. Stocks with betas less than 1.0 rise and fall to a lesser extent than the broad market. Such stocks are considered to possess lower investment risk than the broad market. Typically, the stocks of biotechnology companies with embryonic and noncommercialized technology have high betas, reflecting the risk of the business. Low betas are often associated with mature businesses, such as food companies whose products and technologies are expected to deliver consistent amounts of sales and earrings.

Using beta as a measure of risk, an attempt was made to compensate for the judgment errors that may exist in the qualitative risk assignment previously discussed. For each technology license the beta of the licensee was obtained from Media General Industriscope for the last week in September 1994. When the licensee was not a public company the beta of the licenser was used. When betas were not available for either the licensee or the licenser an industry beta was used, representing the risk of the industry into which the technology was transferred. For the most part, betas were available for the licensee. The scatter plot of Exhibit 13.2 does not reveal obvious correlation.

The scatter plot certainly shows data points where low royalty rates are associated with low betas. At the riskier, right-hand, side of the graph, however, low rates are also associated with very high levels of beta. The middle of the graph shows royalty rates ranging from 3 to 15 percent for betas between 1.0 and 2.0. As with the analysis using qualitative measures for risk, for moderate risk deals (with betas ranging between 1.0 and 2.0) correlation is difficult to find even when you look at the graph with squinted eyes.

A regression analysis, shown in Exhibit 13.3, contributes little toward identifying a correlation between royalty rates and risk. The R-squared is an unimpressive 0.001. An R-squared of 0.80 or maybe even 0.70 would have been more helpful for proving the hypothesis.

A polynomial analysis, shown in Exhibit 13.4, indicates a relationship between risk and royalty rates that is inconsistent with intuition. The polynomial line indicates that low risk (low beta) licensees pay a royalty rate of approximately 6 percent. Moving to the right, as risk increases the royalty rates paid by licensees begins to decrease but then they increase to almost 8 percent as higher risk is expected. Much higher risk (continuing to move

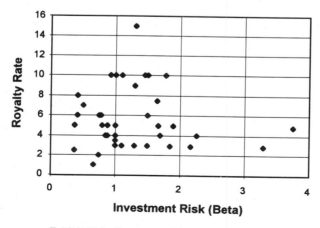

Exhibit 13.2   Investment Risk & Royalty Rates

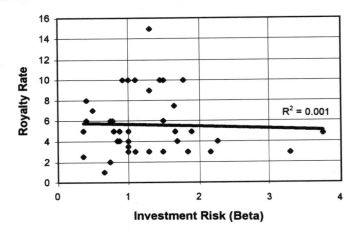

Exhibit 13.3   Investment Risk & Royalty Rates

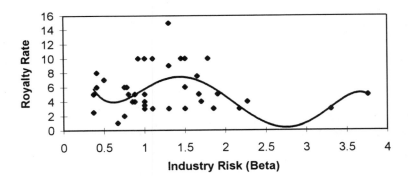

Exhibit 13.4   Royalty Rates & Industry Risk

to the right of the x axis) shows a dramatic decrease in licensee royalty rates, but the rates suddenly increase again at extremely high levels of risk.

Royalty rates cannot be related satisfactorily to the stock market risk associated with licensing companies. The qualitative analysis shows better correlation, indicating that royalty rates are sensitive to the specific conditions associated with specific technology transfers. This analysis indicates that royalty rates cannot be linked with general rules-of-thumb or industry norms. The qualitative analysis could have been even more supportive of the hypothesis if greater inside knowledge about the risks of the specific transactions was known, allowing for better qualitative risk categorization.

The primary reason that a simple correlation could not be identified is because each of the three fundamental factors previously listed has many secondary factors that drive them. Listed among the fundamental factors are additional factors that can skew the royalties when looked at solely from a risk relationship point of view.

- Economic benefits derived from the technology
    benefits derived from complementary assets
    competitor efforts
    consumer reactions
    management competency
    production efficiencies
    commercialization expenses
    commercialization time frame requirements
- Duration of the benefits
    rapid technological obsolescence
    alternate technologies
    validity of patent risks
    changing consumer reactions
- Risk of receiving the benefits
    economic risk
    regulatory risk
    political risk
    inflationary risk
    unexpected conditions and events

This analysis leads to a conclusion that royalty rates must be derived with consideration for the specific business factors that affect commercial success, including specific risk factors.

MARKET TRANSACTIONS IN GENERAL

Information about royalty rates obtained by others in third-party market transactions can show a *typical* royalty rate for an industry but, as this analysis will show, a more precise model is still needed. The bar chart presented in Exhibit 13.5 summarizes royalty rates associated with technology licenses.[2] A total of 95 licenses are represented, involving technology transfers in the telecommunications, semiconductor, and computer industries. The answer to the question What is a typical royalty rate for advanced technology? can be addressed with an analysis of the charted data.

The average royalty rate, weighted by the number of times it showed up in a license agreement, is 5.1 percent. If the high end royalty rates of 20 and

---

[2]The information for this analysis was generously provided by Michael Merwin of Ernst & Young LLP, Chicago, Illinois, and Licensing Economics Review, Moorestown, New Jersey.

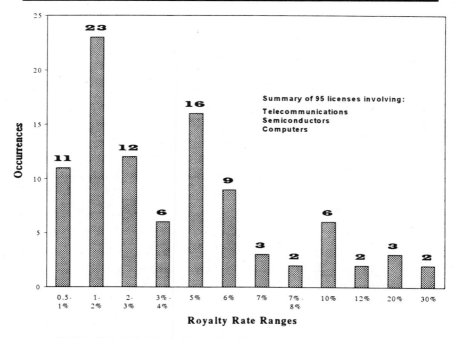

Exhibit 13.5   Third Party Technology Transfer Royalty Rate Distribution

30 percent are eliminated as being anomalies, then the weighted average royalty rate is 4 percent. Based on this analysis, some negotiators are happy to finalize their agreements using a royalty rate of 4 or 5 percent. By using this information we assume that the technology we are attempting to quantify is reasonably comparable to the technology involved in the 95 licenses analyzed. The problem is that a specific technology cannot be comparable to all of the 95 licensed technologies. It can only be similar to some of the transferred technology. Therefore, the market transaction royalty rates should be looked at mostly as general guidance that helps to define the boundaries within which a settlement royalty rate should fall.

More Guidance

The most frequently reported royalty rate was 5 percent, found in 16 of the 95 licenses. The second most frequently negotiated royalty rate was 2 percent, which was found in 14 agreements. Third place went to 3 percent, with appearances in 11 licenses. The fourth most frequently negotiated rate was 6 percent, which showed up 9 times. Fifth place went to royalty rates of 1.5 percent, with 8 appearances. A royalty rate of 1 percent showed up 7 times. The following table, Exhibit 13.6, summarizes the frequency of the most common rates.

Exhibit 13.6 Bar Chart Data—Most Common Royalty Rates

Royalty Rate	Frequency
5.0%	16
2.0%	14
3.0%	11
6.0%	9
1.5%	8
1.0%	7

Our analysis now shows us the average royalty rates negotiated and the number of times specific rates were negotiated. A cumulative analysis provides additional insights:

- 55 percent of the licenses involved royalty rates of 4 percent or less
- 72 percent of the licenses involved royalty rates of 5 percent or less
- 81 percent of the licenses involved royalty rates of 6 percent or less
- 93 percent of the licenses involved royalty rates of 10 percent or less
- 95 percent of the licenses involved royalty rates of 12 percent or less

In this analysis we have developed a general range of reasonable royalty rates. However, something is missing from the analysis. Something important. Something that will allow the market information just presented to be filtered for direct application to a specific technology reflecting specific conditions. We are missing a model that will focus on earning fair rates of return on the investments committed to the project.

An investment rate of return model can yield a royalty rate that allows the licenser to earn a fair rate of return on its investment in the project while returning to the licensee a royalty reflecting the value of the licensed technology and its contribution to the success of the contemplated project. An investment rate of return model that allows a licensee to earn a fair rate of return on its investment in the project is key to filtering the market data. The model must consider the working capital committed to the project and the investment in fixed assets such as manufacturing facilities. Additionally, the model should provide the licensee with a fair rate of return on the investment value of the intangible assets and intellectual property it is contributing to the project in the form of complementary patents, trademarks, customer lists, and distribution networks. Such a model is presented later in this chapter.

INFRINGEMENT DAMAGES—THE ANALYTICAL APPROACH

The analytical approach is a method for deriving a reasonable royalty that was first expressed in a court decision on royalties. While a license negotiation may be independent of any legal actions, insight can be gained from considering the royalty rate models that are used in legal proceedings. The analytical approach, as it is called by the courts, determines a reasonable royalty as the difference between profits expected from infringing sales and a normal industry profit level. The analytical approach can be summarized by the following equation:

Expected Profit Margin − Normal Profit Margin = Royalty Rate

In *TWM Mfg. Co., Inc. v. Dura Corp.*, 789 F.2d 895, 899 (Fed. Cir. 1986), a royalty for damages was calculated based on an analysis of the business plan the infringer had prepared just prior to the onset of the infringing activity. The court discovered the infringer's profit expectations from using the infringed technology from internal memoranda written by top executives of the company. These internal memoranda showed that company management expected to earn gross profit margins of almost 53 percent from the proposed infringing sales. Operating profit margins were then calculated by subtracting overhead costs to yield an unexpected profit margin of between 37 and 42 percent. To find the portion of this profit level that should be provided as a royalty to the plaintiff the court considered the standard profits earned in the industry at the time of infringement. These profit levels were determined to be between 6.6 and 12.5 percent. These normal industry profits were considered to represent profit margins that would be acceptable to firms operating in the industry. The remaining 30 percent of profits were found to represent a reasonable royalty from which to calculate infringement damages. On appeal the Federal Circuit affirmed.

Normal Industry Profits

The problem with the analytical approach centers on answering the question, What's a normal industry profit margin? Normal is hard to quantify. It is meant to reflect the profit margins that might be gained from operating the businesses in an industry without the technology in question. It can also be difficult to find agreement on what constitutes normal profit margins for an individual company. Different subsidiaries or divisions, and even different product lines within the same company, can display wide swings in profitability. Many large companies have a portfolio of businesses. Some of the product offerings are mature products that enjoy large market shares but contribute only moderate profit margins because of selling price competition. Other product offerings are emerging products that have great potential for profits and market share but won't deliver earnings contribution until a later date. Still other products of the same diversified company might contribute huge profits because of a technological advantage but only from exploitation of a small market niche.

The analytical approach can be very useful. It is based on information timely to the license negotiation at hand. It attempts to allocate the profits earned from intellectual property exploitation between the licenser and licensee. The analytical approach is especially useful if a normalized standard industry profit can be properly derived. The analytical approach can provide an order of magnitude indication of a reasonable royalty. The analytical approach, however, can be improved.

A More Comprehensive Analytical Approach

Missing from the analytical approach is any consideration of the amount of complementary assets required for exploitation of the intellectual property. A unique intellectual property might require significantly more investment in manufacturing assets than is typical for an industry, and so the industry standard profit margin might be inappropriate. From another viewpoint, the industry profit requirement for commercializing specific intellectual property requiring massive fixed asset investment might be higher than the profits typically required in a specific industry. This could easily happen if new intellectual property is being introduced into an industry not accustomed to capital intensive activities.

The analytical approach loses sight of the balance sheet. Profits are important but they are not independent of investment in complementary business assets. Otherwise, everyone with an idea would be in business. The profit and loss statement is derived from the management of the investment in the assets reported on the balance sheet. Exploitation of intellectual property requires the integration of different types of resources and assets. Intellectual property by itself rarely spews forth money. The equation of commercialization requires working capital, fixed assets, intangible assets, and intellectual property. A more comprehensive version of the analytical approach should be utilized; enhanced to the extent that the profits to be allocated between the licenser and licensee reflect the dynamic relationship between profits and the amounts invested in the complementary assets.

A company that produces the commodity product is by definition in a competitive environment. The product price is affected by heavy competition and profits margins are thin. In such an environment, an efficient market eventually will stabilize the pricing of the commodity product to a level that allows participants in the market to earn a fair rate of return on the assets invested in the business but no more. A fair return would be earned on the working capital, fixed assets, and intangible assets, but excess profits typically are not earned from the production and sale of a commodity product.

A company producing an enhanced product, using proprietary technology, possesses elements of product differentiation that allow it to charge a premium price. The premium might be due to a trademark that consumers associate with quality. Alternatively, the premium might be derived from special utility offered by the product covered by patented technology. The price premium might even be derived from a combination of trademark and technological advantages. The producer of the enhanced product would earn a profit that represents a fair return on its working capital, fixed assets, and intangible assets, and an excess return from the intellectual property.

The highest amount of royalty that a commodity product producer should be willing to pay to license rights to manufacture and sell the enhanced product is the amount of excess profits associated with the intellectual property. The commodity product licensee would expect to continue to earn a fair rate of return from its investment in working capital, fixed assets, and intangible assets.

The investment returns earned by a commodity product manufacturer on the complementary assets used to manufacture and sell the commodity product can be equated to the normal or standard industry profits. When this amount is subtracted from the total returns earned from commercializing the enhanced product, the difference represents the amount contributed by the intellectual property. Such an amount can be used as a reasonable royalty for damages calculations. This royalty amount might be greater than the licenser and licensee might have negotiated in a hypothetical willing licenser and willing licensee negotiation, but then where is the penalty for forcing the property owner into court? It is also quite likely that the amount is exactly what willing parties would have negotiated.

The analytical approach can work well when the normal industry profit is derived from analysis of commodity products. The analysis requires that the benchmark commodity profit margin be derived from products competing in the same, or similar, industry as the infringing product, for which a reasonable royalty is being sought. The benchmark profits should also reflect similar investment requirements in complementary assets; similar to those required to exploit the enhanced product that is based on the infringed intellectual property. The following equation can provide a reasonable royalty if the above conditions are met:

Enhanced Product Profit Margin − Commodity Product Profit Margin
= Royalty Rate

The exhibit below shows the operating profit margins for a group of personal computer manufacturing companies that arguably are producing commodity products. The products are interchangeable, competitively priced, mass produced, widely distributed, and provide their makers with slim profit margins. The profit margins were derived from information downloaded from the Disclosure database on public corporations via CompuServe. Adjustments were incorporated into the operating profit margins to attempt to isolate the profits derived from the operations of the selected companies. Adjustments were made to eliminate income and expenses associated with nonoperating assets and nonrecurring events when possible. Interest expenses were also eliminated. As a group, the average profit margins of these companies can be looked at as the commodity profit margin for the personal computer industry.

Suppose that we want to derive a royalty rate for a new personal computer that has a proprietary enhancement owned by the mythical company Super PC Ltd. When the profit margins associated with Super PC Ltd. are compared to the commodity group a profit deferential of approximately 6 percent is developed. Exhibit 13.7 shows the profit margins associated with manufacturers of computer systems that can be characterized as commodities along with the profit margins of Super PC Ltd.

It is important to reiterate that the commodity product benchmark profit margin must be derived from an analysis of a product that:

1. Lacks the intellectual property for which a royalty rate is desired and therefore can be described as a commodity product.
2. Participates in the same, or similar, industry in which the subject intellectual property product competes
3. Requires a similar relative amount of investment in complementary assets.

Failure of the Analytical Approach

The analytical approach can fail in instances where the benchmark profit margin that is characterized as normal or that of a commodity contains elements of profitability attributed to other forms of intellectual property.

A simple trademark example is presented to clarify this point. Suppose that an independent communication and check cashing service business uses the trademark Western Union without a license. Assuming that Western Union establishments enjoy 12 percent profit margins on revenues, we are relatively sure that the infringing independent operator enjoyed some bene-

Exhibit 13.7 The Analytical Approach—Personal Computer Industry Operating Profit Margins

Company	1994	1993	1992	1991	Average
Apple	4.3%	5.4%	11.4%	10.6%	7.9%
AST	3.1%	4.3%	10.3%	13.7%	7.9%
Compaq	11.7%	9.6%	7.9%	9.1%	9.6%
Dell	7.2%	−1.4%	6.9%	7.5%	5.1%
Gateway	5.2%	8.6%	9.3%	9.5%	8.2%
Company Avg.	6.3%	5.3%	9.2%	10.1%	7.7%
Super PC Ltd.	*12.0%*	*11.0%*	*15.0%*	*16.0%*	*13.5%*
Profit Differential	*5.7%*	*5.7%*	*5.8%*	*5.9%*	*5.8%*

fit from use of the Western Union name. Suppose further that the profit margins of the independent service business are not easily defined because of poor financial records. Sales records might be available but the profit and loss statement might be impossible to decipher. We might look at the profits from other similar communication and check cashing service businesses as a proxy for a normal profit margin. American Express offers a similar service. Suppose that the profit margins at a typical American Express establishment are 10 percent of revenues. The analytical approach would subtract the 10 percent profit margins associated with the American Express trademark from the 12 percent profit margins associated with the Western Union trademark. The indicated royalty would be 2 percent. The infringing independent operator would then pay 2 percent and get away with the assumed normal 10 percent profit margin. A portion of the supposedly normal 10 percent margin, however, is derived from use of the American Express trademark. Suppose that the profit margins associated with use of the Western Union trademark are 8 percent of revenues. If the 10 percent profit margin of American Express operations are considered normal industry profits then the analytical approach would calculate a deficit royalty rate of 2 percent. Should Western Union then pay the infringer?

The Analytical Approach fails to consider the relationship between relative profit margins and the required investment in complementary assets. Great care is also required when defining a benchmark normalized industry profit margin. An enhanced version of the analytical approach should allocate only the differential profit margins associated with specific intellectual property. This will be accomplished later in this chapter, in the section called Investment Rate of Return Analysis.

INFRINGEMENT DAMAGES QUALITATIVE FACTORS

Another court case listed the important qualitative factors to look at when deriving a royalty rate for damages. Licensing negotiators can also gain insight from considering the implications of these factors. The courts seek to determine the royalty rate the two parties would have negotiated at the time of infringement had they entered into a hypothetical negotiation. In *Georgia-Pacific Corp. v. United States Plywood Corp.*, 318 F.Supp. 1116, 1120 (1970), the court listed fifteen factors that it considered important for deriving a reasonable royalty. These same factors can also provide useful guidance for licensing negotiations that are not part of a lawsuit. These factors traditionally are considered in the context of a lawsuit, assuming that the patent involved in the case is valid and infringed. In a business negotiation a question about the validity of the patent might be an additional factor to consider. The fifteen factors listed by the court are stated below:

1. The royalties received by the patentee for the licensing of the patent in suit, proving or tending to prove an established royalty.
2. The rates paid by the licensee for the use of other patents comparable to the patent in suit.
3. The nature and scope of the license, as exclusive or non-exclusive; or as restricted or non-restricted in terms of territory or with respect to whom the manufactured product may be sold.
4. The licenser's established policy and marketing program to maintain its patent monopoly by not licensing others to use the invention or by gaining licenses under special conditions designed to preserve that monopoly.
5. The commercial relationship between the licenser and the licensee—for example, whether they are competitors in the same territory or in the same line of business; or whether each is inventor and promoter.
6. The effect of selling the patented specialty in promoting sales of other products of the licensee; the existing value of the invention to the licenser as a generator of sales of its nonpatented items; and the extent of such derivative or convoyed sales.
7. The duration of the patent and the term of the license.
8. The established profitability of the product made under the patent; its commercial success; and its current popularity.
9. The utility and advantage of the patent property over the old modes or devices, if any, that had been used for working out similar results.
10. The nature of the patented invention; the character of the commercial embodiment of it as owned and produced by the licenser; and the benefits to those who have used the invention.
11. The extent to which the infringer has made use of the invention; and any evidence probative of the value of that use.
12. The portion of the profit or selling price that may be customary in the particular business or in comparable businesses to allow for the use of the invention or analogous inventions.
13. The portion of the realizable profit that should be credited to the invention as distinguished from non-patented elements, the manufacturing process, business risks, or significant features or improvements added by the infringer.
14. The opinion and testimony of qualified experts.
15. The amount that a licenser (such as the patentee) and a licensee (such as the infringer) would have agreed upon (at the time the infringement began) if both had been reasonably and voluntarily trying to reach an agreement; that is, that amount that a prudent licensee—who desires, as a business proposition, to obtain a license to manufacture and sell a particular article embodying the

patented invention—would have been willing to pay as a royalty and yet be able to make a reasonable profit and which amount would have been acceptable by a prudent patentee who was willing to grant a license.

Two basic elements dominate the list of fifteen considerations—profits and precedents. The focus on precedents looks at the actions of both the potential licenser and licensee with regard to how the specific, or similar, intellectual property has been treated. Past licensing deals are scrutinized, along with royalties previously negotiated. The actions of other parties in the same industry with similar property are also useful precedents for determining royalty rates. An analysis of the license agreements of others, with an eye to established royalties, can serve as a benchmark for establishing a royalty rate to use as the basis of a business license.

Profits are the other basic element of reasonable royalties that the fifteen Georgia-Pacific factors address. What level of profits have been enjoyed from use of the invention? What percentage of sales and market share can be attributed to use of the patented invention? What cost savings result from use of the invention? If the technology is new and yet to be commercialized then the same questions must be answered from the point of view of expected profits, market share, and cost savings.

Considering the Georgia Pacific Factors

Factors 1, 2, 3, and 12 of the Georgia-Pacific decision look at rates established in past licenses of the subject technology or similar technology. Consideration must be given to the types of licenses granted with respect to exclusivity, the scope of the license, territorial limitations, advance license fees, sublicensing rights, cross-licensing of other technology, transference of know-how, and transference of enabling technology and grant-backs of future technology that the licensee may invent. The terms contemplated in a licensing negotiation determine the usefulness of analyzing the established licenses. When licenses comparable to the one being negotiated are available a starting point—and maybe an ending point as well—is provided. Established rates are difficult to ignore without the existence of special circumstances.

In Factors 4 and 5 of the Georgia-Pacific case the court said that the unwillingness of a patent owner to grant a license to the infringer at an industry established rate at the time of infringement is a pertinent factor in establishing a reasonable royalty for damages calculations. Licenses between industry competitors can be expensive. Licensers with monopoly positions are not likely to part easily with a key business advantage. Any reluctance by a patent owner to share its monopoly position is most likely only going to be overcome by a higher royalty rate unless the potential licensee has something else of value to offer as a trade for a cross-license. When negotiations are between competitors a relatively high royalty rate should be expected.

Factor 6 looks at the effect of selling the patented specialty in promoting sales of other products of the licensee. Such additional sales are often called convoyed sales. They represent the sales associated with other products of the licensee that can be expected because of the licensed technology. The convoyed products may not use the licensed technology but the sales often can be attributed directly to the sale of the licensed product. When this condition exists the licenser is going to expect a healthy royalty rate on the licensed product.

Factor 7 considers the duration of the patent and the term of the license. The remaining life of the patent can have a strong bearing on the royalty rate. The potential licensee has to decide if waiting for the patent to expire is a viable business option. But a patent with a short life can also command a high royalty rate. If the patented invention is vital to the plans of the licensee then a high royalty rate for a short time might be tolerable. Typically, a long patent life cannot command a high royalty rate without other important characteristics being present.

Factors 8, 9, 10, 11, and 13 look at the established profitability of the product made under the patent, its commercial success, its current popularity, its utility, and the advantage of the patented property over the old modes or devices that had been used for working out similar results. This is where a financial analysis is important. The comparative questions to answer are How much will the licensee make using the technology? and How much will the licensee make without access to the technology?

Factor 15 considers the amount that a licenser and a licensee would have agreed on at the time the infringement began if both had been reasonably and voluntarily trying to reach an agreement.

While all of the factors listed above can affect the derivation of an appropriate royalty rate, the Georgia-Pacific factors are unassociated with a foundation. The response to various factors might indicate that a higher or lower royalty rate is appropriate but higher or lower relative to what? Without a base these qualitative factors alone cannot provide an answer to the royalty rate question.

INVESTMENT RATE OF RETURN ANALYSIS

Important negotiations deserve thorough analyses. This last section of Chapter 12 presents an approach for determining a royalty rate based on investment rate of returns. This analysis requires consideration of the profits expected from exploitation of the various assets of a business, including the technology that will be licensed. By allocating a fair rate of return to all of the integrated assets of a business, including the licensed technology, a fair rate of return for use of a specific patent can be derived and expressed as a royalty rate.

The basic principles in this type of analysis involve looking at the total profits of a business and allocating the profits among the different classes of assets used in the business. When a commodity-oriented business demonstrates an ability to earn higher-than-expected profits, then the presence of intellectual property, such as patented technology, is identified. An allocation of the total profits derived from using all assets of the company can attribute a portion of the profits to the technology of a business. When the profits that are apportioned to the technology are expressed as a percentage of revenues, royalty rate guidance is obtained.

The investment rate of return analysis yields an indication of a royalty rate for a technology license after a fair return is earned on investment in the other assets of the business. Thus, a royalty rate conclusion that is supported by an investment rate of return analysis allows for payment of a royalty to a licenser while still allowing a licensee to earn a fair investment rate of return on its own, nonlicensed assets used in the business.

Exhibit 13.8 shows a business enterprise as made up of working capital, fixed assets, intangible assets, and technology. This is the collection of asset categories that all companies use to participate in an industry and generate profits. The exhibit also shows that the value of an enterprise, as comprised of its equity and debt, equals the value of the aggregate asset categories.

The value of the components shown in Exhibit 13.8 equals the value of the business enterprise as shown in Exhibit 13.9.

Exhibit 13.10 shows that the profits of an enterprise can be allocated to the different asset categories that comprise the enterprise. The amount of

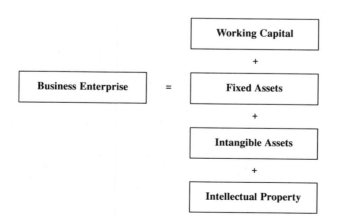

Exhibit 13.8   Composition of a Business Enterprise

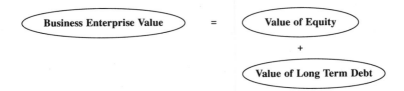

Exhibit 13.9   Value of a Business Enterprise

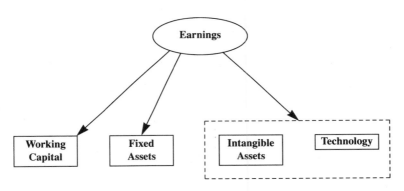

Exhibit 13.10   Distribution of Earnings

profits is directly related to the existence of the different asset categories. Companies lacking any one category of assets would have different profits.

The earnings of a business are derived from exploiting its assets. The number of assets in each category, along with their nature and quality, determines the level of earnings that the business generates. Working capital, fixed assets, and intangible assets[3] are commodity assets that all businesses can possess and exploit. A company that possesses only those limited assets will enjoy only limited earnings because of the competitive nature of commodities. A company that generates superior earnings must have something special—intellectual property in the form of patented technology, trademarks, or copyrights. The distribution of the earnings among the assets is primarily driven by the value of the assets and the investment risk associated with them.

---

[3]Intangible assets can take the form of distribution networks, corporate practices and procedures, manufacturing systems computer systems, assembled workforce, and established relationships with banks, vendors, utilities, government agencies, and unions.

Royalty Rates

The royalty rate to associate with a specific technology equals the earnings derived from the technology divided by the revenues derived with the technology, as shown in Exhibit 13.11.

Specifically, a company lacking intangible assets and technology would be reduced to operating a commodity-oriented enterprise where competition and lack of product distinction would severely limit the potential for profits. Conversely, a company possessing proprietary assets can throw off the restrictions of commodity-oriented operations and earn superior profits. When a portion of the profit stream of a company is attributed to its proprietary assets, an indication of the profits contributed by the existence of the proprietary assets is provided and a basis for a royalty is established when the attributed profits are expressed as a percentage of the corresponding revenues. The total profits can be allocated among the different asset categories based on the number of assets in each category and the relative investment risk associated with each asset category.

An appropriate rate of return to associate with net working capital is determined by considering the investment rate of returns that can be earned from alternate uses of working capital that reflect the same type of invest-

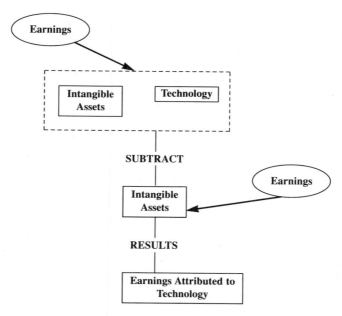

$$\frac{\text{Earnings due to possessing technology}}{\text{Revenues}} = \text{Royalty Rate}$$

Exhibit 13.11   Excess Earnings as a Percent of Revenues

ment risk characteristics. A review of relatively safe investments is considered an appropriate alternative for net working capital. The relative liquidity of net working capital makes this asset component of a business less risky relative to its other asset components.

Fixed assets of a business are machinery, equipment, plants, and the like. An appropriate rate of return for this component of business assets can be approximated by looking at the interest rate at which commercial banks make loans using fixed assets as collateral and also by looking at the interest rates associated with the general rates that leasing companies charge for fixed asset based leases. Another indication of the amount of return that should be attributed to the fixed assets of the company can be derived from reviewing the interest rates associated with corporate debt.

An appropriate investment risk is then derived and assigned to the intangible assets of the business, including the technology to be licensed by using the weighted average cost of capital for the business, the return on fixed assets deemed appropriate, and the return on working capital deemed appropriate. An appropriate rate of return can then derived for the riskier intangible assets of the business, and this serves as a basis for a royalty.

The royalty derived from this analysis includes the technology to be licensed. The exact same analysis for a business not possessing the technology to be licensed will also yield an indicated royalty rate and the difference between the royalty with the technology and the royalty without the technology is the royalty rate to ascribe to the licensed technology.

Hypothetical Example—Super PC Ltd.

Super PC Ltd. is a hypothetical company that produces personal computers for home and business use. The company has a small portion of the market, competes with large companies, and manufactures in the United States. The company achieves superior profits because its products include patented features that allow customers to gain access to information on hard drives that are not connected to the computer. Using a combination of laser and electromagnetic fields, a patented component lets the computer access data on any hard drive placed within 20 feet of a Super PC computer. The company has been able to obtain a premium price for their computers, which are similar to the general market offerings except for the patented hard disk reader.

The following analysis is useful for isolating the amount of income derived from the patented feature and for setting a royalty rate at which to license the invention. Exhibit 13.12 through 13.19 present a working example of the concepts featured in Exhibits 8 through 11.

In Exhibit 13.12, the most recent balance sheets for the company show the working capital, fixed assets, and other assets used in the business for the most recent two years. This schedule indicates the average investment in such assets used to achieve the superior profits.

Exhibit 13.12   Super PC Ltd. Balance Sheets ($000s)

Investment Rate of Return Method
Super PC Ltd.
Balance Sheets

	1994	1995	1994-1995 Average
Assets			
Cash and temporary investments	100,000	320,000	210,000
Accounts Receivable	325,000	410,000	367,500
Inventories	125,000	145,000	135,000
Prepaid Expenses & Other	52,000	62,500	57,250
Total Current Assets	602,000	937,500	769,750
Property, plant, and equipment, gross	275,000	335,000	305,000
Property, plant, and equipment, net	145,000	175,000	160,000
LT Financial Instruments & Other Assets	50,000	50,000	50,000
Total Assets	797,000	1,162,500	979,750
Liabilities and Deferred Credits			
Total Current Liabilities	110,500	226,500	168,500
Total Long Term Liabilities	325,000	240,000	282,500
Total Current & Long Term Liabilities	435,500	466,500	451,000
Shareholders' Equity	361,500	696,000	528,750
Tot. Liab. & Shareholders' Equity	797,000	1,162,500	979,750

Exhibit 13.13   Super PC Ltd.—Calculation of the Business Enterprise Value ($000s)

Investment Rate of Return Method
Super PC Ltd.

	1994	1995	1994–1995 Average
Common Shares Outstanding	100,000	105,000	102,500
Price per Share	17.5	20.5	19.0
Equity Value	1,750,000	2,152,500	1,947,500
Long-Term Obligations	325,000	240,000	282,500
Invested Capital	2,075,000	2,392,500	2,230,000

Figure 13.13 estimates the value of the business enterprise defined as the market value of invested capital as comprised of shareholders' equity and debt. The equity value was obtained from the stock market. Long term debt value is estimated at its book value. The schedule shows the value of equity at over $1.9 billion with debt valued at just under $300,000 for a total enterprise value of $2.2 billion.

Exhibit 13.14 specifically identifies the average working capital and fixed asset values used in the conduct of business. Only $761 million of working capital is needed to support operations.

Exhibit 13.15 shows the revenues and operating income derived from the business—specifically the manufacture and sale of personal computers containing the patented feature.

Exhibits 13.16 and 13.17 estimate the costs of different sources of capital and the weighted average cost of capital for Super PC Ltd. The capital asset pricing model is used to estimate the cost of capital for equity.[4] Debt

Exhibit 13.14   Super PC Ltd.—Average Working Capital and Average Fixed Assets Employed in the Business ($000s)

Investment Rate of Return Method Super PC Ltd. Complementary Business Assets	
	1994–1995 Average
Net Working Capital	601,250
Plant, Property, & Equipment, net	160,000
Total	716,250

Net Working Capital is calculated as current assets minus current liabilities.
Plant, Property, & Equipment, net, is from the company balance sheets.

Exhibit 13.15   Super PC Ltd.—Operating Income Derived from Commercialization of Technology ($000s)

Investment Rate of Return Method Super PC Ltd.—Technology-Based Revenues and Operating Income			
	1994	1995	1994–1995 Average
Revenues	1,350,000	1,625,000	1,487,500
Operating Income	142,500	175,000	158,750

All information in this schedule is taken from the annual report of Super PC Ltd.

---

[4]The Capital Asset Pricing Model and other methods for defining costs of capital are widely discussed in books and articles. An excellent general discussion of this topic can be found in *Valuation: Measuring and Managing the Value of Companies, Second Edition*, by Tom Copeland, Tim Koller, and Jack Murin (New York: John Wiley & Sons). A similar discussion about costs of capital as it relates to intellectual property valuation can be found in Appendix A of the book *Valuation of Intellectual Property and Intangible Assets, Second Edition*, by Gordon V. Smith and Russell L. Parr (New York: John Wiley & Sons).

Exhibit 13.16   Super PC Ltd.—Calculation of Cost of Capital Components

Investment Rate of Return Method
Components of the Weighted Average Cost of Capital

Equity Cost		
Risk-Free Return, Rf	6.83%	(1)
Beta, B	1.17	(2)
Risk Premium, Rm-Rf	7.0%	(3)
Equity Return, Re	15.0%	(4)
Debt Cost	7.55%	(5)

(1) U.S. Financial Data, Federal Reserve of St. Louis, August 11, 1995; yield on long-term treasury securities.

(2) IndustriScope, published by Media General Financial Services; Beta of Super PC Ltd.

(3) Risk premium of equity investments over risk free rate as estimated by R. G. Ibbotson Associates for large companies.

(4) Super PC Ltd. required return on equity caculated by using the Capital Asset Pricing Model; re = rf + B (rm-rf).

(5) Long-term debt costs of Super PC Ltd.

Exhibit 13.17   Super PC Ltd.—Calculation of Weighted Average Cost of Capital

Investment Rate of Return Method
Super PC Ltd.—Weighted Average Cost of Capital

Capital Component	Percent	Pretax Cost	After-Tax Cost	Weighted Cost
	(1)	(2)	(3)	(4)
Equity (a)	87.3%	15.0%	15.0%	13.1%
Debt (b)	12.7%	7.6%	5.4%	0.7%
Weighted Average Cost of Capital, WACOC, (5)				13.8%

(1a) Presents the common equity as a percent of invested capital.
(1b) Presents the debt as a percent of invested capital.
(2a, b) Cost of capital components from Exhibit 13.16.
(3a, b) Cost of capital reflecting effective tax rate of 28.8% for Super PC Ltd.
(4) Cost of capital weighted by capital structure as presented in column 1.
(5) WACOC is the sum of 4a and 4b.

costs are reflected by the bond yield associated with the long term debt of the company. The weighting of the different capital costs relative to the capital structure of the company provides the weighted average cost of capital (WACOC). This is the hurdle rate that corporate investment generally must pass in order to be considered as viable business initiatives. These schedules define the investment rate of return requirements driving the investment decisions and operations of the company. The calculations conclude that the weighted average cost of capital for Super PC Ltd. is 13.8 percent.

Exhibit 13.18 allocates the total operating income of the company among the different categories of assets used in the business. Values for net working capital and fixed assets were taken from the balance sheet schedule. The value of intangible assets and intellectual property equal the difference between the total enterprise value of $2.2 billion and the values for working capital and fixed assets. Incorporated in the $1,468,750 value is the patent invention associated with reading foreign hard disks. Also in this value are the traditional intangible assets of a personal computer company such as engineering drawings, trademark, distribution network, and assembled work force. The schedule shows that 78.7 percent of total operating income can be attributed to the intangible assets and intellectual property of the company after a fair return on working capital and fixed asset investment is considered.

Exhibit 13.19 reflects the $124.9 million of income allocated to the intangible assets and intellectual property as a percent of revenue. The royalty rate of 8.4 percent derived from this analysis is the hypothetical maximum amount that a licenser must consider paying to license not only the subject patented invention but also the other intangible assets and intellectual property of Super PC Ltd.

Exhibit 13.18   Super PC Ltd.—Allocation of Operating Income to Intangible Assets & Intellectual Property ($000s)

Investment Rate of Return Method
Super PC Ltd.—Excess Return from Intangible Assets (IA) & Intellectual Property (IP)

Asset Category	Amount	Percent	Required Return	Weighted Required Return	Allocated Weighted Return	Allocated Operating Income
	(1)	(2)	(3)	(4)	(5)	(6)
Net Working Capital	601,250	27%	8.0%	2.2%	15.6%	24,788
Fixed Assets	160,000	7%	11.0%	0.8%	5.7%	9,070
IA & IP	1,468,750	66%	16.5%	10.9%	78.7%	124,892
Invested Capital	2,230,000	100%		13.8%	100.0%	158,750

(1) Values in column 1 are from Super PC Ltd. Balance Sheet and Invested Capital calculation.

(2) Values in column 2 are the values in column 1 expressed as a percent of Invested Capital in column 1.

(3) Values in column 3 are estimated rates of return to associate with the different asset categories, balancing out to equal the weighted average cost of capital for the entire company as determined in column 4.

(4) Values in column 4 are the column 3 rates of return weighted by the column 2 percentages of invested capital.

(5) Values in column 5 are the weighted returns as a percent of the total return in column 4; showing that 78.7% of operating income is derived from all of the intellectual property and intangible assets of the company.

(6) Column 6 allocates the operating income of the company among the asset categories using the column 5 weights.

**Exhibit 13.19   Super PC Ltd.—Income Allocated to Intangible Assets
and Intellectual Property as a Percent of Revenues ($000s)**

IP & IA Allocated Income (1)	124,892
Revenues (2)	1,487,500
Derived Royalty for All IP & IA (3)	8.4%

(1) Allocated income from Exhibit 13.18.
(2) Average revenues from Exhibit 13.15.
(3) Calculated as (1) divided by (2) representing the maximum royalty that should be paid to license all intellectual property and intangible assets of the company.

Royalty Rate for the Specific Patented Invention

The next step is to answer the question, How much of a royalty rate should be subtracted from the derived 8.4 percent royalty rate to isolate the portion that is attributable to only the subject patents? It must be remembered that the 8.4 percent rate is for all of the intangible assets and intellectual property possessed by Super PC Ltd., including use the subject patented invention.

The answer to this question has been estimated by focusing on a company that operates in a similar industry and has most of the same intangible assets as a typical personal computer company. However, the selected company must be one that does not possess or use the subject proprietary and patented inventions. The company selected should make and sell desktop personal computer systems. The company should possess a well known trademark, a distribution network, and an assembled workforce of trained and productive personnel. Companies such as Dell Computer, Gateway 2000, or Compaq can serve as a proxy for the rate of return earned on all intangible assets and intellectual property *other than* the patented invention. By duplicating the same analysis presented in Exhibits 13.12 through 13.19 for one of these surrogates we can isolate the amount of income to associate with all intangible assets and intellectual property except for the subject patent. When this analysis was concluded, the royalty rate to associate with everything other than the subject patent was 5 percent. The difference between this rate and the 8.4 percent is the royalty rate to associate with the subject patent is −3.4 percent, as shown in Exhibit 13.20.

Benefits of An Investment Rate of Return Analysis

An investment rate of return analysis enhances royalty rate determination models by:

1. Considering the investment risk associated with the business and industry environment in which the licensed technology will be used.

2. Reflecting specific commercialization factors associated with the licensed technology as embedded in forecasts associated with sales, production costs, and operating expenses.
3. Allowing for an investment return to be earned on the fixed assets used in the business.
4. Allowing for an investment return to be earned on the working capital assets used in the business.
5. Allowing for an investment return to be earned on the other intangible assets and intellectual property used in the business *other than* the subject patent.

DISCOUNTED CASH FLOW ANALYSIS

A variation of the investment rate of return analysis can also be used for royalty rate derivation. This alternate method makes use of a discounted cash flow analysis that converts a stream of expected cash flows into a present value. The conversion of expected cash flows is accomplished by using a discount rate reflecting the riskiness of the expected cash flows. In addition to the benefits just listed from using an investment rate of return analysis, the discounted cash flow analysis also reflects the:

• Time period during which economic benefits will be obtained.
• Timing of capital expenditure investments.
• Timing of working capital investments.
• Timing and amount of other investments in intellectual property and intangible assets not associated with the subject technology.

The basis of all value is cash. The net amount of cash flow thrown off by a business is central to corporate value. Net cash flow—also called free cash flow—is the amount of cash remaining after reinvestment in the business to sustain its continued viability. Net cash flow can be used for dividends, charity contributions, or diversification investments. Net cash flow is not needed to continue fueling the business. Aggregation of all future net cash flows derived from operating the business, modified with respect to the time value of money, represents the value of a business.

A basic net cash flow calculation is shown in Exhibit 13.21.

Sales represent the revenue dollars collected by the company from providing products or services to customers. Net sales are the amount of revenues that remain after discounts, returns, and refunds.

Manufacturing costs are the primary costs associated with making or providing the product or service. Included in this expense category are expenses associated with labor, raw materials, manufacturing plant costs, and all other expenses directly related to transforming raw materials into finished goods.

```
┌─────────────────────────────────────┐
│         Royalty Rate Associated      │
│         with all Intangible Assets   │
│         and Intellectual Property of │
│         Super PC Ltd. Including the   │
│     Foreign Hard Disk Reader Invention│
└─────────────────────────────────────┘
```

MINUS

```
┌─────────────────────────────────────┐
│         Royalty Rate Associated      │
│         with all Intangible Assets   │
│         and Intellectual Property of │
│      Surrogate Personal Computer      │
│        Companies Excluding the        │
│     Foreign Hard Disk Reader Invention│
└─────────────────────────────────────┘
```

EQUALS

```
┌─────────────────────────────────────┐
│      Royalty Rate Associated with the │
│     Foreign Hard Disk Reader Invention│
└─────────────────────────────────────┘
```

Exhibit 13.20   Super PC Ltd.—Royalty Rate for Patented Foreign Hard Disk Reader

Gross profit is the difference between net sales and manufacturing costs. The level of gross profits reflects manufacturing efficiencies and a general level of product profitability. It does not, however, reflect the ultimate commercial success of a product or service. Many other expenses important to commercial success are not accounted for at the gross profit level. Other expenses contributing to successful commercialization of a product include:

Research expenses associated with creating new products and enhancing old ones.

Marketing expenses required to motivate customers to purchase the products or service.

General overhead expenses required to provide basic corporate support for commercialization activities.

Selling expenses associated with salaries, commissions and other activities that keep product moving into the hands of customers.

Operating profits reflect the amount left over after nonmanufacturing expenses are subtracted from gross profits.

Income taxes are an expense of doing business and must be accounted for in valuing any business initiative.

Exhibit 13.21   Calculation of Net Cash Flow

NET SALES minus
MANUFACTURING COSTS equals
GROSS PROFITS

GROSS PROFITS minus
RESEARCH EXPENSES and
MARKETING EXPENSES and
GENERAL OVERHEAD EXPENSES and
ADMINISTRATION EXPENSES and
SELLING EXPENSES equal
OPERATING PROFITS

OPERATING PROFITS minus
INCOME TAXES equals
NET INCOME

NET INCOME plus
DEPRECIATION equals
GROSS CASH FLOW

GROSS CASH FLOW minus
ADDITIONS TO WORKING CAPITAL and
ADDITIONS TO FIXED PLANT INVESTMENT equals
NET CASH FLOW

Depreciation expense is calculated based on the remaining useful life of equipment that is purchased for business purposes. It is a noncash expense that allocates the original amount invested in fixed assets. Depreciation is calculated to account for the deterioration of fixed assets as they are used to produce, market, sell, deliver, and administer the process of generating sales. Depreciation accounts for the using up of assets. It is called a noncash expense because the cash associated with the expense was disbursed long ago, at the time that fixed assets were purchased and installed. The depreciation expense is subtracted before reaching operating profit so that income taxes will reflect depreciation as an expense of doing business.

Gross cash flow is calculated by adding the depreciation expense, previously subtracted to calculated operating income, back to the after tax income of the company. Gross cash flow represents the total amount of cash that the business generates each year.

Additions to working capital and additions to fixed plant investment are investments in the business required to fuel continued production capabilities.

Net cash flow is everything that remains of gross cash flow after accounting for the reinvestment in the business for fixed plant and working capital additions.

Value is derived from the net cash flows by converting the expected amounts into a present value using discount rates that reflect investment risk and time value of money as previously discussed in the investment rate of return section of this chapter.

Exhibit 13.22 Quiescent Corporation Discounted Cash Flow Analysis ($000s)

YEAR	1	2	3	4	5	6	7	8	9	10	11
Q Product Unit Sales (000s)	1,500	1,575	1,654	1,736	1,823	1,914	2,010	2,111	2,216	2,327	2,443
Q Product Price per unit	$100.00	$103.00	$106.09	$109.27	$112.55	$115.93	$119.41	$122.99	$126.68	$130.48	$134.39
Q Product Manufacturing Costs per unit	$60.00	$61.80	$63.65	$65.56	$67.53	$69.56	$71.64	$73.79	$76.01	$78.29	$80.63
Sales	150,000	162,225	175,446	189,745	205,209	221,934	240,022	259,583	280,739	303,620	328,365
Cost of Sales	90,000	97,335	105,268	113,847	123,126	133,160	144,013	155,750	168,444	182,172	197,019
Gross Profit	60,000	64,890	70,179	75,898	82,084	88,774	96,009	103,833	112,296	121,448	131,346
Gross Profit Margin	40.0%	40.0%	40.0%	40.0%	40.0%	40.0%	40.0%	40.0%	40.0%	40.0%	40.0%
Operating Expenses:											
General & Administrative	15,000	16,223	17,545	18,975	20,521	22,193	24,002	25,958	28,074	30,362	32,836
Research & Development	750	811	877	949	1,026	1,110	1,200	1,298	1,404	1,518	1,642
Marketing	12,000	12,978	14,036	15,180	16,417	17,755	19,202	20,767	22,459	24,290	26,269
Selling	25,500	27,578	29,826	32,257	34,886	37,729	40,804	44,129	47,726	51,615	55,822
Operating Profit	6,750	7,300	7,895	8,539	9,234	9,987	10,801	11,681	12,633	13,663	14,776
Operating Profit Margin	4.5%	4.5%	4.5%	4.5%	4.5%	4.5%	4.5%	4.5%	4.5%	4.5%	4.5%
Income Taxes	2,565	2,774	3,000	3,245	3,509	3,795	4,104	4,439	4,801	5,192	5,615
Net Income	4,185	4,526	4,895	5,294	5,725	6,192	6,697	7,242	7,833	8,471	9,161
Net Profit Margin	2.8%	2.8%	2.8%	2.8%	2.8%	2.8%	2.8%	2.8%	2.8%	2.8%	2.8%
Cash Flow Calculation:											
+ Depreciation	800	922	1,054	1,197	1,352	1,519	1,700	1,896	2,107	2,336	2,475
- Working Capital Additions	1,250	1,528	1,653	1,787	1,933	2,091	2,261	2,445	2,645	2,860	3,093
- Capital Expenditures	1,000	1,223	1,322	1,430	1,546	1,672	1,809	1,956	2,116	2,288	2,475
Net Cash Flow	2,735	2,698	2,975	3,274	3,598	3,948	4,327	4,737	5,180	5,659	6,068
Discount Factor 14%	0.937	0.822	0.721	0.633	0.555	0.487	0.427	0.375	0.329	0.288	2.366
Present Value of Net Cash Flow	2,563	2,218	2,145	2,071	1,997	1,922	1,848	1,774	1,702	1,631	14,359
Net Present Value	$34,230										

236

Quiescent Corporation Value

Consider the discounted cash flow analysis presented in Exhibits 13.22 through 13.25 as a simple example of using discounted cash flow analysis for royalty rate derivation.

Exhibit 13.22 represents the future net cash flows for Quiescent Corporation as it currently operates. The sales, expenses, and earnings for Quiescent Corporation reflect the commodity-like nature of the business. Product prices are under pressure of strong competition translating to low profitability. Strong competition also severely limits the opportunity for the company to achieve any substantial growth in the future. The present value calculation contained in Exhibit 13.22 shows a value for Quiescent at $34,230,000 using a discount rate of 14 percent. The calculation of the value of the company includes the present value of the net cash flows expected after year eleven. Constant growth, reflecting inflation and minimal volume growth into perpetuity, is reflected at 4 percent. This is captured in the final year discount rate factor used in year eleven. The $34 million value equals the aggregate value of all the assets of the company as previously depicted in Exhibit 13.8. This amount indicates that Quiescent Corp. has earned its required weighted average cost of capital and an excess present value of $34 million.

Quiescent Corporation is planning to embark on a major business initiative with the introduction of a new product using new technology. The technology will be licensed. Exhibit 13.23 represents the present value of the company, including the net cash flows from the existing operations of the company and the net cash flows from the new product initiative. Additional sales, manufacturing costs, and expenses are reflected, as are the additions to working capital and fixed assets required for the new product commercialization effort. The present value of the company increases to $69,999,000. The higher value reflects the added revenues and earnings of the new product at the higher profit margins of the new product. A comparison of Exhibits 13.22 and 13.23 shows that research, marketing, working capital additions, and fixed asset additions are all higher and by more than just a proportional share of the higher sales forecasts. This is especially true for the early years in the discounted cash flow analysis, because the new product initially does not contribute significant sales volume but definitely has expenses.

Investment risk is also expected to increase with the new product initiative and is reflected by using a higher discount rate. The higher rate represents the risk associated with failure of the new product initiative.

Quiescent Corporation Royalty Rate

What royalty rate should Quiescent pay for use of the new product technology? The answer is not found by using the 25 percent Rule previously discussed in Chapter 10. Exhibit 13.24 shows the same analysis as Exhibit

Exhibit 13.23 Quiescent Corporation—Discounted Cash Flow Analysis

YEAR	1	2	3	4	5	6	7	8	9	10	11
Q Product, Unit Sales (000s)	1,500	1,575	1,654	1,736	1,823	1,914	2,010	2,111	2,216	2,327	2,443
Q Product, Price per unit	$100.00	$103.00	$106.09	$109.27	$112.55	$115.93	$119.41	$122.99	$126.68	$130.48	$134.39
Q Product, Manufacturing Costs per unit	$60.00	$61.80	$63.65	$65.56	$67.53	$69.56	$71.64	$73.79	$76.01	$78.29	$80.63
New Product, Unit Sales (000s)	0	25	250	1,000	1,500	1,575	1,654	1,736	1,823	1,914	2,010
New Product, Price per unit	$0.00	$80.00	$80.00	$75.00	$50.00	$51.50	$53.05	$54.64	$56.28	$57.96	$59.70
New Product, Manufacturing Costs per unit	$0.00	$50.00	$51.50	$40.00	$21.00	$20.00	$20.60	$21.22	$21.85	$22.51	$23.19
Q Product, Sales	150,000	162,225	175,446	189,745	205,209	221,934	240,022	259,583	280,739	303,620	328,365
Q Product, Cost of Sales	90,000	97,335	105,268	113,847	123,126	133,160	144,013	155,750	168,444	182,172	197,019
Q Product, Gross Profit	60,000	64,890	70,179	75,898	82,084	88,774	96,009	103,833	112,296	121,448	131,346
Q Product, Gross Profit Margin	40.0%	40.0%	40.0%	40.0%	40.0%	40.0%	40.0%	40.0%	40.0%	40.0%	40.0%
New Product, Sales	0	2,000	20,000	75,000	75,000	81,113	87,723	94,873	102,605	110,967	120,011
New Product, Cost of Sales	0	1,250	12,875	40,000	31,500	31,500	34,067	36,844	39,846	43,094	46,606
New Product, Gross Profit	0	750	7,125	35,000	43,500	49,613	53,656	58,029	62,758	67,873	73,405
New Product, Gross Profit Margin	0.0%	37.5%	35.6%	46.7%	58.0%	61.2%	61.2%	61.2%	61.2%	61.2%	61.2%

Total Sales	150,000	164,225	195,446	264,745	280,209	303,047	327,745	354,456	383,344	414,587	448,376
Total Cost of Sales	90,000	98,585	118,143	153,847	154,626	164,660	178,080	192,594	208,290	225,266	243,625
Total Gross Profit	60,000	65,640	77,304	110,898	125,584	138,386	149,665	161,862	175,054	189,321	204,751
Total Gross Profit Margin	40.0%	40.0%	39.6%	41.9%	44.8%	45.7%	45.7%	45.7%	45.7%	45.7%	45.7%
Operating Expenses:											
General & Administrative	15,000	16,423	19,545	26,475	28,021	30,305	32,774	35,446	38,334	41,459	44,838
Research & Development	2,750	1,821	977	1,324	1,401	1,515	1,639	1,772	1,917	2,073	2,242
Marketing	12,000	19,138	20,636	21,180	22,417	24,244	26,220	28,356	30,668	33,167	35,870
Selling	25,500	27,918	33,226	45,007	47,636	51,518	55,717	60,258	65,169	70,480	76,224
Operating Profit	4,750	340	2,920	16,914	26,109	30,805	33,315	36,030	38,967	42,143	45,577
Operating Profit Margin	3.2%	0.2%	1.5%	6.4%	9.3%	10.2%	10.2%	10.2%	10.2%	10.2%	10.2%
Income Taxes	1,805	129	1,110	6,427	9,922	11,706	12,660	13,692	14,807	16,014	17,319
Net Income	2,945	211	1,810	10,486	16,188	19,099	20,655	22,339	24,159	26,128	28,258
Net Profit Margin	2.0%	0.1%	1.0%	5.5%	7.9%	8.6%	8.6%	8.6%	8.6%	8.6%	8.6%
Cash Flow Calculation:											
+ Depreciation	1,300	1,842	2,154	2,847	3,002	3,230	3,477	3,745	4,033	4,346	3,379
- Working Capital Additions	1,250	1,778	3,903	8,662	1,933	2,855	3,087	3,339	3,611	3,905	4,224
- Capital Expenditures	6,000	5,423	3,122	6,930	1,546	2,284	2,470	2,671	2,889	3,124	3,379
Net Cash Flow	(3,005)	(5,147)	(3,060)	(2,258)	15,710	17,191	18,576	20,073	21,693	23,445	24,034
Discount Factor 16%	0.92933	0.80115	0.69064	0.59538	0.51326	0.44247	0.38144	0.32882	0.28347	0.24437	1.62847
Present Value of Net Cash Flow	(2,793)	(4,124)	(2,113)	(1,345)	8,064	7,606	7,085	6,601	6,149	5,729	39,139
Net Present Value	**$69,999**										

Exhibit 13.24   Quiescent Corporation—Discounted Cash Flow Analysis

YEAR	1	2	3	4	5	6	7	8	9	10	11
Q Product, Unit Sales (000s)	1,500	1,575	1,654	1,736	1,823	1,914	2,010	2,111	2,216	2,327	2,443
Q Product, Price per unit	$100.00	$103.00	$106.09	$109.27	$112.55	$115.93	$119.41	$122.99	$126.68	$130.48	$134.39
Q Product, Manufacturing Costs per unit	$60.00	$61.80	$63.65	$65.56	$67.53	$69.56	$71.64	$73.79	$76.01	$78.29	$80.63
New Product, Unit Sales (000s)	0	25	250	1,000	1,500	1,575	1,654	1,736	1,823	1,914	2,010
New Product, Price per unit	$0.00	$80.00	$80.00	$75.00	$50.00	$51.50	$53.05	$54.64	$56.28	$57.96	$59.70
New Product, Manufacturing Costs per unit	$0.00	$50.00	$51.50	$40.00	$21.00	$20.00	$20.60	$21.22	$21.85	$22.51	$23.19
Q Product, Sales	150,000	162,225	175,446	189,745	205,209	221,934	240,022	259,583	280,739	303,620	328,365
Q Product, Cost of Sales	90,000	97,335	105,268	113,847	123,126	133,160	144,013	155,750	168,444	182,172	197,019
Q Product, Gross Profit	60,000	64,890	70,179	75,898	82,084	88,774	96,009	103,833	112,296	121,448	131,346
Q Product, Gross Profit Margin	40.0%	40.0%	40.0%	40.0%	40.0%	40.0%	40.0%	40.0%	40.0%	40.0%	40.0%
New Product, Sales	0	2,000	20,000	75,000	75,000	81,113	87,723	94,873	102,605	110,967	120,011
New Product, Cost of Sales	0	1,250	12,875	40,000	31,500	31,500	34,067	36,844	39,846	43,094	46,606
New Product, Gross Profit	0	750	7,125	35,000	43,500	49,613	53,656	58,029	62,758	67,873	73,405
New Product, Gross Profit Margin	0.0%	37.5%	35.6%	46.7%	58.0%	61.2%	61.2%	61.2%	61.2%	61.2%	61.2%
Total Sales	150,000	164,225	195,446	264,745	280,209	303,047	327,745	354,456	383,344	414,587	448,376
Total Cost of Sales	90,000	98,585	118,143	153,847	154,626	164,660	178,080	192,594	208,290	225,266	243,625

240

Total Gross Profit	60,000	65,640	77,304	110,898	125,584	138,386	149,665	161,862	175,054	189,321	204,751
Total Gross Profit Margin	40.0%	40.0%	39.6%	41.9%	44.8%	45.7%	45.7%	45.7%	45.7%	45.7%	45.7%
Operating Expenses:											
General & Administrative	15,000	16,423	19,545	26,475	28,021	30,305	32,774	35,446	38,334	41,459	44,838
Research & Development	2,750	1,821	977	1,324	1,401	1,515	1,639	1,772	1,917	2,073	2,242
Marketing	12,000	19,138	20,636	21,180	22,417	24,244	26,220	28,356	30,668	33,167	35,870
Selling	25,500	27,918	33,226	45,007	47,636	51,518	55,717	60,258	65,169	70,480	76,224
Royalty 15.0%	0	300	3,000	11,250	11,250	12,167	13,158	14,231	15,391	16,645	18,002
Operating Profit	4,750	40	(80)	5,664	14,859	18,638	20,157	21,799	23,576	25,498	27,576
Operating Profit Margin	3.2%	0.0%	0.0%	2.1%	5.3%	6.2%	6.2%	6.2%	6.2%	6.2%	6.2%
Income Taxes	1,805	15	(30)	2,152	5,647	7,082	7,660	8,284	8,959	9,689	10,479
Net Income	2,945	25	(50)	3,511	9,213	11,555	12,497	13,516	14,617	15,808	17,097
Net Profit Margin	2.0%	0.0%	0.0%	1.9%	4.5%	5.2%	5.2%	5.2%	5.2%	5.2%	5.2%
Cash Flow Calculation:											
+ Depreciation	1,300	1,842	2,154	2,847	3,002	3,230	3,477	3,745	4,033	4,346	3,379
- Working Capital Additions	1,250	1,778	3,903	8,662	1,933	2,855	3,087	3,339	3,611	3,905	4,224
- Capital Expenditures	6,000	5,423	3,122	6,930	1,546	2,284	2,470	2,671	2,889	3,124	3,379
Net Cash Flow	(3,005)	(5,333)	(4,920)	(9,233)	8,735	9,648	10,417	11,250	12,151	13,125	12,873
Discount Factor 16%	0.92933	0.80115	0.69064	0.59538	0.51326	0.44247	0.38144	0.32882	0.28347	0.24437	1.62847
Present Value of Net Cash Flow	(2,793)	(4,273)	(3,398)	(5,497)	4,484	4,269	3,974	3,699	3,444	3,207	20,964
Net Present Value	**$28,080**										

Exhibit 13.25   Quiescent Corporation—Discounted Cash Flow Analysis

YEAR	1	2	3	4	5	6	7	8	9	10	11
Q Product, Unit Sales (000s)	1,500	1,575	1,654	1,736	1,823	1,914	2,010	2,111	2,216	2,327	2,443
Q Product, Price per unit	$100.00	$103.00	$106.09	$109.27	$112.55	$115.93	$119.41	$122.99	$126.68	$130.48	$134.39
Q Product, Manufacturing Costs per unit	$60.00	$61.80	$63.65	$65.56	$67.53	$69.56	$71.64	$73.79	$76.01	$78.29	$80.63
New Product, Unit Sales (000s)	0	25	250	1,000	1,500	1,575	1,654	1,736	1,823	1,914	2,010
New Product, Price per unit	$0.00	$80.00	$80.00	$75.00	$50.00	$51.50	$53.05	$54.64	$56.28	$57.96	$59.70
New Product, Manufacturing Costs per unit	$0.00	$50.00	$51.50	$40.00	$21.00	$20.00	$20.60	$21.22	$21.85	$22.51	$23.19
Q Product, Sales	150,000	162,225	175,446	189,745	205,209	221,934	240,022	259,583	280,739	303,620	328,365
Q Product, Cost of Sales	90,000	97,335	105,268	113,847	123,126	133,160	144,013	155,750	168,444	182,172	197,019
Q Product, Gross Profit	60,000	64,890	70,179	75,898	82,084	88,774	96,009	103,833	112,296	121,448	131,346
Q Product, Gross Profit Margin	40.0%	40.0%	40.0%	40.0%	40.0%	40.0%	40.0%	40.0%	40.0%	40.0%	40.0%
New Product, Sales	0	2,000	20,000	75,000	75,000	81,113	87,723	94,873	102,605	110,967	120,011
New Product, Cost of Sales	0	1,250	12,875	40,000	31,500	31,500	34,067	36,844	39,846	43,094	46,606
New Product, Gross Profit	0	750	7,125	35,000	43,500	49,613	53,656	58,029	62,758	67,873	73,405
New Product, Gross Profit Margin	0.0%	37.5%	35.6%	46.7%	58.0%	61.2%	61.2%	61.2%	61.2%	61.2%	61.2%
Total Sales	150,000	164,225	195,446	264,745	280,209	303,047	327,745	354,456	383,344	414,587	448,376
Total Cost of Sales	90,000	98,585	118,143	153,847	164,626	164,660	178,080	192,594	208,290	225,266	243,625

Total Gross Profit	60,000	65,640	77,304	110,898	125,584	138,386	149,665	161,862	175,054	189,321	204,751
Total Gross Profit Margin	40.0%	40.0%	39.6%	41.9%	44.8%	45.7%	45.7%	45.7%	45.7%	45.7%	45.7%
Operating Expenses:											
General & Administrative	15,000	16,423	19,545	26,475	28,021	30,305	32,774	35,446	38,334	41,459	44,838
Research & Development	2,750	1,821	977	1,324	1,401	1,515	1,639	1,772	1,917	2,073	2,242
Marketing	12,000	19,138	20,636	21,180	22,417	24,244	26,220	28,356	30,668	33,167	35,870
Selling	25,500	27,918	33,226	45,007	47,636	51,518	55,717	60,258	65,169	70,480	76,224
Royalty 12.8%	0	256	2,560	9,599	9,599	10,382	11,228	12,143	13,133	14,203	15,361
Operating Profit	4,750	84	360	7,314	16,510	20,423	22,087	23,887	25,834	27,940	30,217
Operating Profit Margin	3.2%	0.1%	0.2%	2.8%	5.9%	6.7%	6.7%	6.7%	6.7%	6.7%	6.7%
Income Taxes	1,805	32	137	2,779	6,274	7,761	8,393	9,077	9,817	10,617	11,482
Net Income	2,945	52	223	4,535	10,236	12,662	13,694	14,810	16,017	17,323	18,734
Net Profit Margin	2.0%	0.0%	0.1%	2.4%	5.0%	5.7%	5.7%	5.7%	5.7%	5.7%	5.7%
Cash Flow Calculation:											
+ Depreciation	1,300	1,842	2,154	2,847	3,002	3,230	3,477	3,745	4,033	4,346	3,379
- Working Capital Additions	1,250	1,778	3,903	8,662	1,933	2,855	3,087	3,339	3,611	3,905	4,224
- Capital Expenditures	6,000	5,423	3,122	6,930	1,546	2,284	2,470	2,671	2,889	3,124	3,379
Net Cash Flow	(3,005)	(5,306)	(4,647)	(8,210)	9,759	10,754	11,614	12,545	13,551	14,639	14,511
Discount Factor 16%	0.92933	0.80115	0.69064	0.59538	0.51326	0.44247	0.38144	0.32882	0.28347	0.24437	1.62847
Present Value of Net Cash Flow	(2,793)	(4,251)	(3,209)	(4,888)	5,009	4,758	4,430	4,125	3,841	3,577	23,630
Net Present Value	**$34,230**										

Exhibit 13.26 Summary List of Technology Licenses Royalty Rates & Industry Risk

Licenser	Licensee	Product	Industry	Royalty Rate	Risk
Amgen, Inc.	Sloan-Kettering Cancer Center	Neupogen, cancer therapy	Pharmaceutical	3	Low
Belmac Corp.	Pharmacin Corp.	Erythromycin Antibody	Pharmaceutical	1	Low
Gamma Electronic Systems	Fuscan Laboratory	Psycho-acoustical Audio Tech	Recording Industry	3	Low
IGL Japan	Insituform Group Limited	Trenchless Pipe Rehabilitation	Construction	6	Low
Interline Resources Corp	Western India Group	Oil Refinery Process	Refinery	10	Low
International Systems & Tech.	New York Power Authority	Industrial Pipe Repair Process	Construction	5	Low
Lesnina, Yugoslavian	Snauwaert, Belgian	Tennis Racket Design	Entertainment	3	Low
Mattel	Disney	Lion King Character	Merchandise	10	Low
Stabilator AB, Swedish	Insituform Group Limited	Trenchless Pipe Rehabilitation	Construction	8	Low
Sylva Industries	Ovonic Battery Corp.	Consumer Battery Technology	Batteries	3.5	Low
Spectra-Physics Inc.	Patlex Corp.	Basic Laser Patents	Electronics	5	Low
Various Laboratories	Roche Molecular Systems	Polymerase Chain Reaction	Biotechnology	9	Low
Various Universities	Various manufacturers	Apparel	Novelty	7	Low
Anam Electrical Ind. Co.	Matsushita Electric	Video Tape Recorders	Electronics	3	Moderate
Bradley Pharmaceuticals	Upsher-Smith Laboratories	Lubrin, feminine hygiene	Medical	3	Moderate
Carver Holt Harvey Plastics	American Safety Closure Corp.	Plastic Tamper-Evident Closure	Packaging	5	Moderate
Cyro-Cell International	InstaCool Inc. NA	Blood plasma freezers	Medical	5	Moderate
Electrosource, Inc.	Tracor, Inc.	Coextrusion Lead Battery Tech.	Battery	4	Moderate
Future Medical Technologies	University of Maryland	Salmonella Detection	Agricultural	6	Moderate

Company	Technology/Product		Level
Galverbel SA	Research Frontiers, Inc.	Glass variable light tech	Glass	5	Moderate
Koala Corp.	A&B Booster Inc.	Children's booster seat	Home Furnishings	6	Moderate
Lucky-Goldstar Group	Sinar Mas Group	Polyvinyl Chloride Pipe	Construction	2.5	Moderate
Meridian Diagnostics Inc.	Disease Detection Int'l	Rapid Diagnostic Test Kits	Medical	6	Moderate
Olympus Optical Company	Symbol Technologies, Inc.	Bar Code Capture Products	Electronics	7.5	Moderate
Pfizer, Inc.	Water-Jel technologies	Burn Victim Treatment	Medical	5	Moderate
Sippican, Inc.	Fiberchem Inc.	Chemical Sensor Technology	Environmental	3	Moderate
Ssangyong Motor Co. of Korea	Mercedes Benz AG	Truck and Van Technology	Automotive	2	Moderate
WPS, Inc.	Wisconsin Public Service	Software System	Software for Utilities	10	Moderate
Biopharmaceutics Inc.	Cornell Research Foundation	Alzheimer's diagnostic	Biotechnology	5	High
Deprenyl Animal Health, Inc.	IVAX	Alzheimer Drug Treatment	Pharmaceutical	10	High
DuPont	Molecular Biosystems, Inc.	Nucleic Acid Probe Technologies	Biotechnology	4	High
Future Medical Technologies	Human Medical Laboratories	Microorganism Body Fluids Filter	Medical	3	High
Futurex Inc.	TRW Electronic Products	Communication Encryption	Communications	4	High
German Investors	Carrier Inc.	Bioptron lamp therapy	Medical	4	High
Hailey Energy	Langdon Medical Inc.	Cytology Device	Medical	9	High
Hauntrepreneurs	Haunted Hayrides	Hayride Franchises	Entertainment	10	High
Lasermedics, Inc.	CB Svendsen	Low energy laser	Medical	3	High
Mitsui Toastsu Chemicals	Southwall Technologies, Inc.	Transparent Thin Film Circuit	Electronic Materials	4	High
National Fire Coding Systems	PNF Industries	Fire Prevention Coating	Wood	10	High
Savyon Diagnostic	Devaron, Inc.	Rapid diagnostic test kits	Pharmaceutical	15	High
USSR Joint Venture	Energy Conversion Devices	Photovoltaic Solar Products	Energy	3	High

The information for this analysis was provided by Licensing Economics Review, Morristown, New Jersey.

13.23 but includes an expense line for royalties. Introduction of a 15 percent royalty rate is applied to the sales of the new product based on multiplying 25 percent times the 60 percent gross profit margin of the new product. The net present value of the entire company drops to $28 million. This value is less than the value of the company before it embarked on the new product initiative. This level of royalties diminished the value of the entire company. At this level the company would be better off not introducing the new product. A licenser getting this level of royalty would be getting compensation for the licensed technology and part of the value of the original company. The licenser would be overcompensated for the technology.

The highest amount of royalty Quiescent should be willing to pay for the licensed technology is shown in Exhibit 13.25. A royalty of 12.8 percent of the sales associated with the new product yields a present value of $34,230,000—the initial value of the company. At this royalty the company has earned a return on the additional investment required (at the higher discount rate) to commercialize the new product technology and not a penny more. A royalty rate of less than 12.8 percent would increase the value of the company.

CONCLUSION

Intellectual property value is without comparison. It is the central factor in the creation of business value. The enormous size of recent infringement damage awards is partial proof. Indications of a reasonable royalty for technology are available from a wide variety of analytical methods and models. Considering the importance of intellectual property, royalty rates based on industry norms and rules of thumb are not enough.

Part III

Intellectual Capital

14

A Model for Managing Intellectual Capital

Patrick H. Sullivan

The ICM Group

Leif Edvinsson

Skandia

INTRODUCTION

What is intellectual capital? Is it, as one company has defined it, "what walks out the door at the end of the business day"? Is it the people? A firm's know-how? Does it include Sony's know-how about miniaturization? Does it include Hewlett-Packard's know-how in identifying, manufacturing, and marketing hardware products so quickly that more than 40 percent of their sales comes from products less than two years old? Or Intel's ability to create and develop new, faster, and more productive computer chips?

Intellectual capital is a topic of increasing interest to firms that derive their profits from innovation and knowledge-intensive services. In many cases, these "knowledge firms" find that the marketplace values them at a price far higher than their balance sheets warrant. What is the true value of a company like Microsoft? It's more than the tangible assets; the company's value is in its intangible intellectual assets as well as its ability to convert those assets into revenues. The market premium for Microsoft and other knowledge companies is for the intellectual capital as well as the firm's ability to systematically leverage it. But, surprisingly, few managers in knowledge firms can define intellectual capital, what it is, where it resides in their firm, and how they manage it to produce the profits that so excite the market.

Definitions of intellectual capital are just now beginning to emerge as the interest in the topic spreads. Tom Stewart, author of *Fortune* magazine's series of articles on the subject says, "[It] is something you can't touch but which makes you rich." Larry Prusak, Ernst & Young's spokesperson on intellectual capital, defines it as "intellectual material that has been formalized, captured, and leveraged [to produce a higher-valued asset]." Mobil's Ted Lumley sees it as "knowledge used to increase economic order in the business process." Dow Chemical's Gordon Petrash defines intellectual capital as "knowledge with potential for value." And Hughes Space and Communications Company's Arian Ward believes that intellectual capital is fundamentally the sum of the company's "islands of knowledge" and that the challenge is to link and coordinate knowledge workers for the benefit of the firm.

These definitions seem to agree that intellectual capital is a stock of focused, organized information (knowledge) that the organization can use for some productive application. But the existence of a stock of intellectual capital is not enough to account for the high value the marketplace puts on many knowledge companies. Indeed, it is the ability of companies to *leverage* their intellectual capital that is perhaps a greater key to profitability. This was recognized early by Skandia of Sweden, where Leif Edvinsson, Director of Intellectual Capital, initially described intellectual capital as the sum of human capital and structural capital, including customer capital.

This chapter discusses managing and leveraging intellectual capital. It explains how intellectual capital is but one component of the value-creation machinery of a knowledge firm. It identifies the components and then describes how managing the firm's intellectual capital, in the context of the other parts of the value-generation equation, can be accomplished.

THE KNOWLEDGE FIRM

Companies that use their knowledge as a source of competitive advantage are called knowledge companies. Knowledge companies derive their profits from the commercialization of the knowledge created by their human resource— their employees. In some cases, knowledge companies differentiate themselves from the competition through their knowledge. Knowledge companies are found in many industries. In the product field they include computer companies and other high-technology firms, software companies, and manufacturers of new or differentiated products. Knowledge companies in the services industry include law firms, consulting firms, financial services firms, and media companies (newspaper, periodicals, television, and radio).

Knowledge companies contain two kinds of capital: intellectual and structural. Both have as their basis the human resource, the most dynamic of all of the components of a knowledge company for a long-term stability to the firm's revenue-generating capability. All firms have structural capital, and it is the structural capital, not the intellectual capital, that provides the most visible financial asset. Structural capital includes all of the firm's tangible balance-sheet assets. These assets include the infrastructure that provides support for the firm's intellectual capital and the complementary business assets that are so necessary to maximizing profits for the firm.

KNOWLEDGE

A discussion of intellectual capital is best understood if one has a clear understanding of *knowledge* in the business context. Business knowledge generally is of two kinds: that which is codified and that which is tacit. This distinction is very important strategically. Knowledge that is codified can be written down, transferred, and shared. Codified business knowledge is definable and can be protected by the legal system, whether as trade secrets, patents, copyrights, or semiconductor masks. If not protected by intellectual property law, codified information is often easy to imitate. In contrast, tacit knowledge, or know-how, is by nature difficult to describe. It can be demonstrated but rarely codified. Tacit knowledge gets transferred through demonstration and on-the-job training. Process knowledge, in manufacturing firms in particular, is often tacit. Relationship knowledge, often found in service firms, is also usually tacit. As with many things, the tacit knowledge position can be both an advantage and a disadvantage. Because it is difficult to transfer, tacit know-how is inherently protected. Once transferred, however, there are few means for the original owner to re-assert ownership.

Three other dimensions of knowledge are worth mentioning. The first is whether it is observable in use or not. Some technologies can be used without being observed by others. Process technology is often of that kind. Product technology is different; to sell it, you have to reveal it to others. A second dimension is the complexity or simplicity of the technology. And third we must note whether a technology can stand alone or whether it has value only when embedded in some kind of integrated system. Whether a technology is autonomous affects the way you manage its commercialization. Exhibit 14.1 summarizes the descriptive dimensions of knowledge.

There is a relationship between the degree of codification of knowledge and the amount of value it can be said to command. For example, there is a difference between *knowing about* something and *knowledge*. Knowing about involves having an awareness of a subject or pieces of information about it. Knowing about something is perhaps the first step in the creation of knowledge assets that can be leveraged. Knowledge, in contrast, implies a specific or delineated set of knowings. It tends to have a central focus or theme, and for this reason it is represented by the definition or codification that takes place just before an idea or innovation can be committed to pen and paper.

Once defined and described, on paper or on a blackboard, an idea be-

Exhibit 14.1   Types of Industrial Knowledge

	Tacit	Codified
Definition	Knowledge that is difficult to articulate and may be embedded in ways of doing things	Knowledge that is written down in some medium
Ownership	Ownership resides with the holder of the know-how; it is difficult to copy and/or transfer	Technology is easier to protect using the mechanism of the law, yet also easier to transfer
Examples	Experience Lore Group skills	Blueprints Code Formulae Computer Programs

comes useful. Its potential value is increased because it becomes available to others for improvement, refinement, and use. In fact, there is a relationship between the degree of codification of an idea and its relative value.

INTELLECTUAL CAPITAL

We define intellectual capital as knowledge that can be converted to value. This definition is very broad, encompassing inventions, ideas, general knowledge, designs, computer programs, data processes, and publications. It is not limited to technological innovations, or to just those forms of intellectual property identified by the law (including patents, trademarks, and trade secrets.) For the manager, intellectual capital (IC) has two major components: *human capital* and *intellectual assets*. The distinction between these two kinds of IC is of particular importance to owners of knowledge companies. Unlike human resources, which are not interchangeable and cannot be owned by shareholders, intellectual assets are and can be. For this reason, it is clearly to the advantage of the knowledge firm to transform the innovations produced by its human capital into intellectual assets to which the firm can assert rights of ownership. One major task of IC managers is to transform human capital assets into intellectual assets. To facilitate this transformation, it is important to understand the differences between human and intellectual assets.

Human Capital

The human capital of the firm may be defined as the capabilities of employees to solve customer problems. The firm-wide human capital resource is the know-how and institutional memory about topics of importance to the company. This resource includes the collective experience, skills, and general know-how of all of the firm's employees. It is a resource because it can generate value for the company, yet it would be difficult for the company to deliver this value without the employees themselves. For example, a law firm might count its staff of lawyers as its primary human capital. The lawyers appear in court and advise clients on legal matters. It is difficult to see how a law firm could provide such legal services to its clients without the carrier of skills, the lawyer.

Other companies use their human resources to create value, but not necessarily directly. A software company may use its programmers to create a new software program. The program, once codified, becomes an intellectual asset that is then reproduced, manufactured, and sold to customers. In this case, the human capital does not create value directly, as the lawyer does; he or she does it indirectly, by creating an intellectual asset that is subsequently manufactured and sold.

Gaining access to the power of a firm's human capital often means knowing what piece of information is relevant, which employee has it, and the speed with which it can be shared. Access to relevant information becomes more problematic as firms grow and become complex. When companies are small it is easy for everyone to know what information is relevant to a situation and how to gain access to the knowledge possessed by the human capital. As companies grow and the size of the human capital pool increases, such information is less widely shared and becomes more compartmentalized. In the days before re-engineering dramatically downsized the middle-management ranks, middle managers were often the most knowledgeable people in the firm about what was happening, what was relevant, and who had the relevant information or skill. Now middle managers are largely absent and firms are struggling to figure out who knows what. Technologies such as e-mail and the Internet facilitate the rapid exchange of information, but they do not help identify the relevant information and who has it.

One solution has been to create a set of yellow pages that directs the user to the people in the firm who know about particular topics of interest. The Swiss pharmaceutical company Hoffman LaRoche has developed a set of yellow pages that they call Rudi, named after an employee who was not important in the firm's hierarchy but nevertheless was the person people went to learn about how things really worked.

In an ideal world the corporation would evolve to possess some form of *collective intelligence*, a term coined by George Por, in which all members of the organization were aware of and had access to all of the relevant knowledge. In small groups this often occurs naturally. As groups increase in size, diversity, and number of locations, increasingly sophisticated information technology is often used to store and organize the firm's collective intelligence.

Intellectual Assets

Intellectual assets, the second component of IC, are the codified, tangible, or physical descriptions of specific knowledge to which the company can assert ownership rights and that they can readily trade in disembodied form. Any piece of knowledge that becomes defined, usually by being written down or input into a computer, qualifies as an intellectual asset and can be protected. Intellectual assets are the source of innovations that the firm commercializes. Exhibit 14.2 shows how parts of a firm's IC are made up of know-how (tactic knowledge) and intellectual assets (codified knowledge).

In firms that commercialize their intellectual assets, the production of such assets usually triggers a process that catalogues, lists, or somehow identifies them. Some subsequent process or activity is often used to determine which intellectual assets are to receive some form of investment and commercialization. In technology firms, intellectual assets are routinely reviewed with a view toward legally protecting those that meet some predetermined criteria.

Intellectual assets receiving legal protection become *intellectual property* (see Exhibit 14.3). Intellectual property law, the body of law that deals with the protection of intellectual assets, recognizes five forms of legal protection in the United States: patents, copyrights, trade secrets, trademarks, and semiconductor masks. For each form of protection, the nature and amount of protection available varies, as does the degree to which that protection applies to an innovation.

Intellectual assets, by definition, are potentially prosecutable through legal means. Indeed, regardless of whether formal legal protection is sought, they are usually protected by the trade secret provisions of the law. Not all

Exhibit 14.2   Two Components of Intellectual Capital

	Human Resources	Intellectual Assets
Definition	Knowledge and know-how that can be converted to value	Specific knowledge to which ownership can be asserted
Examples	• Experience • General Know-how • Skills • Creativity	• Technologies • Inventions • Processes • Data • Publications • Computer Programs
Repository	• People and organizational routines and procedures	• Tangible form (e.g. documents, CD ROM, etc.)
Protection Methods	• Umbrella agreements between employer and employee • Contracts	• Patents • Copyrights • Trade secret laws • Semiconductor masks

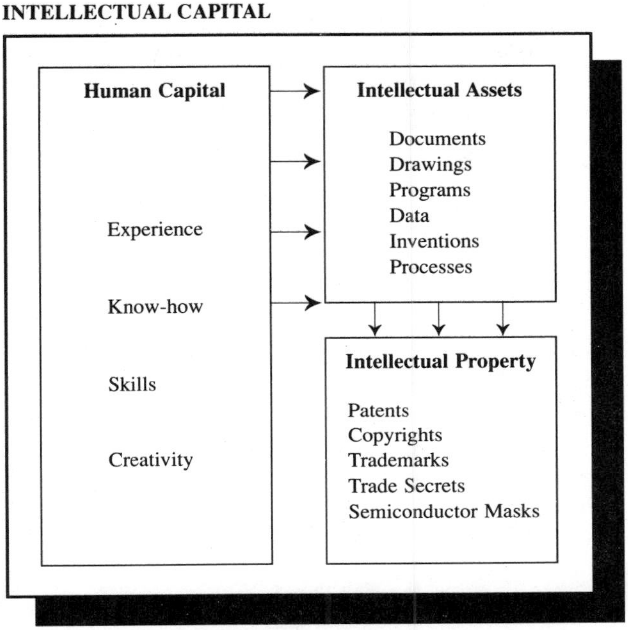

INTELLECTUAL CAPITAL

Exhibit 14.3   Relationships Among Elements of Intellectual Capital

intellectual assets will be legally protected by the firm. Nevertheless, both intellectual assets and intellectual properties are commercializable.

The transition between the three elements of intellectual capital are shown in Exhibit 14.3.

STRUCTURAL CAPITAL

Human capital by itself is of little value. Picture, for a moment, a group of skilled people, huddled together on a hillside, thinking great business thoughts. But without the supporting resources of a firm they have no ability to do anything with their ideas. They have no paper with which to write things down; there is no production staff or manufacturing facility; there is no telephone to call potential customers. In short, the human capital lacks the firm's supporting resources, called *structural capital*.

Structural capital is the support or infrastructure that firms provide to their human capital. It includes both direct and indirect support, and for each there are both physical and intangible elements. Direct support, which is the support that touches the human capital directly, includes both physical support such as computers, desks, and telephones, and intangible support such as information systems, computer software, work procedures, marketing plans and company know-how. Indirect support (which is the support that touches the people who touch the human capital) includes physical elements such as buildings, lights, electricity, and plumbing, and indirect elements such as strategic plans, payroll systems, costing structures, and supplier relationships. Indeed, structural capital provides the environment that encourages the human capital to create and leverage its knowledge. The structural capital is the part of the firm that remains when the human capital goes home.

In knowledge companies, structural capital should be designed to maximize intellectual output. For example, the physical surroundings of such firms should promote creative and productive thought. Their rooms should be designed for collaborative work, with whiteboards and easels easily at hand, with computers and enabling tools easily accessible, and with design rooms as well as conference rooms in abundance. In addition to hard supporting assets, structural capital also consists of soft assets—files of lessons learned, information on best industry practices, and business intelligence about customers' needs in new products and services.

Physical structural capital takes on different forms depending upon the firm and the industry. For example, in a prestigious law firm it may involve walnut-paneled offices, a library, and an extensive computer-assisted research system. In a think tank, it might include clean, well-lighted workrooms with throw rugs and comfortable chairs and lots of wall space to write on. It might include an operating budget that allows for attendance at creative conferences and sabbaticals for intellectual introspection and renewal. Structural capital allows the human capital to be all that it can be.

Intangible structural capital is in many ways even more important to the firm than its physical counterpart. The intangible elements include the firm's culture, history, and even that portion of the intellectual assets that relate to the management of the firm. Whereas the firm's human capital is normally thought of as the source of knowledge that becomes commercialized, other elements of intellectual capital determine the direction the company will take and its vision for the future; these include the firm's mission, its values, and its business objectives. Yet another component of intangible structural capital is the relationships the firm has with its customers, sometimes referred to as *customer capital*.

An interesting debate concerns the degree to which intellectual capital is embedded in the firm's structural capital. Indeed, it makes sense to say that a good portion of the intellectual capital of knowledge firms focuses on the administrative and business affairs of the firm rather than its product and service affairs. The results of the former's efforts are lodged with the structural capital and form a major portion of its intangible elements.

The debate most often arises when one attempts to draw the interface between intellectual and structural capital. Any ambiguity between structural and intellectual capital was largely resolved by Hughes' Arian Ward, who said that definitions are often confining and confusing. His preference is not to carefully define things, but rather to differentiate. In this spirit, the firm's structural capital should be considered to be the abode of the portion of its intellectual capital that relates to business and administrative activities.

COMPLEMENTARY BUSINESS ASSETS

Complementary business assets are assets of the firm that are used to create value in the commercialization process. Typically, for knowledge companies, the business assets of the firm complement the innovations developed by the firm's human capital. These complementary business assets typically include manufacturing facilities, distribution networks, customer lists, supplier networks, service forces, and organization capabilities. Complementary assets may be thought of as the string of assets through which the technology must be processed in order to reach the customer. Obvious complementary assets are manufacturing capabilities, warehousing capabilities, distribution networks, and sales outlets. Complementary assets could also be other complementary technologies, customer lists, trademarks, or customer relationships. No matter how exciting an intellectual asset itself may be, it will have little commercial value unless paired with the appropriate complementary assets.

There are two kinds of complementary assets. The first are business assets that are widely available—*generic complementary assets*. They can be bought or contracted for on the open market and may be used in commercializing a wide range of technology applications. The second kind, which offer more leverage, are called *specific complementary assets*. Suppose an inventor devised a unique product with large market appeal. If this product could be made using manufacturing equipment that is available in the marketplace, then its manufacture would involve the use of generic assets. If, however, the product required some manufacturing process or technique that was unique to the technology or the product's design, so that generic manufacturing equipment was not capable of producing it, then that specific manufacturing capability would be a specific complementary asset. A specific complementary business asset can be used strategically; it can be used as a barrier to competition; it can be licensed out as a source of income; it can be sold; it can be used to attract joint venture partners. Most important, it can be used to protect a technology from competitors when legal protection is either not desired or not available.

Specific complementary assets, then, are a source of value in addition to the value created by the innovation. The use of a business asset in the commercialization process adds value to the innovation on its way to the marketplace. It is this additional value that the owner of the complementary asset can capture and retain for him or herself. The value realized by the manufacturing process can be captured as profit by the owner of the manufacturing system, the value of distribution can be captured as profit by the owner of the distribution system, and so on. Where the business assets are unique to the innovation, their owners can charge a greater premium for the value they add to the innovation. Thus complementary business assets are also a source of hidden value; in fact, they provide a greater value to the firm than their book value as tangible assets.

Specific complementary assets are usually created in conjunction with the commercialization of a specific application of an intellectual asset. They are therefore unique, and they are often themselves protectable. In effect, controlling the specific complementary assets is equivalent to controlling the underlying intellectual asset and the ultimate commercial value of an intellectual asset. This has the advantage of protecting a technology without having to reveal the technology itself. Patenting does not provide this advantage.

AN IC MODEL OF THE KNOWLEDGE FIRM

With this definition of complementary assets, it is now possible to describe the knowledge firm more fully in terms that allow a contemplation of all the sources of value developed by its intellectual and structural capital. As Exhibit 14.4 shows, the intellectual capital of the firm has three major elements in its make-up: human capital, intellectual assets, and intellectual property. A knowledge company's intellectual capital is enabled by the firm's structural capital, which includes both tangible and intangible assets. Indeed, that portion of the firm's intellectual assets pertaining to business and administrative infrastructure may be viewed as an intangible element of the structural capital.

The firm's structural capital includes as part of its tangible assets the business assets that complement the innovations produced by the IC. These complementary business assets not only process, refine and bring innovations to market, they also add value and bring profits to the firm themselves.

SUMMARY

Past business lore held that three conditions were sufficient for success in the commercialization of an innovation. If the innovation met a market need, was legally protected, and could be brought to market before any competitors could respond, then large profits were not only possible but highly likely. However, many innovators acted on this maxim and did not achieve success.

Today, successful knowledge firms recognize that intellectual capital is a major source of value. A recent cover story in *Fortune* magazine discusses

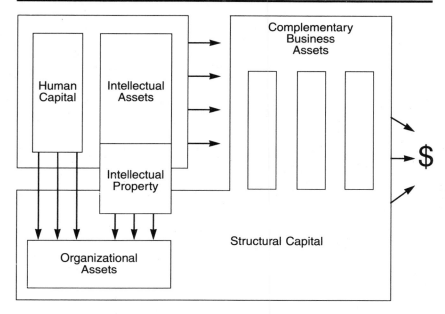

Exhibit 14.4   Model of the Knowledge Firm

this business asset. Firms that profit from their intellectual capital know that there is more to successful technology commercialization than meeting these three conditions. This chapter has focused on the infrastructure behind the first of these bits of lore: creating the innovation.

We have also learned that there are two major sources of value for knowledge firms. The first is the innovations created by the firm's human capital. These become company property when they are converted into intellectual assets, and when legally protected they become intellectual property. Innovations, when coupled with complementary business assets, the second major source of value for knowledge firms, are commercialized and make their way into the marketplace where they are sold as products or services.

The definitions and descriptions have made clear the relationship between human capital, intellectual assets, and intellectual property, and the desirability of converting innovations from the realm of human capital to that of intellectual assets should now be apparent.

GLOSSARY

Human Capital: Human capital is the organization's human element. It includes owners, employees, contractors, suppliers, and all other people who collectively bring to the firm their skills, know-how, and individual abilities.

It represents the capabilities of the firm to solve problems. Human capital is one of the major elements of an organization's intellectual capital.

Intangible Assets: An accounting term defined as: non-physical benefits that contribute to future cash flows. (The benefit has already been obtained or is owned by an entity which controls the access of others to it.)

Intellectual Assets: Intellectual assets are the codified, tangible, or physical descriptions of specific knowledge to which the organization may assert ownership rights. Intellectual assets are one of the major elements of an organization's intellectual capital.

Intellectual Capital: Knowledge that can be converted to value.

Intellectual Property: A legal term describing the intellectual assets for which legal protection has been obtained.

BIBLIOGRAPHY

Stewart, Thomas A. (1992). "Emergence of Intellectual Property Exploitation Strategies," *Licensing Economic Review*, July/August, p. 216.

Stewart, Thomas A. (1994). "Your Company's Most Valuable Asset: Intellectual Capital," *Fortune*, 3 October, p. 68–74.

Sullivan, Suzanne P. (1993). "Insights Into Commercializing Technology," *Les Nouvelles*, March, p. 30–35.

Teece, David J. (1986). "Profiting from Technological Innovation: Implications for Integration, Collaboration, and Licensing and Public Policy," *Research Policy* 15: 285–305.

15

Developing an Intellectual Capital Management Capability at Skandia

Leif Edvinsson

Skandia

Patrick H. Sullivan

The ICM Group

Intellectual Capital (IC) is receiving increasing attention as we move into what is coming to be called the "knowledge era". The importance of intellectual capital for knowledge-intensive companies may have historically been understated. For these firms the "hidden value" represented by their intellectual capital may be greater than the value of their financial assets. This value difference, initially explored by Professor Tobin in his series of articles on what is known as "Tobin's Q," is the difference between the market value of the firm and its book value. For knowledge companies this gap may be attributed to the firm's stock of intellectual capital. Valuing such firms through the normal financial measures is very much like measuring an iceberg by the mass it displays above water; there is a lot that isn't visible. Financial and managerial accounting both focus on the tip of the iceberg.

The ability to manage this hidden value requires that knowledge firms go beyond traditional methods. Standard accounting and financial reports are no longer adequate to provide measures of results. Traditional management methods and techniques do not necessarily apply. Indeed, the management of a knowledge firm's hidden value might be referred to as managing its not-visible assets. Such a negative definition, however, ignores the driving forces for the creation of value for the firm and the ability of that value to be converted into financial capital. The ability of knowledge firms to manage and improve their hidden value has in the past few years become known as intellectual capital management (ICM).

This chapter describes the efforts to develop an intellectual capital management capability at Skandia, Sweden's largest insurance company. It reports on some of the findings, definitions and perspectives developed by Skandia on its way to managing its intellectual capital.

INTELLECTUAL CAPITAL

Skandia, where Leif Edvinsson is Corporate Director of Intellectual Capital, has worked to define the importance of intellectual capital to the firm while developing effective ways of managing it. When Skandia began thinking about ICM, they could find very little in the literature to provide guidance. For this reason Skandia developed its own framework for understanding ICM so that it could begin managing what for many years had been perceived as the firm's hidden value—its intellectual capital.

Skandia recognized that managing this hidden value meant managing a series of invisible assets. Seeking to make these assets more visible, Skandia created a framework of its own to describe the major elements of hidden value it wished to manage. The firm developed a simple formula to describe its view of IC:

$$IC = \text{Human Capital} + \text{Structural Capital}$$

This definition emerged during the firm's development process when they conducted an inventory of their own hidden value in one of the company's most rapidly growing units, Skandia Assurance and Financial Services (AFS). The inventory, conducted in 1992, revealed that the firm had over fifty value-laden activities that were not relevantly accounted for in the accounting and financial systems. In order to create a capability for managing these activities, they devised a clear and simple set of dichotomous definitions. First, all hidden value activities relating to human beings were to be categorized as human capital issues. All others were to be defined as structural capital. Under this simple set of definitions, the human capital value-laden activities were those involving individual human beings and the capabilities they provided to Skandia for the achievement of its mission. Structural capital, by way of contrast, represented the firm's organizational capabilities for achieving its mission. Although with hindsight, the firm may find these definitions oversimplified, the framework proved to be very useful as a starting point.

THE IC CHALLENGE

As the firm further developed its thinking about IC and its management, it also uncovered several important insights:

- Human capital is not the only source of hidden value. There is also significant hidden value tied up in Skandia's structural capital.
- The firm doesn't own its human capital, whereas it does own the structural capital.
- The real core of value creation for Skandia is based on three sub-components of intellectual capital:
  (1) the innovativeness of the firm's human capital
  (2) the customer relationships the human capital has developed and institutionalized.
  (3) the company's infrastructure and its capabilities.

These insights led to several self-imposed challenges. The first challenge was how to convert much of the value in the firm's human capital (the capital the firm didn't own) into structural capital (the capital they did own). This led Skandia to research and understand knowledge creation and knowledge transfer. As a result of these efforts the company is now learning how to challenge its human capital as well as how to convert their innovations into structural capital.

The second challenge was how to combine both the human and structural capital hidden values so as to achieve new levels of hidden value for Skandia. Here the economist's concept of complementary assets was useful. It helped Skandia to understand that some portions of the structural capital actually complemented the innovations developed by the firm's human capital. These complementary business assets, related businesses, distribution channels, customer lists, et. al., when matched with specific innovations from the human capital often provided Skandia with additional or leveraged measures of hidden value.

The learning which emerged from Skandia's second challenge caused them to seek out and identify firm-unique combinations of human and structural capital that provide some unique or market-powerful capability that increases the firm's hidden value.

The third challenge was how to capitalize on Skandia's identification of the three core sub components of its IC. Although still developing and implementing new insights into how to manage this third challenge, Skandia has learned that leadership and vision are keys to success. Skandia created a special inquiry into the need for leadership in managing intellectual capital. It convened a group of IC pioneers, drawn from a diversity of backgrounds and interests, in Mill Valley, California, in 1994 to explore the meaning of "leadership" in an IC context. In a powerful several days of collective thinking, it became clear that in order for value to be created in knowledge company environments it is important that there be a set of explicit, clearly expressed organizational values to guide the collective efforts of the human capital. "Values" are different from "value". Whereas the first describes what is important and what creates meaning for the organization, the second is a measure of what is created within the context of the firms' values.

The importance of values, context, and value to the creation of new hidden value through intellectual capital created yet one more insight for Skandia. It allowed the firm to realize that although values and value creation are of fundamental concern to the firm's top-level management, it is at the same time unremarkable and invisible to the day-to-day management activity of the firm's middle managers. This insight has led Skandia to focus more of its management attention on developing linkages between these two management levels in order to better grasp the leverage that management can provide through a careful and pervasive explanation of the firm's context and values to Skandia's intellectual capital.

THE PARADOX OF INTELLECTUAL PROPERTY

The managers of any firm's intellectual property (intellectual assets that are legally protected, such as through patents and copyrights) inevitably use the legal system of rights as the point of reference. But how is this frame of reference related to the idea of value creation? Should the focus of the intellectual property manager be protection oriented or relationship oriented? The answer lies in the firms' business mentality, i.e., the value system. The role of intellectual property should be consistent with the business strategy as well as with the organization or the firm's structural capital. The paradox implicit in the management of a firm's intellectual property, however, begins with the notion that value creation and value-leveraging flourish with the release of innovation. The more that human and structural capital can be interconnected, linked, cycled, and recycled, the more value there is to release. But traditionally the management of intellectual property has focused on protecting the hidden value of the firm, or building fences around it. How can these two apparently conflicting concepts exist in the same organization at the same time? The new wave of IC managers will need to develop responses to this paradox in order to be successful.

CONCLUSIONS

The real bottom line for Skandia's long-term earnings and business sustainability is the need to focus on more than the financial dimensions of the business. Skandia uses its ICM model, called the Skandia Navigator, to develop indicators for navigating into the future. The indicators focus management attention on finances, customers, process employees and on renewal and further development. Skandia has found the most challenging of these is renewal and development because not only must they renew and develop but they must also develop new metrics to measure the degree to which their efforts are producing desirable results. This need to develop new metrics has placed Skandia in the forefront of companies working to develop new approaches to accounting that focus on the future, not the past. These new metrics focus on value creation and new ways for communicating about the employees, the customers and the shareholders.

Skandia is also creating a new stream of investments for the "soft" management areas, such as knowledge development, information technology, creation of strategic alliances and virtual businesses. Management of these newly defined activities is based on a set of newly defined values. Skandia's work over the past several years has produced a set of key insights which the firm believes it can summarize:

- Intellectual capital produces value through creating business applications from the innovations of the firm's human capital.
- Applications linking Skandia's human and structural capital are more powerful than applications arising from only one or the other form of capital.
- Intellectual capital management is about visualizing, releasing, linking, relinking, recycling and renewal.
- Intellectual property management is only one component of ICM.
- To be successful with ICM we must learn how to deal with the paradox between the need to release intellectual capital and the need to protect it.

Application of these insights has been powerful for Skandia. In the past five years Skandia's AFS has seen its sales increase tenfold. The IC component of Skandia's stock price and the productivity of its employees have both increased more than 300%. Imagine what would happen if principles such as those developed at Skandia were applied across the broad range of western industries. We believe the results of such an evolution could be staggering!

16

The Future of Intellectual Capital Management

Russell L. Parr

AUS Consulting and Intellectual Property Research Associates

Patrick H. Sullivan

The ICM Group

Society has evolved through a series of ages to arrive at where we are today, the age of information. Although the information age gets a lot of attention, information itself is not a primary creator of value. Knowledge underlies the creation of value, and the leveraging of knowledge is what allows society to progress both socially and technologically. We may more properly say that we have arrived at the age of knowledge and knowledge management.

Being successful through periods of transition requires a new perspective on old problems. Success in the future will have less to do with the value creators of the past, natural resources and geography, and more to do with innovations and knowledge, the stuff that is often miscategorized as *information*. We see around us companies, even countries, desperately working to produce new knowledge and innovations that can be commercialized and converted into value. This drive to innovate using intellectual capital has become a major activity in the world we live in. The creation, codification, and leveraging of knowledge is already a major economic force in society, and humankind's ability to create more useful knowledge and to leverage that use will eventually define its success.

We broadly define intellectual capital as knowledge that can be converted into profit. Intellectual capital has been described as having three major components: human capital, intellectual assets, and intellectual property. Human capital, or brain power, creates innovations and these, once written or codified, become intellectual assets. Some intellectual assets, usually those perceived to offer the greatest potential commercial value, are protected legally and become intellectual property. Firms commercialize intellectual property in any number of ways. They may out-license it, they may use it in conjunction with the assets of another firm in a joint venture, they may use it in negotiations to gain access to markets held by others through an alliance, or they may commercialize their innovations entirely by themselves.

This book is about licensing, which is one form of turning a firm's intellectual property into profits. But what about the way we will produce our innovations in the future? Will this change? Will the current pace of creating new intellectual assets and properties continue? Will it increase? Will approaches to the management and commercialization of intellectual capital change? Can we expect to see licensing continue as a major conversion mechanism for converting ideas into cash? In thinking about these questions we believe we have been able to see a few glimpses of the future. In this, our final chapter, we will present what we believe the future holds for the world of intellectual capital.

INTELLECTUAL CAPITAL CREATES CORPORATE VALUE

Rewards are already apparent for companies heavily involved in commercializing their intellectual capital. In a recent article, *Fortune* magazine developed a list of the companies it believed were creating the most Market Value Added (MVA). MVA asks whether a company has increased or diminished the capital entrusted to it by shareholders and lenders. It asks whether the enterprise has created wealth. MVA is calculated as the difference between the amount of capital invested and the market value of the cor-

Exhibit 16.1   Top Ten Value Creators

1995 Rank	The Top Wealth Creators	Market Value Added (millions)	Total Return to Investors (1984–94)
1	Coca-Cola	$60,846	28.9%
2	General Electric	$52,071	17.2%
3	Wal-Mart Stores	$34,996	25.1%
4	Merck	$31,467	25.1%
5	Microsoft	$29,904	51.9%
6	Procter & Gamble	$27,830	19.3%
7	Philip Morris	$27,338	23.7%
8	Johnson & Johnson	$24,699	22.4%
9	AT&T	$22,542	14.5%
10	Motorola	$21,068	22.8%

poration. If a company's MVA is less than all the capital that was put into it—if its MVA is negative—the company has wasted its capital. If the company's MVA is positive, its managers have created value. Exhibit 16.1 shows Fortune's list of the top ten MVA producers.

Nine out of the ten companies—the exception is Wal-Mart—are directly dependent upon intellectual property for their profits. Technological innovation dominates the future success of General Electric, Merck, Microsoft, Johnson & Johnson, AT&T, and Motorola. Trademarks set the stage for Coca-Cola, Procter & Gamble, and Philip Morris. These companies are on the list because they create, nurture, and manage their intellectual property very well.

Managers Are Now Driven By Intellectual Property.   Mergers were big news in the 1980s but there is a significant difference between what is driving the renewed interest in business combinations today. The biggest acquisition of all time was Kohlberg Kravis Roberts' $25 billion takeover of RJR Nabisco in 1989. This leveraged buyout had nothing to do with expanding market share or economies of scale. It had nothing to do with combining core competencies. It was a financial restructuring of a company comprised of valuable business units. The deal was based on swapping equity for debt, thus restructuring the risk of ownership. The future of acquisitions will be strategically based. In this new era of mergers and acquisitions, knowledge, technology, and intellectual capital will be the leveraging tools, not financing. The entertainment industry is an example of the new focus. It is going through a consolidation phase where the distributors of entertainment are combining with the creators of entertainment. The intellectual property of creation is being combined with the intangible asset of distribution. This combination was also behind the joint venture named DuPont-Merck. The drug development program of DuPont needed access to a distribution network and expertise in gaining FDA approvals. Merck needed new drug inventions—its research pipeline was running dry. The combination brought invention from one party and commercialization knowledge from the other. These combinations have little to do with financial restructuring. The coveted coin of the realm is intellectual capital.

Lack of Attention is Dangerous.   Use it or lose it. NASA has been considering the next generation of launch vehicles it will build to replace the aging and complex space shuttle. Once suggestion that initially met with excitement was a plan that would upgrade the Saturn V booster rockets that put the Apollo spacecraft into orbit for the moon. This plan was argued as being a simple and inexpensive solution for meeting many of the large payload launch requirements that are anticipated. Not only would this plan be less expensive, but because it was tested and used during the Apollo missions it was known and reliable.

Unfortunately, NASA no longer possesses the intellectual capital required to use the Saturn V. Drawings, tooling, and dies have been lost. Worse, the engineers and experts who knew the Saturn V launch system have moved on, retired, or died. The valuable intellectual capital the nation created to reach the moon is gone. The technology of only two decades ago is now lost. Intellectual capital is not permanent. Corporate managers should take note.

Leadership

The new business environment will place new challenges on leaders. Companies must learn to create, use, absorb, and nurture new knowledge from various sources. This will blur organizational lines of authority and will make former distinctions between companies, customers, suppliers, and competitors less clear. The fixed and immutable borders that used to define corporations will have to become permeable so that the firm's intellectual capital may create the most value from the knowledge it is now able to access.

During the past two decades corporate organizations have evolved in response to the importance of different elements of business activities. The value of employee education, training, productivity, and retention was recognized, and as a result personnel managers moved into essential corporate positions. Data processing managers, similarly, who once had been relegated to helping the accounting department manage accounts payable, receivable, and cash flow, have now become critical to all aspects of business operations. Their value to their firms has vaulted them into positions where they are now known as the Chief Information Officers.

The importance of intellectual property is even greater than ever. It can command premium product prices, reduce production costs, create new products and even new industries. Intellectual assets can allow a start-up company to dominate a market or can bring a one-time giant to its knees. Intellectual assets are at the heart of all modern business strategies.

Licensing managers will become Chief Intellectual Property officers and they will be central to all strategic initiatives of corporations. CIPOs will likely report directly to CEOs and many will sit on boards of directors.

A New Model for Knowledge Creation

We have a vision for knowledge creation. Because it is a vision it is incomplete and we cannot yet say how it will come to fruition. An earlier chapter in this book shows that the structure of intellectual capital has implications for how it is created and managed. In this model a firm's human capital (its employees) develops innovative ideas; when the ideas eventually are written down or drawn they become intellectual assets. When firms protect these intellectual assets the protected assets become intellectual property. In other words, the firm extracts value from its intellectual capital.

In our current management–employee environment, management styles range from paternal and controlling at the one end to leader-like and open on the other. Employee response to these managerial styles similarly varies from reluctant response to enthusiastic self-activation. The diagram in Exhibit 16.2 shows this relationship. It also shows the relationship between managerial philosophy and employee response, and characterizes the intellectual capital output.

We have identified several philosophies of management in Exhibit 16.2. The paternalistic manager believes that employees are childlike and must be treated as children. Managers with this philosophy are directive and controlling and employees often respond grudgingly. Theory Y Managers believe that employees are eager to work and need only tools and guidance in order to perform. Although managers see themselves in a superior–subordinate relationship, employees are self-actuated along directions prescribed by management. Under the stewardship management philosophy, managers see themselves as overseers of the firm's assets where employees are managerial partners as well as producers. Managers and employees share responsibility for results.

These three models of organizational behavior demonstrate an increasing sophistication as the dominance of management diminishes from one to the next. As employees are allowed to assume increasing responsibility for their focus and results, the need for managers diminishes.

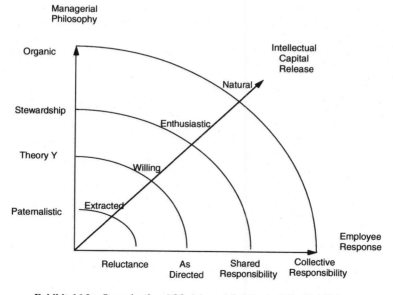

Exhibit 16.2   Organizational Models and Intellectual Capital Release

The ultimate in sophisticated management is the complete absence of managers. Firms that achieve this position find that all members of the organization know not only their roles and functions but also the roles and functions of all other employees and components of the firm. Knowledge is created spontaneously by employees and immediately sent to the location in the organization that needs it. Knowledge is also created spontaneously in response to a real or perceived need or opportunity for commercialization.

The Organic Organization. There are no managers in this organization. Every employee knows what is needed and when. The organization requires no leadership, no direction, no supervision. All of the employees understand and support the firm's vision, goals, and objectives. They individually and collectively operate in a manner that produces the desired results. Intellectual capital output in this case may be characterized as *natural*.

Organic organizations already exist, at least in spirit, although they may not operate exactly as described above. For example, shuttle astronaut crews operate organically. All members of the crew are highly trained specialists, with a complete understanding of their own work and that of their colleagues. Each is skilled and competent in his or her own role and can also fill in for anyone else in the crew. Each one knows what information or result is needed by the others and they work in a mutually supportive way to produce results before they are acquired. Unlike the firm model, shuttle crews do have a captain, whose role is largely to provide focus in emergencies and to communicate with organizations outside of the spacecraft.

Organic organizations are perhaps the ultimate in organizational sophistication. We have learned how to create such organizations already and have done so where the size of the organization is small, the goals and directions of the group are clearly defined, and the members of the group are highly trained and educated. As we move into the future, we believe that this kind of organization will become more prevalent, particularly in knowledge organizations. We believe it is a model to which firms engaged in intellectual capital commercialization can aspire.

The Paradox of Protection

The current practice of protecting innovations before commercializing them has its roots in the past. For millennia farmers have been protecting their crops and animals from marauders using a simple fence or a roving patrol. When craftmanship developed, masters protected their work by marking it distinctively, as a way of declaring to the world that the quality of the product could be identified with their names. With the age of exploration nations jealously guarded the wealth of their colonial empires. Spain restricted access to its rights to the riches of the new world. England licensed crown companies to be the sole extractors of profits from specific pieces of English territory. The Dutch formed the Dutch East India company to limit the access of others to the riches of the Spice Islands. For hundreds of years, nations, firms, and individuals have learned that limited access to resources was a way to protect their wealth and ensure profits.

Intellectual property, of course, has characteristics that differentiate it from physical property. Does limiting access to legally protected ideas make as much sense as the historical practice of limiting access to physical assets? Put another way, does limiting access protect innovations as surely as it does for physical assets?

Winston Churchill, in *The History of The English Speaking Peoples*, makes the case that the evolution of England as a great nation is fundamentally the story of the evolution of legal rights for its people. We discuss elsewhere in this book how intellectual assets are legally protected and become intellectual property. The owners of legally protected property have rights, including the right to prevent others from using the protected property commercially. The rights of ownership to intellectual property have dramatically increased in value over the past decade, driven largely by judicial actions in United States courts.

Knowledge is most useful to society when it is available to create new knowledge. Yet society, in an effort to encourage the creation of knowledge, has created a system that discourages its free and open dissemination. Some believe that our system of intellectual property protection can hardly be characterized as inhibiting the free and open dissemination of information. After all, they might say, just because some knowledge is copyrighted doesn't mean it isn't freely available. Indeed, they argue, the very existence of the copyright guarantees that it will can be published and distributed widely.

But knowledge moves rapidly. It ignores boundaries and limits. People seek out and find knowledge regardless of rules that govern its use or dissemination. Despite our copyright laws, the existence of ubiquitous and low-cost copying machinery has made rigorous enforcement of copyrights virtually impossible. Further, the Internet and its relatively free access to information makes our current protection system even more subject to abuse. And access to the ideas of others is the mother's milk of innovation. Albert Einstein, when asked how he conceived the theory of relativity, is reported to have responded that he stood on the shoulders of giants.

The very legal system that has increased the value of knowledge to the owner has, by that same act, limited its value to society by limiting free access. Under our current scheme of rights, however, opening up access to ideas would reduce the incentive innovators currently have to generate and develop new ideas and through the legal monopoly provided by patent law to profit from their use. Without for a moment suggesting that innovators should not profit from their ideas, we believe that there is a paradox implicit in our intellectual property system. While we applaud the protection and access to profits the current system provides to the innovators, we lament the loss to society of the stimulation lost by limited access to ideas that are protected.

Implications of The New World

What are the implications of this new world of knowledge? We believe that there are great implications for the human capital—the people who generate the innovative ideas that firms codify and convert into intellectual assets. We believe that the relationship between knowledge employees and companies will change dramatically. We also believe that there will be major implications for the nature and kind of reimbursement individual innovators can expect to receive from the use of their ideas in the marketplace. Finally, we believe that intellectual assets will be recognized as providing significant value to the firm. Firms will become much more active and skilled in developing profits from their intellectual assets, especially by avoiding litigation and establishing more business alliances for cross-licensing and profit sharing.

As firms become more aware of the value of their intellectual assets they will realize that they can exercise only limited control over the source of those assets, their human capital. We believe that companies will work harder to extract ideas from their human capital. So long as an idea remains inside the brain of an employee, the firm doesn't have real ownership rights, but the employee may. Firms must press to have ideas written, drawn, or otherwise codified, because until that takes place, the firm cannot assert rights of ownership. In some firms, particularly those where the employee–management relationship is or continues to be paternalistic or controlling, the human capital will find ways of distance itself from the firm and protect its rights to the innovations it creates for the firm. We believe groups of knowledge employees will form collectives or idea-producing companies to sell their ideas. In this view of the future, the human capital may separate itself from the rest of the firm in order to receive benefit for itself.

In other firms, those that want to be progressive with their human capital intact, their management style will evolve to become more organic and eventually reach a stage where the firm's human capital becomes the management, the employees, and the owners.

Litigation of intellectual property cases has increased over the past decade with the increase in the value of intellectual property. Indeed, IP law has become one of the fastest growing segments of the legal profession. Major law firms are opening IP practices, acquiring IP boutique firms, and seeking out law school graduates with an interest in IP law. The cost of litigation, of course, falls upon the clients. Businesses are realizing that litigation is very expensive, and further, that it may be avoidable. Large and sophisticated firms avoid litigation, choosing to litigate only those cases that they have a good chance of winning and finding ways of settling the others.

As the value of intellectual assets increases the possibility of disputes over the rights to income from those assets will also increase. We believe that firms will develop business strategies as alternatives to litigation in the resolution of disputes over intellectual property. They may, for example, take actions before disputes can arise by developing early business alliances with competitors in which innovations are cross-licensed and profits are shared. This strategy may reduce the firm's total expected income from an innovation but by avoiding litigation costs may allow for greater profits. After infringement has already taken place, firms may become more amenable to licensing the infringer and accepting payment for past infringement rather than face the cost of litigation. But whatever approach firms take, we believe that they will become more sophisticated in the management of their ownership rights and create business solutions that are less costly than litigation.

Summary and Conclusion

In this chapter we have offered our ideas about what the future may hold for intellectual capital and its management. As intellectual capital increases in value around the world, its management will continue to become increasingly important to firms. We believe that intellectual assets are the value-generators of the future and that the next century will bring significant changes in the laws affecting ownership and exploitation rights. We expect technology itself to be a major force in framing how access to information will occur, and thereby how the owners of rights to information and knowledge are compensated. Business will become much more sophisticated in their management of how the intellectual assets are created, improved, and brought to market, and also in their ability to minimize the litigation costs that today eat into profits.

We believe that licensing, as a mechanisms for extracting value from intellectual assets, is sucl a flexible mechanism that its use will increase dramatically. Further, we expect to see more firms engaging in out-licensing to extract increasing measures of value from their available intellectual assets. In short, we believe that licensing will become a bigger part of the firm's business strategy rather than primarily a legal activity. And we expect to see the creation of professional associations such as the Licensing Executives Society rise as the need for more and different of licensing activity becomes apparent.

Finally, we believe that the future of society will be in large measure determined by our collective ability to create innovative solutions to the problems of humankind. Although most of these solutions will be cultural, societal, political, and spiritual, some will be commercial. We commend the practice of intellectual capital management and licensing to the emerging generations of bright young people, who will find no greater challenge than that offered by this new and societally important field of endeavor.

Appendix

Recent Technology Transfers and Royalty Rates

As discussed in the main text, royalty rate negotiations can benefit from knowledge about the amount of royalty rate that others in different industries are getting for their technology transfers. To that end royalty rates are summarized in this appendix, covering different industries to provide examples and guidance for new licensing agreements. The licensing transactions are presented, categorized by industry and product type. The information shows that royalty payments in market transactions typically are based on a percentage of net sales. The information also shows that sometimes the royalty rate is a flat amount, and sometimes it changes over time or is tied to an aggregate amount of royalty payments. Sometimes license fees are high, low, or not part of the deal at all. Royalty rate agreement is limited only by the imagination of the negotiating parties.

The following information was obtained from *Licensing Economics Review*, 155 Gaither Drive, Moorestown, New Jersey 08057, a monthly journal dedicated to reporting the financial information associated with licensing transaction involving technology, trademarks, and copyrights. The information was obtained from sources that are considered to be reliable but no attempt has been made to verify the information. Users of this information should proceed accordingly. The information was derived from licenses occurring between November 1990 and July 1995, representing the most comprehensive compilation of the *Licensing Economics Review* data base.

AUTOMOTIVE

Mercedes Benz AG licenses technological know-how to Ssangyong Motor Company of Korea for use in manufacturing small trucks, vans, diesel engines, and transaxles. Ssangyong committed to invest $1 billion by 1996 to build the necessary manufacturing plants. Mercedes Benz will receive 80 million marks as a down payment and a running royalty of **2% of sales per unit**.

Hyundai Motor Co Ltd., of South Korea, started production of sub-compact Excel on a knock-down kit basis in Thailand. Hyundai will provide United Auto Sales, the largest car maker in Thailand, with auto parts to assemble 4,000 Excels in the first year of the agreement and 7,000 by the second year at its Bangchan plant. The Thai company will pay **$50 per unit in technology royalties**. Plans are to assemble 10,000 Excels a year beginning in 1995.

Editors' Note: South Korean vehicle manufacturers paid out $67 million in royalties in 1992, down 48 percent from $99 million in 1991. The Korea Automobile Manufacturers Association said Britain was the largest recipient of royalties, at $23 million, while Japan accounted for $16 million.

CHEMICALS

Churchill Technology Inc. signed a Supply License in the United Arab Emirates for the supply of the raw material to produce its revolutionary biodegradable plastic, "Vertix." The product will be sold at a price equal to or less than the lowest net price available to any licensee for the raw material of their required specifications, performance, and volume. On December 6, 1994, the company also sold a license for the territory of the UAE to Al Khobra Chemical Trading Est. of Dubai based on a Master License agreement by which territorial licenses to produce Vertix are priced by reference to per capital consumption of plastic. While the company acknowledges that the population of the UAE represents a limited opportunity, at 2 million, the deal still generated an **up-front license premium of $448,488 with an additional 4% ongoing royalty on sales**, which applies to domestic sales and exports that are not limited to the territories under license.

Fibercem Incorporated licensed its fiber optic chemical sensor technology to Sippican, Incorporated, for use in environmental markets in the areas of ocean, ground, and surface water detection and monitoring. Fibercem will also continue to market the technology in the same markets under its own label. Sippican agreed to pay a licensing fee of $25,000 and also agreed to pay an additional $500,000 for sensor research and development funding in three payments. In addition, Sippican agreed to pay a **5% royalty on its gross sales** of Fibercem developed products along with a **3% royalty on "accessory" products** that are made for use with a Fibercem sensor. Fibercem indicated that it will manufacture sensors for both its own product lines and that of the licensee. Sippican is a privately owned corporation located in Marion, Massachusetts, specializing in oceanographic instrumentation.

Editors' Note: The above reference to gross sales is atypical of royalty rate bases. Typically royalty rate bases are represented by net sales and not gross sales. Licensing agreement sections usually provide the definition of net sales as gross sales less discounts and product returns. Sometimes the definition includes subtraction of shipping expenses from the gross selling price, depending on the type of product and industry practices. In this instance gross sales were identified as the royalty base.

Interline Resources Corp. formed a joint venture company with Whelan Environmental Services, Ltd., of Birmingham, England, to construct a $2.2 million used oil re-refinery in Stoke, England. The used oil re-refinery, with a capacity to process 24,000 gallons of used oil per day, will be the first re-refinery in the United Kingdom. Interline will own 40 percent of the joint venture, called Interline UK, Ltd., and Interline Resources Corp. will receive a **royalty of 6 cents in U.S. currency per gallon of used oil processed by the re-refinery.** The joint venture will sell the processed used oil as a lubricating base oil or for other uses. Interline's construction division, Gagon Mechanical, will build the re-refinery at its Sandy, Utah, location and supervise installation of the plant at the site in Stoke. Whelan will contribute $750,000 to the joint venture and has already commenced site improvements at Stoke. The targeted completion date is August 1995.

The joint venture company was also appointed as Interline's marketing agent in the Netherlands, Belgium, Portugal, and Spain. As marketing agent, the joint venture will pursue licensing agreements for Interline with companies in those countries. The agreement includes the construction of one re-refinery, but leaves open the possibility of building additional plants in the United Kingdom. Interline licenses a proprietary technology for used oil re-refining and for cleaning contaminated hydrocarbons. Besides the end product of a lubricating base oil, the finished product can be sold as a diesel extender and a clean-burning industrial fuel, and the byproducts from the Interline re-refineries are environmentally safe. The first re-refinery utilizing this technology is being constructed in Dubai. The oil re-refining division of Interline has previously signed exclusive licensing agreements with Western India Group for 10 Middle Eastern and Far Eastern countries, and with Quaker State Resources for the United States, Canada, and Mexico.

Southwall Technologies, Inc., granted a license to product transparent conductive thin films and flexible circuit base materials using proprietary sputtering technology to Mitsui Toatsu Chemicals, Inc. The license agreement is an extension of an ongoing relationship between the two companies. Mitsui agreed to pay a $3.8 million fee for the license, which provides the company with exclusive manufacturing rights for certain electronic products in Japan. The license agreement also calls for the payment of annual royalties based on product sales. The royalty rate, in any calendar year, on products that are covered by the license is calculated on a sliding scale as follows: **5% on the first $5 million of sales; 4% on the next $5 million and 3% on any other sales in a calendar year.** Beginning in 1996 Mitsui will guarantee annual minimum royalty payments of $300,000 with the minimum amount escalating at a rate of 5% each year until the expiration date of the license agreement at the end of 2006.

COMMUNICATIONS

Amusements International Ltd., through its wholly owned subsidiary, 4D Sound Corp., has successfully concluded the company's first licensing agreement of its proprietary 4D Sound technology. Amusements International said under the five-year agreement, Soundelux agreed to sell 200 units in the first year, 350 units in the second, 500 units in the third, 650 units in the fourth and 1,000 units in the fifth year. The average retail price of each unit is about $10,000. Under the performance contract Amusements International will get a **10% royalty of gross sales of all products incorporating the audio technology**. Soundelux, an industry leader in the development and implementation of commercial audio for the motion picture and theme park/attraction industries, has been awarded the exclusive rights to manufacture, supply, and install 4D Sound technology to specific commercial audio applications. Soundelux may apply the 4D Sound technology to movie theaters, amusement rides and attractions, theme parks, arenas, hotels, and restaurants. The contract awards Soundelux the international territories of the United States, Asia, Australia, and South America. Royalties from each Soundelux project involving 4D Sound will be paid directly to 4D Sound Corp. Soundelux's recent movie Soundtrack and audio production credits include Oliver Stone's *Natural Born Killers*, Sylvester Stallone's *Cliffhanger*, and *The Crow*, by Mirimax, just to name a few. Recent audio credits for theme park attractions include Jaws, Backdraft, Earthquake, and the Kongfrontation attractions at Universal Studios; The Batman Stunt spectacular at three Six Flags Parks in the United States; and the Wayne's World attraction at two Paramount theme parks.

4D Sound (U.S. and International Patent Pending) technology shatters traditional audio concepts and accomplishes what the entertainment industry has been attempting to create over the past 50 years—full dimensional sound that is perfectly balanced no matter where you are in the room. Unlike surround products that use up to eight speakers to fill a room, 4D Sound can achieve full sound through a front and rear speaker technology. The company anticipates licensing agreements for multimedia computer applications, home theater and television speaker systems, car audio, and live performance speaker systems.

Amusements International Ltd. is a publicly traded company operating in the rapidly expanding international amusement and entertainment industries. Over the past decade the company has expanded its operations to include the development of water theme parks and themed attractions in North America, Asia, Europe, and Australia.

InterDigital Communications Corporation and its subsidiary, InterDigital Technology Corporation (InterDigital Technology), entered into a worldwide, royalty-bearing patent license agreement with Sanyo Electric Company, Ltd. Sanyo is a leading developer, manufacturer, and distributor of consumer electronic products including Time Division Multiple Access (TDMA)-based digital wireless telephones. Under the agreement, Sanyo will pay InterDigital Technology **$2.75 million** as a royalty advance and has agreed to pay a royalty on various types of digital wireless telephones including those built in accordance with the TDMA-based IS-54, GSM, PHS, and PDC standards. Sanyo will use the technology in its personal handy-phone system. A Japanese newspaper said that Sanyo is paying an advance of $2.75 million and a patent royalty of **$15 a phone**. Sanyo is one of many Japanese electronics makers gearing up for what is expected to be very tough competition in the personal handy-phone system market. Personal handy-phones are similar to cellular phones but lack their range. They require a dense network of relay stations that will make them an option mainly for urban dwellers. Their expected low price will cause the market to take off quickly, Japanese government and industry planners believe. Virtually all of Japan's major electronics makers plan to make the equipment, but the Sanyo spokesman said his company has an edge because it is the top maker of analog cordless telephones.

Network Computing Devices Inc. entered into an agreement with a major telecommunications provider to license various communication software products. NCD will be **paid minimum royalties of $15 million** over the next several years, subject to completion of the products and their acceptance by the telecommunications provider. Network Computing Devices, Inc., provides information-access solutions for client–server computing environments. NCD is the leading worldwide supplier of X Window System terminals, with a broad family of color and monochrome units, and PC-X server software products that integrate MicroSoft Windows- and DOS-based PCs into X/UNIX networks. The company's Z-Code Division supplies a family of cross-platform electronic mail and messaging software for open-systems environments.

CONSTRUCTION

Insituform of North America, Incorporated, reported that NuPipe International, a wholly owned subsidiary, signed an exclusive agreement to license a trenchless pipeline rehabilitation technology to Nordisk Rorrenovering AB of Sweden. American Underground Technology Limited, in Australia, will also receive an exclusive agreement to use the technology in Australia. The licensees paid an initial licensing fee that was undisclosed and each have agreed to pay royalties of **8% on new contract volume**, subject to a minimum royalty payment, throughout the life of the 20-year license agreement. The NuPipe process begins with a folded pipe manufactured from PVC, which is stored on a reel and heated at the installation sight. The heat makes the replacement pipe flexible so it can be inserted into an existing manhole and pulled into place. A special rounding device is inserted in the upstream end of the NuPipe and propelled by pressure to the termination point. The rounding device expands the NuPipe tightly against the walls of the host pipe. Rehabilitated systems achieve a strong, seamless, jointless, corrosive-resistant PVC pipe that is installed in an existing underground system without requiring excavation.

Insituform also completed an acquisition of Gelco Services, Inc., and various affiliated entities. The acquired companies are licensees of the Insituform® and NuPipe® processes in northern California and northern Nevada, Oregon, Washington, Idaho, British Columbia, Alaska, Hawaii, Guam, and portions of Montana. The acquisition was accomplished through the purchase of the shares of Gelco Services, Inc., Gelco NuPipe, Inc., GelTech Constructors, Inc., and MarTech Insituform Ltd., and related assets, for an aggregate purchase price of $18 million, $9 million of which was paid by Insituform in cash from its bank line and the remainder in notes. Jean-Paul Richard, ITI's President and Chief Executive Officer, stated, "The acquisition of Gelco, with its present management being maintained in place, will greatly contribute in increasing ITI's contracting skills as it pursues its strategy of becoming a major installer as well as licensor of its own technologies. Also, this acquisition allows ITI to achieve a greater control over the growth of Insituform and associated technologies over the entire western part of North America."

Lucky-Goldstar Group, of South Korea, signed a $10 million contract with Sinar Mas Group to make polyvinyl chloride products. A 50–50 joint venture was formed and will be called P. T. Sinar Lucky Plastics Industry. A plant will be built in Indonesia and will produce polyvinyl chloride pipe. The products will provide Indonesia with construction materials for water supply and sewage facilities. Lucky-Goldstar will provide the manufacturing, production, and facilities design technology. Sinar will pay a running royalty of **2.5% of net sales** over the next five years.

Total Containment Inc. reached a settlement regarding its patent covering, among other things, the retractability of its Enviroflex piping system. The company received an unfavorable decision from the U.S. Patent and Trademark Office relating to its and Exxon Corp.'s U.S. Patent No. 4,971,477. In a press release, however, the company said that it has reached a settlement of this action with Keith Osborne, an officer with Buffalo Environment Products Corp., a Total Containment competitor based in Maryland. The settlement provides for the granting of an exclusive worldwide license to Total Containment for the practice of any and all inventions covered by Osborne's patents, in exchange for Total Containment abandoning its rights to appeal the aforementioned decision. Osborne will retain rights similar to those granted to Total Containment. Osborne also is required to terminate his existing license with Ameron and Ameron's sublicensee, Environ. For the granting of this license, Total Containment will **pay Osborne $5.45**

million, $1.5 million of which will be in company stock. In addition, a **royalty of 3% on future sales** of Enviroflex systems will be paid. This royalty is similar to the 3% royalty that Total Containment currently pays Exxon. These royalties will be discontinued, as the patent is expected to be abandoned. Total Containment also said that it will advance $1.5 million to Osborne as a prepaid royalty. Total Containment said that the $5.45 million will be capitalized as a license under long-term assets of the company and amortized over 17 years from the date of issue of the related patent. Simultaneously, the Enviroflex patent carried on the books of the company at a value of $1 million after taxes will be written off in the fourth quarter.

Utilex Corporation and Dow Corning signed a definitive agreement under which Utilex became the exclusive licensee of the Dow Corning Cablecure technology. The cablecure process uses a proprietary method to treat and restore failing underground electric cables. Under terms of the agreement, Utilex paid $2 million in cash and will pay a royalty of **50 percent of the pretax profits from the sale of cablecure services**. Utilex also issued warrants to Dow Corning to purchase up to 353,846 additional shares of its common stock at an exercise price of $8.13 per share. The warrants will become exercisable if revenues from cablecure business reach certain milestones during the first eight years of the agreement. This agreement is unique because the running royalty payment is based on a split of profits rather than a percentage of revenues. This agreement adds another proprietary technology to the Cablecure repertoire of skills for renovating underground utility infrastructure possessed by Utilex. The company provides services for the replacement and renovation of underground utilities in the United States and Canada through a network of regional sales and services centers. It also conducts operations in Europe and Asia through its wholly owned subsidiary in the United Kingdom and through business associates throughout Europe and Japan.

Editors' Note: This agreement involves a royalty payment based on a percentage of pretax profits of the licensee. Such royalty arrangements are very rare because disputes can arise about the reasonableness of the expenses subtracted from revenues in reaching the profit royalty base.

CONSUMER GOODS

Koala Corporation entered into an agreement to acquire molds and related equipment used in manufacturing "Booster Buddy" booster seats currently manufactured and sold by A & B Booster, Inc., of Fort Myers, Florida. Koala also acquired a pending patent application related to the "Booster Buddy" booster seat, all rights related to the "Booster Buddy" trademark, and the goodwill related to the assets acquired. The purchase price was $35,000 cash plus royalties and warrants. Koala is obligated to pay a **royalty equal to 6**

percent of sales of booster seats during the next 36 months. Additionally, Koala is obligated to issue to the seller or its assigns, warrants to purchase 100 shares of common stock for each whole multiple of $10,000 of sales of "Booster Buddy" booster seats during the next 36 months. Such warrants are exercisable at $6.50 per share until January 1, 1998. The "Booster Buddy" seat is specially designed and engineered for use by children in movie theaters, auditoriums, and similar settings. The reversible design fits children from two to seven years old. Unique features include a convenient carrying handle, a cup holder, and   recessed candy/popcorn holder. Koala Corporation develops, designs, manufactures, and markets infant and child protection products for use in commercial, institutional, and recreational settings.

Phase-Out of America Inc. said it has agreed on a restructured licensing arrangement with Products and Patents Ltd. Based on a revised agreement, Phase-Out has acquired the Phase-Out Product patent together with the worldwide marketing and manufacturing rights in exchange for six million restricted shares of Phase-Out's common stock. Phase-Out said that the previous agreement provided for U.S. marketing and manufacturing rights exclusively. In addition, Phase-Out will make a royalty payment to Products and Patents of **$1.00 per product unit**. With this development, Phase-Out will change its name to Phase-Out International Inc. Five million of the Phase-Out shares received by P&P will be distributed to the P&P shareholders as a dividend. Phase-Out is a public company that has developed a patented smoking cessation product.

Workforce Systems Corp., the manufacturer for the Thaw Master meat thawing tray, and that Naturale Home Products Inc. received an initial order from Linens 'N Things for the thawing trays. The value of the order was not disclosed. Workforce Systems said that Naturale Home Products is the developer and marketer of the Thaw Master. Workforce said it owns a 15% stake in Naturale Home and receives a **royalty of from 30 cents to 50 cents on each Thaw Master** sold by Naturale in addition to the profit on the contract manufacturing.

ELECTRONICS

Atrix International, Inc. entered into a nonexclusive license agreement with American Innovations, Ltd., of Austin, Texas. The agreement grants American Innovations a nonexclusive license to make, use, or sell its licensed products under Atrix's patent for remote metering. In consideration for the license, American Innovations has agreed to pay Atrix a **5.5% royalty on all net sales** made by American, from the date they received notice until the expiration of the patent. Atrix President and Chief Executive officer, Steven D. Riedel, said, "This greatly enhances the validity of the patent and adds to the list of companies paying royalties for its use. The company has patent license agreements with Scientific Atlanta, Monitel Corporation, Interactive Technologies, Schulmberger, and now American Innovations. Currently, the company has two outstanding lawsuits against Landis and Gyr and Badger Meter regarding patent infringement and has notified numerous others of potential infringement."

Atrix is a leading edge manufacturer of remote metering and copy control products. The company is also a manufacturer of toner vacuums, vacuum filters, and printed circuit board transport cases for the office machinery industry. In addition, the company distributes tools, custom tool kits, and instrumentation for field service organizations throughout the world.

Aura Systems, Inc., licensed patented technology associated with high definition television technology (HDTV) to Daewoo Electronics Corporation, a Korean manufacturing giant. The specific technology licensed is called the Actuated Mirror Array (AMA) technology. Under terms of the agreement, Daewoo pays a royalty of **1.8% of its net selling price** of the display systems to Aura. The license agreement requires a minimum payment of $40 per unit for large-screen HDTV systems selling for $2,000 or more. For HDTV systems that sell for less than $2,000, the 1.8% royalty applies without the $40 per unit minimum.

Gamma Electronic Systems Incorporated signed a license agreement with Fusan Laboratory Incorporated for the exclusive distribution rights to B.A.S.E. audio technology, a patented system using a psychoacoustical technique that brings a natural sonic ambiance to audio material. It has a wide range of applications in professional recording studios, broadcasting stations, film sound tracks, and consumer audio playback systems. The terms of the agreement include up-front licensing fees, minimum annual performance criteria, and a minimum of **3% royalty on sales**. The B.A.S.E. system has been used on movie productions including *The Hunt for Red October*, *Total Recall*, and *Star Trek V*.

IBM received royalties from dozens of Taiwanese companies that pay a royalty rate of **3% of sales** for AT and XT clones that are sold in the United States. The royalty rate for sales of clones that are sold outside of the United States is 2% of sales.

MTC Electronic Technologies Company, Ltd., acquired all rights to an AC-DC voltage converter with isolation capabilities. The converter was designed to be configured as an integrated circuit device and is composed of discrete electronic components. MTC acquired its exclusive worldwide rights to the converter through a 70% owned subsidiary, which simultaneously sold rights for the converter to MTC in exchange for royalties equal to **6% of the net sales** of the converter. The remaining 30% of the worldwide rights is owned by the engineers who designed the converter. The converter device is designed to perform the functions of a traditional power transformer as well as to convert voltage from AC to DC. Traditional power transformers are inefficient, heavy, and costly. Two power transformers are traditionally employed in electronic devices with one used to step voltages up and down while the other is used for isolation. The converter accomplishes both tasks. In addition to being smaller and saving on space and weight, the converter is designed to be more efficient. The commercial status of the product is embryonic. The company has not done customer-based testing, nor has it finalized productions plans nor completed any market research.

Ovonic Battery Company, Inc., entered into license agreements involving its battery technology. The company has granted Sylva Industries, Ltd., a division of Gold Peak Industries of Hong Kong, a nonexclusive license to make small consumer batteries in Hong Kong, Singapore, Taiwan, The People's Republic of China, Malaysia, and Indonesia. The license also allows Sylva to use and sell the consumer batteries worldwide. The agreement requires Sylva to pay Ovonic an initial payment of $1 million. In addition, Sylva will pay running **royalties of 3.5% of net sales** until five years after the expiration of an improvement period and 2.0% of net sales thereafter for the remainder of the license. Ovonic Battery Company, Inc., is a subsidiary of Energy Conversion Devices, Inc. Ovonic batteries, unlike conventional batteries, contain no toxic materials and have over twice the energy of nickel cadmium (NiCd). The batteries also can be made in any size ranging from button cells to batteries for energy storage at utilities. In addition, the batteries do not have a memory effect. The battery technology of Ovonic is based on nickel metal hybrid technology. Some of the companies around the world that are converting to this new technology include Varta Batterie A. G., Gates Energy Products, Hitachi Maxell, Ltd., and Sovlux. The company has also formed joint ventures with entities in the USSR and India.

Research Frontiers Inc. entered into a license agreement with Sanyo Electric Co., Ltd., of Japan. The license agreement gives Sanyo the nonexclusive right to manufacture and sell flat displays worldwide using Research Frontiers' patented suspended particle device technology. Sanyo will repay Research Frontiers a **royalty of 5 percent of net sales** of licensed products.

Sony and Phillips receive a **3 cent** royalty for each compact disk (CD) sold around the world. The royalty was initially negotiated in 1982 and it is indexed for inflation in many countries. Some manufacturers in some countries still pay the initial amount of 3 cents.

Symbol Technologies Inc. formed a joint venture with Olympus Optical Company Ltd. to sell and support bar-code data capture products in Asia. The joint venture will be called Olympus Symbol Inc. and will be financed on an equal basis by both partners. Symbol Technologies Inc. will receive a **10% royalty on revenues** from the venture in addition to its equity ownership stake. After five years of operation the royalty rate will drop to 7.5%. Symbol Technologies Inc. has also licensed its one-piece integrated laser scanning terminal for reading bar codes and collecting data to Electromagnetic Systems Inc. for a **royalty on sales of 7.5%**.

Editors' Note: Texas Instruments has earned more than $900 million in *royalties from technology licenses in less than ten years. In fact, the licensing operations of TI are more profitable than its core business, which is subject to the extreme competitive pressures found in the electronics industry.*

IBM earned more than $500 million from patent royalties in 1994, a jump of more than 42% from the $350 million earned in 1993. IBM has portfolio of about 30,000 worldwide patents, including 10,000 in the United States.

ENTERTAINMENT

ACTV Inc. agreed to grant an exclusive license to Greenwich Entertainment Group for "Amazing Space" interactive children's theaters. ACTV owns the concept of the theaters. In a press release, ACTV said it will receive an **8% royalty** of admission fees to the theaters for the first $1 million of revenue per theater and a **10% royalty** on amounts more than $1 million per theater. ACTV also will receive a guaranteed minimum royalty payment of $200,000 in 1996, $500,000 in 1997, $1 million in 1998, $1.25 million in 1999 and $1.5 million in 2000 and each year thereafter. The company said it also acquired a "small stake" in Greenwich Entertainment.

Greenwich Entertainment, based in Greenwich, Connecticut, will open the first Amazing Space complex this fall in the Mall of America in Minneapolis and plans to form a national chain. The chain will incorporate themed educational exhibits and play areas with interactive learning. According to William Eberle, Chairman of Greenwich Entertainment Group, "Our concept is to create an area within the mall environment which is fun and educational for children and their parents. The key elements in these play areas will be a 30-minute movie which will match the theme of our exhibits in the play area and will be individualized for children utilizing ACTV's software. The design of the play area within 'The Amazing Space' will conceptually mirror a museum. Children will gravitate to distinct exhibits or pods, and play and learn within them. Unlike other children's play areas, parents will be able to participate with their children in exploring. 'The Amazing Space,' will also have a separate area from which to watch their children as they explore the exhibits."

Advancing Gaming Technology Inc. (AGTI) signed an exclusive ten-year licensing agreement with Dyerling Ventures Limited for the United Kingdom, Ireland, and South America. Dyerling is directly affiliated with a network of established contract suppliers of bingo and casino products to gaming operations throughout the United Kingdom and South America. The exclusive licensing agreement calls for AGTI to supply electronic bingo systems, including hardware and software, for sale and distribution by Dyerling in its licensed territories. Dyerling will pay a one-time **licensing fee of USD $750,000 plus an ongoing royalty payment of 10% of the gross revenues earned from the products and 30% of the gross profit earned from the**

products in the licensed territories. In ratifying the agreement, AGTI has received the initial down payment of USD $150,000, with the remainder to be paid within four months of initial shipment of product to each market. Preliminary arrangements have been made with a major leasing firm to support financing for the manufacture and supply of equipment to these new markets. Details of this arrangement will be announced subsequent to completing the transaction.

The average attendance at the 1,000 bingo clubs is 5,000 people each week per hall, or approximately 260 million bingo players per year. AGTI anticipates, based on U.S. experience, that roughly 20% of bingo players from the 1,000 bingo clubs will participate in electronic bingo. The company expects to supply Dyerling in excess of 140 electronic bingo units per hall for a total of 140,000 units during the first three years of the license agreement. AGTI will receive a net minimum fee per unit of USD $0.80 per day. Once these 140,000 units are placed and operating on a daily basis, AGTI could derive USD $110,000 per day or USD $40.5 million per year.

Bingo is a popular and widely accepted form of gaming in the United Kingdom, Ireland, and South America. Total bingo industry revenues for the United Kingdom and Ireland are higher than in the United States. Bingo is presently played using the traditional paper and marker format in most areas. Through electronic bingo systems, AGTI participates in a profit-building capacity in a noncompetitive business environment. Advanced Gaming Technology Inc. designs, manufactures, markets, and services patented and proprietary gaming systems, including technologically advanced electronic bingo systems. The company is a major supplier of electronic gaming systems, offering increased play potential and revenue to gaming operations.

FIRE RETARDANTS

United Fire Technology, Inc., entered into a license agreement with Yuanchen, Inc., for the Far East Territories of Taiwan, Hong Kong, Thailand, Indonesia, Malaysia, the Phillipines, and Singapore regarding its fire retardants. Yuanchen, Inc., whose clients include governmental agencies and multinational industrial corporations, projects the first product sales in Taiwan, where the city of Taipei recently experienced a devastating fire, killing 68 people and destroying over a half a billion dollars in property. Yuanchen, Inc., projects the Far East market to substantially exceed one billion dollars in the next ten years.

The License Agreement provides for a **$500,000 set-up, training, and license fee**, with an initial order of raw materials of a minimum of $500,000. UFTC will earn a **3% royalty on all retail sales** within the Territories. It is anticipated that the fire retardant products will become mandatory for all commercial business including hotels, nightclubs, and retail outlets. UFTC products include environmentally safe fire extinguishing products, substantially superior to current products, for all four classes of fire.

Recent tests proved the extinguishing products to be over ten times more effective than current products. The fire retardant formulations will fireproof fabrics to over 2000 degrees(F)—a cigarette burns at 400 degrees(F).

FOOD

Advanced Oxygen Technologies Inc. entered into a agreement with W. R. Grace & Co. to sell its proprietary oxygen control technology. The deal calls for $335,000 in cash and a **2.0% royalty** for the next 12 years on sales of products incorporating the company's technology. Advanced Oxygen Technologies said that it expects most of Grace's near term will be focused in the area of oxygen scavenging for food and beverage packaging. This technology removes residual oxygen from packages, contributing to overall freshness of food and beverages, the company said. Specific applications include crowns and closures for bottled foods and beverages, bag-in-box fitments and bags, plastic films and coatings for cans, and aseptic packages. The company said that following the sale its only material assets will be its status as a publicly held corporate shell and its net operating loss carryforward, which approximated $22 million on June 30, 1994.

AquaSciences International exclusively licensed its in-store bottle water purification vending systems to Critical Industries Inc. Critical will promote, market, install, and service the AquaNatural Systems. AquaSciences receives a **2 cent per gallon royalty** for each gallon sold, a percentage of sales on products, and a percentage of licensing and royalty revenues internationally over the 20 year duration of the license agreement. AquaSciences also said that it would continue its ongoing research and development of water purification technologies, and that its marketing plan calls for the installation of about 2,800 systems in the United States during the first three years. It estimates that this would result in the sale of over 100 million gallons by the third year of the agreement. Plans include licensing of the AquaNatural System internationally with concentration on Europe and Mexico.

Golden Valley Microwave Foods Incorporated signed a licensing agreement that settled an outstanding patent infringement case with Hunt-Wesson Incorporated, a wholly owned subsidiary of Conagra Incorporated. The license covers the use of Golden Valley's patented microwave popcorn packaging technologies. Under terms of the agreement, Golden Valley immediately began to receive a cash **royalty of one cent on each bag of microwave popcorn** sold by Hunt-Wesson, including its Orville Redenbacher's brand. Payments will be split between Golden Valley and its original licensee, General Mills Incorporated. Golden Valley's portion of the cash royalties are expected to exceed $2 million on an annual basis.

Vitafort International Corporation designs nutritionally enhanced food and beverage products and then plans manufacturing and marketing systems for the new products. Vitafort has licensed the technology associated with a new line of eggs with increased polyunsaturated fats to Nulaid Food Inc. Vitafort will receive a **royalty of $0.05 per carton of a dozen eggs and $0.01 per pound on sales of egg byproducts**.

GLASS

Eftek Corp. completed an agreement for Allwaste Recycling Inc. to license recycling technology owned by Eftek's International Cullet Exchange Inc. unit. Eftek said in a press release that the license involves the unit's "three-mix" mixed-color cullet for commercial production of amber and other colored glass containers. Under the agreement, Allwaste has exclusive rights to license the technology to existing North American glass container manufacturers and others. The agreement runs for at least two years with renewal considerations. Eftek said it would get a "substantial" share is sublicensing fees and a **royalty fee of $5 a ton** on three-mix cullet either sold by Allwaste or bought by manufacturers licensed by Allwaste to use the technology.

Research Frontiers, Inc. signed an option license agreement with Glaverbel SA. The agreement gives Glaverbel, one of Europe's largest flat glass manufacturers, an option to enter into a license agreement to manufacture and sell, in Europe, Research Frontier's technology covering automotive glass windows (including sunroofs) for nonmilitary transportation vehicles that use variable light transmission technology, also called smart windows. If the option is exercised Glaverbel will pay a **royalty of 5% of net sales of licensed products** and a minimum royalty of $150,000 each year. The option fee is costing Glaverbel $90,000. If the license goes into effect Glaverbel will also receive an option to extend the territory covered by the licenses to include all countries except Korea. If the expanded territory is licensed, the minimum annual royalty increases to $250,000 through 1995 and then increases to $375,000 thereafter.

MEDICAL

Amgen, Inc. made a lump-sum payment to Memorial Sloan-Kettering Cancer Center to reduce future royalties associated with U.S. sales of Neupogen, a drug that boosts production of white blood cells for chemotherapy patients. Amgen announced that the payment will require the company to take a one-time after-tax charge during the current quarter of $46 million. The original agreement with Sloan-Kettering had Amgen paying 5% of sales on the first

$100 million of U.S. sales, 6% on sales over $100 million to $250 million, and 7% on sales over $250 million. The new agreement provides for a **3% royalty payment only in years when sales exceed $350 million**.

Aprogenex Inc. amended the U.S. license agreement of its prenatal genetic abnormalities test product, GenSite, with Dianon Systems Inc. The amendment changes the pricing terms for future sales to Dianon to **$35 per test before Food & Drug Administration approval and $60 per test after FDA approval**. The original agreement, from June, 1993, priced the tests at $10 plus a royalty fee before FDA approval and $20 after approval. The amendment also changed the period of Dianon's exclusive license to four years beginning after a certain milestone is reached or FDA approval. Originally, Dianon's exclusive license was for four years after a certain date.

BioSpecifics Technologies Corp. entered into a license and supply agreement with a Swiss pharmaceutical company, Solco Basel AG, to sell Collagenase ointment. The contract grants Solco the exclusive right to sell Collagenase ointment in a number of countries, particularly Switzerland, Austria, all countries of the former USSR and Middle Eastern countries such as Saudi Arabia, Egypt, and Jordan. Solco is a well-established firm in these areas and has a highly developed sales operation. Solco is focused on the wound-healing market and the addition of Collagenase ointment represents an important expansion of its product line. The contract specifies an up-front payment of **$150,000 and a payment of $15,000 per licensed country** upon receipt of government approval and authorization to market Collagenase ointment, totaling an additional $150,000. Besides buying Collagenase ABC powder, the active ingredient used to make Collagenase ointment, Solco will pay BioSpecifics a royalty on sales of Collagenase ointment. Solco will also bear all governmental fees connected with the registration. The agreement runs for 10 years from the first market introduction of Collagenase ointment in each country.

BioSpecifics Technologies Corp. produces the FDA-approved enzyme Collagenase ABC, the essential constituent of Collagenase Santyl(R) ointment, and licenses it for domestic and international sales. Collagenase Santyl is an ethical topical drug used for treatment of dermal ulcers, pressure sores, and burn wounds. In addition to Collagenase ABC, BioSpecifics is engaged in various stages of research, development, clinical testing, and licensing of additional pharmaceutical products.

Biota Holdings Ltd. said that the first widely available anti-influenza drug in the world and a diagnostic test that identifies the viral infection could be available after 1998. The influenza compound GG-167, which is undergoing tests around the world by British pharmaceuticals giant Glaxo Wellcome Plc, was expected to be submitted for approval to the US Food and Drug Administration (FDA) and other regulators in late 1996 or 1997 and marketing approval might be gained by the end of 1998. Glaxo Wellcome holds the worldwide marketing and development rights to the drug and is conducting all the research. Under a deal signed in 1990, Biota is entitled **to 6% of the gross revenue** of the drug, which analysts have estimated could sell A$500 million (US$360 million) a year. Influenza reportedly affects 10 percent of the world's population each year, and kills 10,000 people annually in the United States alone. Clinical trials of the drug, which would be administered by an inhaler into the lungs and possibly through a nasal spray, showed that it seemed to have so significant side effects.

Disease Detection International (DDI) has provided a nonexclusive license to Meridian Diagnostics Incorporated that will allow Meridian to manufacture and sell six rapid diagnostic test kits for pregnancy, strep throat, toxoplasma rubella, cytomegalovirus, herpes simplex I, and herpes simplex II. DDI received a $110,000 license fee and another $100,000 as an advance against future royalties which are set at **6% of Meridian sales**.

Future Medical Technologies International purchased a patented device from Human Medical Laboratories, Inc., that filters microorganisms from body fluids. Future Medical made an advanced cash payment of $372,000 and 150,000 shares of unregistered common stock. Future Medical will also pay a **3% royalty based upon net profits** with a lifetime cap of $5 million.

Editors' Note: This is another example of a rare arrangement where royalty payments are directly related to revenues.

Future Medical Technologies Incorporated and the University of Maryland at College Park entered into licensing and collaboration agreements. The agreements give Future Medical exclusive worldwide rights to test and commercialize recently developed nonagar based media formulations for use in detecting and/or selectively growing salmonella. Future Medical believes that incorporating this new media into the company's microbiological "Qualture" product line will offer an unusual advantage not usually available in a market which is estimated to perform 12 million and 15 million tests annually. The rights that have been granted to Future Medical are subject to a royalty free nonexclusive license permitting the United States government to practice all licensed inventions for U.S. government purposes. During each of the 4 years of the license agreement, Future Medical will pay annual **escalating royalty rates of 2%, 3%, 4%, and 5% of net sales**, respectively, for all licensed products that the company sells. In the fifth and subsequent years under the license agreement Future Medical will pay an annual royalty of 6% of net sales for all licensed products sold by the company. If sales of the licensed products are made by any authorized sublicensee of Future Medical, then Future Medical will pay 50% of all revenues received from sublicensees to the university. Future Medical Technologies Incorporated markets a device (the "Qualture") that is designed to separate and filter microorganisms from specimens of urine, blood, spinal, joint, and other body fluids for identification, quantification, and presumptive diagnosis of infectious diseases. Moreover, the device works in a time period substantially shorter than present conventional procedures.

Hailey Energy Corp. licensed the worldwide exclusive rights to manufacture and market a new cytology device from Langdon Medical Inc. The device enables doctors to diagnose a number of common cancers and other diseases earlier, faster, and more accurately than current methods. The device allows what was once a $3,000 to $5,000 hospital biopsy procedure to be conducted in a doctor's office for around $600. The terms of the agreement call for the issuance of restricted common stock of Hailey Energy Corp. equivalent to just under 10% of the outstanding stock to Langdon Medical. Hailey will also pay a **9% royalty based on the average retail prices** of product sales less bad debt and return allowances. In addition to the royalty and stock, Hailey agreed to pay Langdon a $300,000 licensing fee. Hailey Energy Corp. operates two primary business: 1) exploration and development of oil and gas reserves and 2) manufacturing and marketing specialty medical products.

Hambrecht & Quist's Timothy Wilson says that investors have a "huge buying opportunity" with BioChem Pharma Inc. But one Toronto analyst urged just the opposite when the stock's price began to creep up on rumors of the European 3TC test results. The analyst says that other drugs being developed for use in combination with AZT and further down the regulatory pipeline than BioChem's 3TC. Even if 3TC is successfully developed, the analyst says, the pricing of BioChem stock has run away from reality. BioChem—the discoverer of 3TC—will only receive **a 12% royalty** from Glaxo Holdings plc, which licensed the drug in 1990 and has been conducting trials. The analyst warns that BioChem stock will get hurt over the next year with positive developments on some of the other combination drugs being groomed for market. Conversely, Hambrecht & Quist's Wilson says that the most convincing part of the data was results showing that patients who had been treated with AZT alone and then switched to the 3TC/AZT combination quickly normalized with patients who had been on the combination since the beginning.

Life Medical Sciences Inc. signed a letter of intent on July 13, 1994 to sell its Sure-losure(TM) skin stretching system product line to MedChem Products for $4,000,000 in cash, a $500,000 interest free loan and a **royalty of 10% on net sales** for ten years. The company said the 10% royalties due could exceed about $50 million over the 10-year period. The agreement permits the company to benefit from the growth of this and future Sure-Closure(TM) products while concentrating its development activities on Cariel(TM) and other proprietary technologies. Life Medical Sciences is a medical technology company developing wound closure products, including Cariel(TM), a wound gel for accelerated healing of difficult and nonhealing wounds. Cariel(TM) is currently undergoing Phase II and Phase III human clinical trials in Europe. The company also owns rights to patented medical polymer technology.

Medco Research, Inc., is a company that develops new treatment and diagnostic drugs and focuses research on cardiovascular diseases. The company recently entered into a license agreement with the Japanese pharmaceutical company Fujisava. The licensing agreement covers the heart disease treatment Adenocard. Medco received a 1-A classification from the FDA and granted an exclusive license for the United States and Canada to Fujisava. Medco will receive **a royalty of 25% of net sales,** which it will split on a 50–50 basis with a university research foundation. Another Medco Research, Inc. drug, Adenoscan, is currently in the stages of final review by the FDA. When cleared for marketing the drug will also be sold in the United States and Canada under an exclusive licensing agreement with Fujisava. **A royalty rate of 25% will be paid on net sales** to Medco. No royalty split is involved with the Adenoscan product.

Molecular Biosystems, Inc. (MBI) amended its supply and license agreement with E. I. duPont De Nemours & Company. The agreement covers proprietary nucleic acid probe technologies that are owned by MBI. The renegotiated agreement was originally established in April, 1986. Previously duPont had an exclusive license but under the new agreement will retain only a nonexclusive right to these technologies. MBI will continue to manufacture nucleic acid probe agents for duPont as it did under previous agreement. **The royalty rate on duPont's net sales was lowered from 5.5% to 4%** to reflect the change of duPont's licensing rights from exclusive to nonexclusive. This represents a reduction in the royalty rate of 27%. Molecular Biosystems, Inc., is a San Diego, California, company recognized as a leading biochemical firm developing proprietary medical products that diagnose human disease. The company is also a leading developer and supplier of direct, nonradioactively labeled nucleic acid probe products. The company is also developing diagnostic imaging products including Albunex, an injectable contrast agent for use in ultrasound imaging.

Pfizer Inc. obtained a license to manufacture and sell Water-Jel sterile burn dressing products in the United States and Canada from Trilling Medical Technologies Incorporated. Pfizer agreed to pay a **royalty of 5% on sales** of Water-Jel products and 5% on sales of any new products that are developed using the technology. Pfizer also promised to pay a 2% royalty on net sales on each new Pfizer product that makes use of Trilling's nine licensed trademarks.

Editors' Note: The entire deal fell through within six months when Trilling received notification of possible patent infringement by the licensed technology from an unaffiliated company. Pfizer immediately withdrew from the deal.

Roche Molecular Systems, a unit of Roche Holding, Ltd., expanded the licensing policy for its Ploymerase Chain Reaction (PCR) diagnostic and testing services to include all laboratories. Previously licenses were available to specific laboratories, including SmithKline Beecham Plc. The new license agreements will be based on royalty rates of **at least 9% of sales.** PCR replicates a single DNA strand millions of times in under two hours. This allows scientists to amplify and identify certain DNA segments. PCR is used in medical tests for conditions such as infectious disease, genetic disease, and cancer, and in other applications including food testing, environmental research, and identity testing. The expanded licensing policy follows Roche's reportedly $300 million acquisition of the PCR technology from Cetus Corporation.

Surgidyne Inc. has provided a unit of Baxter Healthcare Corporation with exclusive worldwide marketing rights for its autotransfusion products. The products involve capturing a surgical patient's blood during an operation and reusing the blood during and after the operation. The licensed system employs a battery-powered vacuum controller with disposable collection and reinfusing products. Baxter will pay Surgidyne a **royalty of 20% on sales up to $2 million** in royalties after which the royalty rate on sales drops to 5%.

OIL REFINING

Interline Resources Corp. signed an exclusive licensing agreement for its contaminated oil reprocessing technology with Gadgil Western Corp. (formerly called Western India Group) for Bahrain and Singapore. For the rights to these countries, Gadgil Western has agreed to pay Interline **$1 million** by August 31, 1995. For all fuel products produced, Gadgil Western will pay Interline a gross **royalty of 2 cents per gallon**. Gadgil Western intends to use Interline's technology in an 82 million gallon per year refinery in Bahrain and a 165 million gallon per year refinery in Singapore. The royalties from these plants would contribute to the anticipated $6 million per year royalties announced in June.

Interline's breakthrough technology allows Gadgil Western to operate fuel oil re-refineries that upgrade low-value, heavy refinery hydrocarbons to middle distillates, such as gasoline and diesel fuels. Gadgil Western has been operating the first Interline refinery since June in Dubai, United Arab Emirates. The refinery has a capacity of about 13 million gallons per year. The licensing agreement now brings the total of countries in which Gadgil Western can exclusively use Interline's technology to 12. In December 1993, Interline signed a licensing agreement with Gadgil Western for 10 Middle Eastern and Far Eastern countries.

Interline owns a patented technology for processing and cleaning contaminated hydrocarbons, including crank case oil, refinery bottoms, waste crude streams, and other heavy oils. The finished products from Interline's technology can be sold as base lubricating oils, clean-burning industrial fuels, diesels, and other middle distillates. The byproducts from the Interline re-refineries are environmentally safe. In addition to licensing its patented re-refining technology, Interline is a diversified oil and natural gas company. Interline also has a wholly owned subsidiary, Gagon Mechanical, which builds Interline's re-refineries and participates in industrial and commercial construction.

SOFTWARE

BLOC Development Corporation reached an agreement in principle for the sale of its F3 Forms Software subsidiary to a group of private investors including F3's President, Geoffrey Cronin, and other outside BLOC stockholders. Total consideration to BLOC for the sale of F3 is expected to be $1 million payable in cash and an interest bearing note. In addition, BLOC will receive up to **$1 million in royalties on future sales** of F3-based products. BLOC Development Corporation, through its Tiger Direct direct marketing subsidiary, sells the latest business productivity and utility software, hardware, and peripherals, and is one of the largest CD-ROM resellers in the country.

Innovative Tech Systems entered into an exclusive five-year OEM agreement with Integraph Corp. Under the terms of the OEM agreement, Intergraph Corp. will have exclusive OEM distribution rights with respect to Innovative Tech Systems' SPAN$^{(TM)}$ software. Intergraph Corp. will market, sell, and distribute the SPAN$^{(TM)}$ software under the IFM$^{(TM)}$ software tools for Facilities Management brand. Intergraph will distribute the IFM$^{(TM)}$ suite of products through a worldwide sales channel that generated over $1 billion of revenue in 1993. Most analysts expect Intergraph to report sales of over $1 billion in 1994. Innovative Tech Systems will continue to aggressively develop, support, and market the SPAN$^{(TM)}$ family of software products worldwide through its direct sales force and resellers. Under the terms of the agreement with Intergraph Corp., Innovative Tech Systems has agreed not to act as an OEM supplier for any other third party. The financial terms of the OEM agreement provide for Innovative Tech Systems to **receive 30 percent royalties on all sales** of IFM$^{(TM)}$ products. Minimum royalties during each year of the agreement must be $1.5 million in order for Intergraph Corp. to maintain exclusive OEM distribution rights. In addition to the minimum royalties of $1.5MM per year during the term, the agreement also calls for increased royalties based on the previous year's sales. Innovative Tech Systems Inc. is the developer of SPAN$^{(TM)}$, an industry leading software solution for the effective planning and management of an organization's facilities. Intergraph Corp. is the world's largest company dedicated to supplying interactive computer graphics systems.

Macromedia, the leader in multimedia software tools, announced that run-time licenses for Authorware Professional and Director for the Windows and Macintosh platforms will be offered royalty-free. As part of the **royalty-free** policy, the Macromedia run-time software license will require developers to include the Made with Macromedia logo on their software. This will identify the product as having been created using Macromedia tools. The Made with Macromedia brand will be developed by Macromedia through advertising, trade shows, public relations, direct mail, and other marketing

.communications. Developers will benefit from the Made with Macromedia brand awareness as well as several specific marketing programs.

Software developers making games for use with gaming machines built by Sega and Nintendo pay the machine makers a royalty on sales ranging from **$9 and $12 per unit.** One of newest game makers, 3DO, was planning to change the rules and charge software developers a royalty of only $3 per unit. Financial strains at 3DO may force the company to change its plans. More information can be obtained from The New York Times, *For 3DO, a* *Make-or-Break Season*, Section 3, page 1, December 11, 1994.

Wisconsin Public Service Corporation, a public utility, licensed management information software to WPS Development Incorporated and will receive a royalty equal **to 10% of all software licensing fees** received by WPS Development, Incorporated. The software program, known as the IFM system, involves numerous computer applications useful for natural gas, electric, sewer, water, and other utilities. Wisconsin Public Service Corporation is not involved in the business of developing and marketing or otherwise servicing computer program designs, and so WPS Development Incorporated has entered into a license agreement whereby it can sublicense the IMF system to others. The agreement runs until December 31, 1996.

TOYS

Toy makers are playing a large role in Hollywood. The amounts spent by movie studios to promote new pictures dwarf the amount of advertising that a toy maker could afford in promoting new toys. By licensing toys from Hollywood they get the promotional benefits associated with the movie. Building awareness for new products is very expensive. Toy companies see movie related products as new products that already have tremendous recognition.

Typically, toy makers spend about 14% of sales on advertising, says Seth Siegel, co-chairman of Beanstalk Group, Inc., a New York licensing agency. Licensing gives them more for their buck, he says, even though licensing fees are rising. Disney first licensed products in the 1930s, and by the 1960s Mickey Mouse and Donald Duck commanded a royalty rate of 5%. The figure was up to 8% by the late 1980s. For Pocahontas merchandise, Disney gets a hefty **12% royalty**. Small wonder, then, that toy companies are playing a bigger role in Hollywood. A Disney animator says that one scene in *Pocahontas*—when the raccoon Meeko briefly braids the star's hair—was created after a suggestion from Mattel, which wanted to be able to make Braided Beauty Pocahontas dolls. Disney denies that Mattel dictated the scene, saying that the film always comes first. Still, the braiding of the two industries seems clear to others. "It's a given in the industry that movies and TV programs are routinely designed with merchandising in mind," says

Weston Anson, president of Trademark & Licensing Associates, Inc., in La Jolla, California. In *Batman Forever*, Kenner got Warner Bros. to put the Riddler in tights because baggy pants don't look good on toy action figures, says Rick Watkins, a former Kenner toy-development manager.

Another reasoning for licensing's success is the continuing failure of traditional toys to excite buyers. That includes old-fashioned dolls, an area where innovations continue. There are dolls that cry, burp, and drool. However, sales of one-trick dolls have been down the past two years, to $331 million in 1994 from $460 million in 1992. Analysts say development cutbacks, along with marketing that boosts licensed products, stack the odds against the new creations.

WASTE MANAGEMENT

Tirex America Inc. received the second $25,000 payment under its purchase agreement with Ocean/Ventures III Inc. of Toms River, New Jersey. Ocean/Ventures III is under common ownership and control with the solid waste recycling firm Ocean County Recycling Center Inc. Under the terms of the agreement, on or before August 31, 1997, Ocean/Ventures III will purchase eight Tirex TCS-1 Cryogenic Tire Disintegration Systems ("TSC-1 Systems") at a price of $1,750,000 each, for an aggregate purchase price of $14,000,000. With payment of this second installment, Ocean/Ventures III has paid $50,000 or a $200,000 contract deposit, full payment of which is due on or before July 31, 1995. The $200,000 deposit will be applied toward the prices of the first four systems purchased.

TSC-1 Systems are intended to be used to break down waste tires into their recyclable component materials of rubber crumb, steel, and nylon cord, which can be sold for multiple uses in many products and industry applications. Ocean/Ventures has agreed to pay Tirex America Inc. a **2% royalty on revenues from the sale of all byproducts** of the tire disintegration process.

Index

Footnotes are referenced by an n following the page number.